Mindful Leadership Coaching

Mindful Leadership Coaching

Journeys into the interior

Manfred F. R. Kets de Vries
*Distinguished Clinical Professor of Leadership Development and
Organizational Change, INSEAD, France, Singapore & Abu Dhabi*

First published 2014 by
PALGRAVE MACMILLAN

Palgrave Macmillan in the UK is an imprint of Macmillan Publishers Limited, registered in England, company number 785998, of Houndmills, Basingstoke, Hampshire RG21 6XS.

Palgrave Macmillan in the US is a division of St Martin's Press LLC, 175 Fifth Avenue, New York, NY 10010.

Palgrave Macmillan is the global academic imprint of the above companies and has companies and representatives throughout the world.

Palgrave® and Macmillan® are registered trademarks in the United States, the United Kingdom, Europe and other countries.

ISBN 978–1–137–38232–0

This book is printed on paper suitable for recycling and made from fully managed and sustained forest sources. Logging, pulping and manufacturing processes are expected to conform to the environmental regulations of the country of origin.

A catalogue record for this book is available from the British Library.

A catalog record for this book is available from the Library of Congress.

Typeset by MPS Limited, Chennai, India.

Contents

Preface

One day an old Chinese sage lost his pearls. Distraught, he sent his eyes to search for his pearls, but his eyes did not find them. Next he sent his ears to search for the pearls, but his ears did not find them either. Then he sent his hands to search for the pearls, but they likewise had no success. And so he sent all of his senses together to search for his pearls, but none found them. Finally he sent his not-search to look for his pearls. And his not-search found them!

— *Chinese fable*

Introduction

A coaching session with Freud

During the summer of 1910, when Freud was vacationing with his family beside the North Sea in Holland, Gustav Mahler visited him for a consultation. Mahler had contacted Freud because of feelings of depression, and serious relationship problems with his wife Alma (associated with sexual dysfunction). As his wife would write in her autobiography, Mahler was not at all well. He dwelled constantly on the past: his troubled childhood, his perception of being an outsider in Vienna, his concerns about not being understood as a composer, and his morbid fascination with death.[1] He was also troubled by responsibilities as the world's leading conductor. These preoccupations, which he transformed into major themes in his music, were having a destructive effect on his marriage. His depression was deepened by the probability that Alma – fed up with his neurotic behavior – was about to leave him for a younger man, the budding architect, Walter Gropius. Mahler decided to consult Sigmund Freud about his troubled state of mind.

Although (according to Freud's biographer Ernest Jones) Freud was always very reluctant to interrupt his holidays, it was difficult for him to refuse seeing a man of Gustav Mahler's stature.[2] The composer's "maddening doubt" had led him, however, to put off the meeting on three previous occasions, making it necessary for Freud to give Mahler a kind of ultimatum. Freud made clear that the end of August would be the last chance to have a consultation, as he was leaving then for Sicily.

The two men met at a restaurant in Leiden and after the meal continued their discussion walking along the canals. They talked for over four hours, the longest therapeutic session Freud ever conducted. Writing much later to Theodor Reik, in 1934, Freud noted, "I analyzed Mahler for an afternoon in the year 1910 in Leiden. If I may believe the reports I achieved much with him at that time. The visit appeared necessary for him, because his wife at that time rebelled against the fact that he withdrew his libido from her. In highly interesting expeditions with him through his life history, we discovered his personal conditions for love, especially in his Holy Mary complex (mother fixation). I had plenty of opportunity to admire the capability of the psychological understanding of this man of genius. No light fell at this time on the symptomatic façade of his obsessional neurosis. It was as if you would dig a single shaft through a mysterious building."[3] Mahler, on his part, sent a telegram to Alma the day after the meeting: "I'm filled with joy. Interesting conversation…" Although Mahler had no knowledge of psychoanalysis, Freud noted that he had never before met anyone who understood so quickly what psychoanalysis was all about. Whatever happened during their session, apparently it changed Mahler's life.

Perhaps Mahler told Freud the story of his troubled childhood, how he was first initiated to music, and the pleasure he derived from it. Perhaps he described how his ability to compose music gave him a sense of victory over his tyrannical father.[4] Perhaps he talked about the terrible, painful relationship between his father and his mother: his father's violence toward his mother and his mother crying, and running out of the house. Perhaps he spoke about his helplessness – all tragic themes that he would iterate in his music.

As to Freud's response, perhaps he made some observations about Mahler's relationships with women, explored the infantile patterns behind them, discussed his striving for perfection, his "Holy Mary" complex, and its possible link with Mahler's sexual dysfunction. Perhaps he speculated that in his striving for perfection, Mahler had sacrificed his relationships with other people, in particular his wife. Mahler wrote, "Others wear the theater out and take care of themselves; I take care of the theater and wear myself out."[5]

While individual four-hour consultations are highly unusual, psychoanalytical interventions (unlike coaching) normally extend over a considerable period of time, often many years. Traditional psychoanalysis has always advocated longer treatments but from the beginning, both longer and shorter forms of treatment have been available within psychoanalysis. Freud's treatment of Mahler has been taken as a prime example of one of Freud's shorter interventions. It seems that although it was only four hours in total – albeit in a single session – Mahler's meeting with Freud had some effect. Mahler's impotency disappeared, and the marital relationship apparently improved. Unfortunately, Mahler died the following year.

In her autobiography, Alma Mahler also recounts the meeting between Freud and her husband, mentioning that Mahler contacted Freud out of fear of losing her.[6] It seems that Freud had told her husband that he recognized his mother, an abused woman, in every woman he met. But Mahler's relationships with women had always been complicated. Later in her book, Alma writes that when she met him Mahler was still a virgin at the age of 40, despite attempts at seduction by several experienced women. Moreover, before their marriage Mahler had written to Alma stipulating that she must give up her own musical ambitions, including composing. The only music to be talked about in his house was his own. (Much later, he partly changed his mind about this requirement.) In that letter, he also wrote that her main task would be to make him happy. Alma should be there only for him – it was almost as if she should behave as an extension of himself.

We can infer from a number of these comments that the couple seemed to be caught in a kind of sado-masochistic relationship, a way of dealing with each other that both needed in order to retain their identity. It seems to have been a very engulfing relationship – all or nothing, life or death, either merging and disappearing inside one another or losing each other. Perhaps the only satisfying, fruitful, and constructive relationship Mahler ever had was the one with his music.

Considering it was so successful when it did take place, why did Mahler cancel his appointment with Freud three times? Perhaps, at an unconscious level, he had a modicum of understanding about what made him so creative. Was he afraid that his talk with Freud would challenge him to face his inner demons? And as these conflicts were so much part of him, would dealing with them impact his ability to compose? Would analyzing his problems cause his fountain of creativity to run dry? Perhaps Mahler's initial reluctance to see Freud had something to do with his own realization that his personal conflicts had been channeled successfully into his compositions.

We can speculate that the effectiveness of Freud's intervention may have been the result of his making a number of supportive observations. Freud recounted that he was quite impressed by Mahler's psychological insight. Whatever happened during that walk, on his return to Vienna, Mahler was remarkably positive about his conversation with Freud, as if it had finally given him a solution to his miserable state of mind. After the meeting with Freud, Alma stopped seeing Walter Gropius (or at least kept her liaisons secret) and Mahler encouraged and praised her compositions. Furthermore, the annotations in the manuscript of Mahler's unfinished 10th Symphony resemble an open love letter to Alma. Whatever happened during the meeting with Freud, it must have reminded Gustav why he loved his wife, and what role she played in his life.[7] In one way or another, Freud helped stabilize their relationship until Mahler's death in 1911.

Everybody has a coach

The Freud-Mahler encounter can be viewed as an example of a remarkably effective coaching session. It demonstrates how much work can be done in a short intervention. Yet many more years would go by before coaching interventions (not necessarily the sort of in-depth interventions like the Freud-Mahler encounter) would be widely practiced. In the early 1980s, leadership coaching started to gain momentum, but the widespread adoption of executive coaching practices began only around a decade later. Of course, as the Freud-Mahler example illustrates, as long as people needed guidance, some form of coaching had been always available, albeit under other names. In the early days, however, having a coach was a kind of a dirty little secret. It was something you didn't want to talk about. If you had a coach, it usually meant you were in some sort of trouble. Being advised to undertake coaching meant you were being given a final chance to do something about whatever it was you were doing wrong. Initially, coaching was stigmatized.

Nowadays, leadership coaching is cast in a far more positive light. In fact, the pendulum has swung to the other extreme and having a coach has become a status symbol. It means you're successful, that you're someone who your organization is investing in for the future. Coaching is no longer a reactive process. Today's fast-track executives proactively seek some form of coaching and nearly every senior executive seems to have a coach.

One of the reasons for the current popularity of coaching is that many executives have realized that leadership coaches offer expertise that is not necessarily found inside the company. Another, which probably accounts more for its attractiveness, is that most find it easier to confide in an objective outsider. External coaches are more likely to offer a confidential relationship within which executives can discuss delicate issues freely, let their defenses down, and explore blind spots, biases, and shortcomings.

The higher executives climb on the organizational ladder, the less they can depend on technical skills and the greater their need for effective interpersonal skills and emotional intelligence. This is where leadership coaches can make a major contribution. For example, there are many

"The higher executives climb on the organizational ladder, the less they can depend on technical skills and the greater their need for effective interpersonal skills and emotional intelligence"

unspoken rules about appropriate executive styles for top-level positions. These rules are not always easy to decipher. Leadership coaches can help executives decode these rules and understand what is expected of them in terms of behaviors and attitudes. Coaches can help their clients to enhance their style, explore future options, and discuss their ideal and actual organizational impact. They can also facilitate their learning, help them to clarify their goals, and guide them in getting things done.

Coaches can draw their clients' attention to repetitive problems that they may not have recognized. They can help their clients realize that what they once regarded as strengths could easily turn into weaknesses as they climb the organizational ladder. They can also help them to become more effective with colleagues, subordinates, bosses, and other stakeholders and take a serious look at behaviors that may adversely affect these relationships. They can help come to terms with behaviors that cause difficulties, and find more effective ways of functioning.

For example, the most common reasons why executives go astray are difficulties in anger management: being too domineering; reacting inappropriately when things are not to their liking; not handling failure well (not admitting error, covering up, or listing excuses); the inability to influence their people constructively; being too far removed from their people; or living an unbalanced lifestyle. At its most basic level, the role of a leadership coach is to help the executive acknowledge and deal with realities that might otherwise be avoided, denied, or accepted with resignation. In addition, coaches may help them recognize defensive routines within their organization, and do something about them.

Effective leadership coaches contract with their clients with the objective not only to improve their clients' performance, but also to guide them on a journey toward personal transformation and reinvention. They can help their clients break free from an unsatisfying or conflict-laden role and plan for new roles. Coaches can expand their clients' horizon of possibilities, eliciting powerful new commitments, transforming their view of themselves, and fostering new ways of being and acting.

"Coaches can expand their clients' horizon of possibilities"

The coach also has a role in helping executives to build shared understanding, that is, learn how to think and interact better in a work setting, through courageous conversations, assisting them in giving constructive feedback. Coaches may help executives to create better functioning teams and design organizational cultures that will get the best out of their people.

But practicing as an effective leadership coach requires a considerable amount of psychological skill and insight. Coaches need to acknowledge not only what is immediately perceivable but also developments under the surface. We need to listen with the third ear, paying attention to transference and countertransference phenomena. We need to identify the unconscious redirection of feelings from one person to another. We need to pay attention to the dynamics within the intrapersonal and interpersonal field.[8] As leadership coaches, we need to be aware of the dynamics that occur when others open up to us, and when we need to open up to them. As with any kind of close relationship, coaching creates a new dynamic with associated past behaviors, patterns, and old ways of thinking. In more traditional leadership coaching, these issues would usually remain in the background; in in-depth coaching these dynamics are identifiers, and used as additional information to help the client.

However, many coaches fail to realize that when these dynamics become activated, they have the potential to derail the coach's efforts. If these unconscious relationship needs are strong, they can work in unfortunate ways that undermine the coaching activity. As these dynamics often involve painful and contradictory feelings – touching us and our clients where we feel most vulnerable – they are often difficult to address. But they need to be addressed, verbally or non-verbally, if we want to be effective in our coaching assignments. This necessitates a degree of mindfulness.

Mindful leadership coaching

Nan-in, a Japanese Zen master during the Meiji era (1868–1912), welcomed a university professor who came to inquire about Zen.

Nan-in served tea. He filled his visitor's cup, then kept pouring.

The professor watched the cup overflowing until he no longer could restrain himself. "Stop! It's full! You can't get any more tea in this cup!"

"Like this cup," Nan-in said, "you are full of your own opinions and speculations. How can I help you learn unless you first empty your cup?"

Coaching in depth requires the ability to listen carefully to whatever the client is trying to convey with an open mind – like the Japanese professor in the Zen story, the coach has to start with an empty "cup." In this kind of coaching context, mindfulness means drawing the client's attention to the experience of the present moment in an open and non-judgmental manner. This can be viewed as a distinct state of consciousness, distinguished from the normal consciousness of everyday living. Mindfulness leads to wiser judgment about what is and isn't important. Taking a reflective pose, rather than resorting to a flight into action, gives clients room to roam

"Mindfulness leads to wiser judgment about what is and isn't important"

from perspective to perspective, from one incomplete thought to the other, until those thoughts begin to crystallize and become the basis for insight and growth. At the same time, we can also roam in our thoughts, trying to make sense of what is happening to us, without trying to achieve premature closure. While most of what we achieve is by "doing," mindfulness achieves its ends by "not doing," simply by taking the time to observe – before doing.

Although mindfulness is at the heart of Buddhist meditation, the practice has also been part of Western traditions and has been used in psycho-therapeutic interventions, under different names, since the earliest days of psychoanalysis. For example, Sigmund Freud referred to a state of "evenly suspended attention,"[9] indicating that when working with clients, psychotherapists should allow their own unconscious activity to operate as freely as possible and suspend the motives that usually direct their attention. Mindfulness is what made Freud so effective.

Mindfulness on the part of leadership coaches seems to achieve its success by allowing them to see thoughts and emotions as just that, rather than things to rule our lives or believe in uncritically. In that respect, mindful-ness is very similar to the concept of countertransference in a psychoana-lytic context.[10] Countertransference can be viewed as the response that is elicited in the recipient (coach) by the other's (client's) unconscious transference communications. This response includes both feelings and associated thoughts. The aim of mindful interventions, using these countertransference feelings, is to help us to become more aware of our thoughts and bodily sensations, and in so doing be able to cope better with day-to-day emotions and problems.

The early advocates of a mindfulness approach to leadership coaching viewed its main benefit as increasing the effectiveness of leadership coaches. Mindfulness, however, is not limited to the behavior of the coach. It works both ways. Clients will also benefit from learning and practicing mindfulness. Although the burden is on coaches to be mindful in their work, they should help their clients to acquire mindfulness skills at the same time.

So, what is mindfulness? Mindful consciousness is quite different from the ordinary consciousness that is appropriate for our day-to-day activities, where attention is actively directed outward, in regular space and time, normally in the service of some agenda or task, and ruled by habitual response patterns. Mindfulness helps us to become more aware of the unhelpfulness of some thoughts. It helps us direct awareness inward and focus on the present moment. Mindfulness makes us aware of what is, as opposed to what needs to be done – to experience non-doing, or non-effort. In a state of mindfulness we self-consciously enable ourselves to suspend agendas, judgments, and common understanding. In being mindful, we are being several things all at once: passive, alert, open, curious, and exploratory.

In addition to the passive capacity simply to witness experience as it unfolds, the purpose of mindfulness is to allow us to have a different, less conflict-ridden relationship with our thoughts, emotions, and bodily sensations. The expected outcome is an increase in well-being – to have more control over our own mind as we spend less time dealing with difficulties and focus more on constructive activities. Thanks to mindfulness, what were once seen as difficulties may disappear altogether.

For example, at times, we may experience very strong emotions, feeling mad, bad, sad, or glad. These emotions may incapacitate us. They may become overwhelming and make us feel that we are no longer in control of our mind and cannot cope. Taking a mindful pose will enable us to become familiar with these feelings and see them in a very different perspective. Mindfulness will give us more insight into our emotions, boost our attention and concentration, improve our relationships, and enrich our work with clients. Although it might appear that mindfulness requires us to relinquish control, paradoxically, it gives us greater control over our mind. No wonder that mindfulness helps our sense of balance, improves our sense of well-being, and enriches our enjoyment of life.

Unfortunately, many leadership coaches are far from mindful. They enter the profession because they've never been listened to themselves and become leadership coaches in the hope that by giving important advice to powerful people, they will finally be heard. It's doubtful that this mindset will be of any real benefit to the client. Like the parable of the overflowing teacup, a mind full of its own agenda will sabotage their efforts to let others express themselves. It will not take very long for their clients to realize that the coach isn't really listening – which will spell the end of the relationship. Only when leadership coaches listen to their clients with a truly open mind will their clients feel listened to, and the coach deliver value.

When mindfulness is used appropriately, it can be a very powerful and effective method to bring about personal insight and change. Being mindful will help coaches unravel negative thoughts and painful emotions. It will help us and others free ourselves from unnecessary fears and unhelpful, habitual patterns.

Leadership coaching in depth

"Mindfulness, and the capacity to coach in depth, are closely intertwined" Mindfulness, and the capacity to coach in depth, are closely intertwined. When coaching in depth, we use an extra lens, and an essential part of this extra lens is the clinical paradigm. Effective leadership coaches are like gardeners. The presenting problems are weeds; we've got to get to the roots to prevent them from popping up again.

The clinical paradigm pertains to a method of analysis that frames whatever we are observing. The term "clinical" indicates that the paradigm is applied to real-life situations. The goal of applying the clinical paradigm is to help people to revisit past experiences and expand their freedom to explore new challenges in life by helping them to become more aware of their choices in the here-and-now.

"if we are to function in a healthy way, we must not be strangers to ourselves" As my digression in mindfulness has indicated, if we are to function in a healthy way, we must not be strangers to ourselves. We need to free ourselves from the bonds of past experience, and find new ways of coping.

The clinical paradigm is built on a number of premises. The first is the proposition that *rationality is an illusion*. "Irrational" behavior is a common pattern in our lives. However, the kind of irrationality we observe always has a "rationale," or meaning, to it. Understanding this rationale will be critical in making sense of our own and other people's "inner theater" – the core themes that affect our personality and leadership style.

Much of what happens to us is *beyond our conscious awareness*. What we see isn't necessarily what we get. All of us have blind spots. There are many things we don't want to know about ourselves and to preempt this kind of knowledge, we resort to *defensive processes and resistances* to avoid experiences that we find disagreeable. Unfortunately, many people derail due to the blind spots in their personality. However, exploring our efforts at avoidance will give us a snapshot of our own and others' personality. It is important to realize that these resistances come to the fore due to conflicts within ourselves; we need to accept that inner dissonance is part of the human condition. We also need to recognize that most psychological difficulties were, at one point in time, adaptive solutions to the problem of living. To have a better understanding of unconscious patterns, our defensive reactions, and our blind spots, we need to explore our inner theater and pay attention to repetitive themes and patterns in our lives.

All of us are the product of our past and *the past is the lens through which we can understand the present and shape the future*. Because of the heavy imprinting that takes place in the early stages of life, we tend to repeat certain behavior patterns. As the saying goes, "The hand that rocks the cradle is the hand that rules the world." The blueprint for our personality structure is the developmental outcome of our early environment, modified by our genetic endowment. Whether we like it or not, there's a continuity between our past and present.

Exploring the relationship between our past and present will be very illuminating, as it will enable us to become liberated from habitual, ingrained behavior. And as there are repetitive themes in our life and the lives of others, the scripts of our inner theaters will be reactivated in our current relationships. To understand our behavior we need to identify these recurrent themes and patterns. Problematic relationship patterns, which are technically transference and countertransference reactions, provide a great opportunity to explore and work through difficult issues in the here-and-now. Adaptive and non-adaptive aspects of our operational mode will be affected by the way in which our original attachment relationships evolved.

Nothing is more central to who we are than the way we express and regulate emotions. Emotions determine many of our actions and emotional intelligence plays a vital role in who we are and what we do. Intellectual insight is not the same as emotional insight, which touches us at a much deeper level. To understand others, and ourselves we need to explore the full range of experienced emotions. These emotions will also play an essential role in why we do what we do, why we take on certain roles, and why we are passionate about certain things.

A personal diversion

At the beginning of the 20th century, the Harvard psychologist and philosopher William James distinguished people as being either "once-born" or "twice-born."[11] According to James, "once-borns" are individuals who do not stray from the straight and narrow. They are tied to familiar territory where they have always felt comfortable. Conversely, "twice-born" people go to great lengths to reinvent themselves, often as a result of dramatic changes in their life. On reflection, they come to realize that their life is too predictable, and that if they do not embark on change, they will sink into a state of living death. The implication is that "twice-born" people actively use difficult changes in their external life to help them come to peace with their inner demons.

In William James's mental framework, we start our life's journey simply by being physically born. However, we may be spiritually and intellectually challenged – in other words, "reborn" – when faced with unexpected adversity, such as a dramatic life crisis. "Twice-borns" – people who have undergone an experience of fundamental, moral, and spiritual upheaval (a near-death experience, for example) – may transcend their self-limitations. They may succeed in escaping their self-imposed mental prison and discover imaginative ways of dealing with adversity. "Twice-borns" are given a new lease of life. The ability to reinvent themselves changes the way they relate to other people and the world around them.

Fairly recently, I have had two near-death experiences: a terrifying accident on the top of a snowy mountain on the Kamchatka Peninsula of the Russian Far East, followed by an almost fatal hospital infection. These experiences created in me a greater awareness of what being "twice-born" really means. It taught me something about mindfulness. It also brought home to me – more than once – how to make the best of the precious gift that life really is. It brought a deep recognition of the fragility of life.

I am a disciple of what Sigmund Freud described as "the impossible profession." As well as being a professor of leadership development and change, I have a parallel life in which I am a psychoanalyst. In that respect, it might be said that I am a kind of shaman – shamanistic interventions being, of course, the original template of all coaching. Throughout human history, shamans have bridged the world of the living and the world of the spirits. Shamans would ensure that the right ceremonies were enacted in the right way to put the world to rights. Shamans were the explorers of the magnificent hidden universe that lies beyond this visible one. They brokered our search for another dimension of seeing. In this context, it's clear that there are many similarities between the role of the shaman and the role played today by people in the helping professions – which include leadership coaching.

As a practitioner in a helping profession, I have spent many years working with executives who are trying to become more effective but also want to retain their humaneness. On a micro level, I try to help individuals to make sense out of their lives. On a more macro level, my life's task has been to bring the human dimension back into the organization – to create the kinds of organization that bring out the best in people, that retain a human quality. Unfortunately, in my work, I have seen too many organizations that resemble gulags.

I have also seen it as my task to do everything in my power to prevent dysfunctional, pathological leadership. One of my motives for this was that I was born in occupied Holland during the Second World War, a period that wrought immeasurable human tragedy. So it should not come as a surprise that the terrible consequences of pathological leadership have always been at the top of my mind. I have always been curious why some people in a leadership position abuse the power that comes with the job. What is the fundamental difference between the Mugabes and the Mandelas of this world? Lord Acton's words have been much quoted – "Power corrupts, and absolute power corrupts absolutely" – but that does not make them any less true. When the sirens of power beckon, some people cannot resist the call.

However, we should never underestimate the altruistic motive that is part of our human DNA. *Homo sapiens* evolved rapidly to become the most sophisticated species on earth largely because of our ability to engage in cooperative behavior. We should not give up on humanity. I believe there is reason to hope for the best – surely that is the meaning of the story of Pandora's box?

Without hope, there is no life. As Napoleon Bonaparte said – and he should know – "Leaders are merchants of hope." Leaders need to speak to the collective imagination of their people to create a group identity, to help people become better than they think they are, a task that I have taken very seriously in my work as a leadership coach. I help people to have dreams about the future. And I like to see people acting on those dreams.

True enough, when I look at the world around me, I don't see many signs of the kind of leadership that transforms people, leaders who help people to live fully and with hope. On the contrary, delusional, wishful thinking seems to be more *de rigueur*, leaders who try to appeal to our tendency toward wishful thinking. There are not many "twice-born" leaders among us. Far from it: we are currently faced with leadership meltdowns everywhere as political leaders exhibit behavior that should be excised from the leadership equation. Unfortunately, in this age of greed and anxiety, short-term expediency prevails, while bold, imaginative leadership is sorely missing. "Twice-born" thinking is notable by its absence. Often, the only thing to be noted is how one form of pathological leadership is replaced by another. In spite of this depressing picture, however, I have not given up on my work with leaders. My hope is that a new generation of leaders will rise to the challenge. I am certainly prepared to do all I can to help them move forward.

"There are not many 'twice-born' leaders among us"

As I suggested earlier, we are not rational decision makers. We all have many blind spots that need attention. To become aware of these blind spots, we do well to pay heed to the words written above the Temple of Apollo in ancient Delphi: "Know thyself." This observation is as relevant today as it has ever been. If we want to develop more effective leaders we have to start with ourselves. But as I have discovered, to paraphrase Goethe, what is often hardest to see is what is right in front of your eyes.

The most exemplary leader of our age, Nelson Mandela, once said, "You can never have an impact on society if you have not changed yourself." To get this message across, I often use metaphors to describe the key actors and primary forces that take the stage in the inner theater that plays in all of us. I tell the leaders I work with that we all have to manage the elephants, hedgehogs, and Ouroboros we harbor within ourselves.

Metaphorically speaking, the elephant is our character, a part of us that can have a powerful and uncontrollable effect on our actions. We often fail to understand what the elephant inside us is doing. It has many faces. For example, the elephant is quite narcissistic. We have a tendency to view ourselves through rose-colored spectacles. The elephant is also paranoid. We are inclined to look at the world with suspicion, an outlook that can have dire consequences. The elephant is into tit-for-tat when it has been wronged. It doesn't take hurts easily. Finally, the elephant is lazy. It is very reluctant to change its behavior. And while the elephant is alive and creating havoc in all of us, it is only by acknowledging its existence, and playing "judo" with it (i.e. using its strength against itself), that we can learn to live with it.

And what about hedgehogs? The great German philosopher Arthur Schopenhauer drew an analogy between humans' and hedgehogs' unease with social proximity. In cold weather, hedgehogs cluster together for warmth but soon find that their spines hurt each other. Yet when they withdraw, they very quickly get cold again. Eventually, after a lot of shuffling and reshuffling, they find the optimum distance for warmth and comfort. For human hedgehogs, this conundrum – our simultaneous need for closeness and distance – is a fundamental reason why people often find it so difficult to work successfully in groups, teams, organizations, and civil society.

The third animal in our inner menagerie is a mythical one, the Ouroboros, usually depicted as a serpent or dragon swallowing its own tail. The Ouroboros symbolizes the cyclical nature of the universe: creation out of destruction, life out of death. The Ouroboros eats its own tail to sustain its life, in an eternal cycle of reinvention and renewal.

The Ouroboros symbolism should remind leaders that things cannot remain the same eternally, that there are times when they have to break with the past. Unfortunately, there are far too many leaders who fit Albert Einstein's alleged definition of insanity: "doing the same thing over and over again, expecting different results." Some people don't seem to know that when we find we are riding a dead horse, the best thing to do is to dismount.

Group coaching for change

The ability to work effectively as a leader is essential in 21st-century organizations. The price tag of dysfunctionality can be staggering. And as leaders in this century, more than ever, need to be effective team players, ways to make that happen take on overriding importance. To enable better team dynamics, in much of my research and writing I have made a plea for leadership group coaching as an experiential training ground for creating more effective leaders. My leadership group coaching model (incorporating the life case study), has been developed over more than 20 years of delivering programs to senior executives, and is now successfully applied all over the world. It is a process whereby people are gently nudged to take an inner journey, and to reinvent themselves.

As I said earlier, one of the hats I wear is that of a psychoanalyst, and in that guise I have focused on the darker side of leadership and organizational life. After researching and writing extensively about dysfunctional leadership and organizations, I began to pay more attention to functionality – what makes for effective leadership. It is now more than a decade since I truly went into the leadership development business, having been the founder of a leadership development center that has become one of the largest in the world – and the largest in leadership group coaching. Through my work in this center, I have been trying to make human hedgehogs more effective and humane. I have helped them dissect the elephant. I have also encouraged them to face the Ouroboros. I have been trying to help leaders create what I have called authentizotic organizations – places of work in which people feel at their best. In this kind of organization, people find meaning in their work, celebrate the people they work with, have pride in what they are doing, and trust the people they work for and with. Such a view of organizations may be idealistic, but (as I said before) without hope, there is no life.

For many years, I taught the core Organizational Behavior course in various MBA programs around the world. I always enjoyed giving this course. I felt it was a gift to be able to guide young men and women in making wise choices about their interpersonal relationships and career. I wanted to help them understand better their own elephant, hedgehog, and Ouroboros.

In my final class, I used to show the students *Wild Strawberries*, a 1957 black-and-white masterpiece directed by Ingmar Bergman. *Wild Strawberries* tells the story of an old man, Isak Borg, who is making two journeys – one from Stockholm to Lund to receive an honorary doctorate, the other more personal, a trip into his inner world. Helped by a combination of dreams, daydreams, fantasies, and various encounters on the way to the ceremony (including one with his very icy mother) he obtains a remarkable insight into his personal inner theater, the quality of his interpersonal relationships, and the kind of muddles and mistakes he has made during his life's journey. We really come to understand his elephant, his hedgehog, and his struggles with the Ouroboros. In spite of all the setbacks he encounters, it is a journey of hope. Even at his advanced age, and guided by the various people he meets on this journey, he opens up to change. One of the messages of the film is that it is never too late – but as we all know, a *sine qua non* in any change process is the will to change yourself.

A goal I have set myself as a teacher is to help people feel better in their skin – to help them attain a modicum of happiness. In that respect, I am a believer in the notion that happiness is not just a question of good health and a bad memory, but more importantly, having something to do, someone to love, and something to hope for. Happiness doesn't come as a result of gaining something we don't have but by recognizing and appreciating the things we do have.

> "Happiness doesn't come as a result of gaining something we don't have but by recognizing and appreciating the things we do have"

The ancient Greeks believed that our life's journey lies at the intersection of the Moerae, or Fates, three goddesses who spin our inescapable destiny; the goddess Fortuna, symbolizing luck and chance; and the daemon, which represents our inner theater, guiding our steps. The way these various dramatic personae interact will always be a work in progress. And in dealing with this work in progress, it is not good enough to complain about the poor hand of cards we may have been dealt. The challenge of life is to make the best out of a poor hand. True leadership shows itself in tough situations. And as I said earlier, many of today's leaders fail that test miserably. They badly need to get in touch with the Ouroboros inside them. Great leaders, however, ponder the question what they would like to leave behind as a legacy in life. How do we want to be remembered? I believe that true leaders take the kinds of action that will benefit the next generation.

About this book

Over the past few years there has been an explosion of interest in leadership coaching in terms of the number of practicing coaches, and the number of individuals and organizations seeking out leadership coaching relationships. This rise in demand in coaching has been met by a rise in the amount of published work in this field. This book tries to be different from most of these by applying a lens of psychodynamic mindfulness to look at leadership coaching.

This book is intended primarily for those who want to learn more about leadership coaching, including executives looking for coaching possibilities, human resources professionals charged with creating a coaching initiative, scholars studying the leadership coaching field, and coaches themselves.

This book takes an in-depth, mindful look at the coaching process. It focuses on the diversity of individual and organizational learning and change with a deep appreciation of the complexities of the human mind. It explores not only the strategic and behavioral benefits of leadership coaching, but also its potential to serve as a foundation for adult development and transformation. The insights provided in this book will help coaches and executives to use frameworks for transforming attitudes, beliefs, and behaviors.

As I have mentioned before, this book is written for people interested in coaching who want to know more about how clinical insights can help the people they work with. In writing this text, I have tried to demystify the language around psychodynamic thinking and mindfulness, applying many of its concepts to the leadership coaching practice. I will illustrate that the main idea of the clinical approach is to work with the coachee's past, present, and future in order to provide insight about the reasons for specific behavior patterns.

I also will try to clarify how the careful use of the clinical approach in coaching will enable a deeper understanding of what's happening "below the surface." I strongly believe that these kinds of clinical interventions can deliver real benefits to organizations in that they contribute to a deeper understanding of the significance and meaning of personal patterns and the inner structure of a person's personality, complex human relationships (including deeply buried and repressed emotions), and the role of teams, group dynamics, and organizational processes. Through a skillful application of the clinical approach, my hope is that the reader will acquire the kind of knowledge – and mindfulness – that creates a solid basis for more effective performance in the future. In addition, by furthering this kind of awareness and insight, such an approach will be helpful in dealing with situations that are not resolved by more conventional interventions.

In this book, I will also dwell on the fact that to coach people successfully, it will be essential for both the coach and coachee to understand the degree to which their actions are affected by what is going on below the surface. This necessitates an exploration of the clients' own personality, their implicit underlying values, the experiences that have shaped their character, and the kind of effects they have on others. Furthermore, I explore how these dynamics influence the undercurrents operating in teams or organizations. Such deeper understanding will help the people who are being coached to function in a more effective manner in whatever situation they will find themselves. Thus in the summing up, the clinical approach to coaching will help people to remove the kinds of individual and organizational defensive screens that typically distort the quality and reality of cooperative relationships at work. By doing so, it will open a way towards constructing a more fulfilling and complete life in the organization.

This book falls into two parts. The first five chapters deal with important presenting issues in leadership coaching and the remaining chapters discuss coaching aims and techniques. Chapter 1 deals with attachment, a subject of unequivocal importance. If we want to better understand human functioning, we need to understand attachment patterns. Chapter 2 examines forgiveness, the capacity which differentiates mediocre executives from great ones. Victim and rescuer roles always come to the fore in coaching relationships. The "games these people play" are explored in Chapters 3 and 4. Chapter 5 deals with people I describe as "SOB executives" – in this case, SOB stands for seductive operational bully and describes the dysfunctional behavior that nevertheless manages to bring this type of executive considerable success. This touches on a very sensitive theme of organizational life – we should all beware the psychopath in the C suite.

In the second part of the book, I change focus and address a number of critical coaching concerns, supported by case examples. The subject of Chapter 6 is the journey an individual takes toward coaching – what it takes to become an executive coach and, in particular, what it takes to be able to deal with groups. Chapter 7 is about helping executives to learn how to play and creating a safe space in which they can do so. These are skills all coaches need to have. Without playfulness, there will be no change. Tipping points and the dynamics of change are discussed in Chapter 8. Finally, in the concluding chapter, I present a number of concerns I have about the future of coaching, after discussing perhaps the best-known and oldest coaching example we know about – the relationship between Aristotle and Alexander the Great.

My aim, in touching on these various themes, is to help the leaders of the organizations of the future understand the importance of a coaching culture to organizational success. The creation of organizational cultures where people have voice will enable them to deal with the diversity of the workforce, markets, and suppliers and help them appreciate how these elements will affect strategies, productivity, market penetration, customer service, recruitment costs, turnover rate, and other organizational dynamics. Organizations that recognize the benefits of leadership coaching can profit in many different ways: improved interpersonal skills; out-of-the-box thinking; better conflict management; more effective team behavior; an improved ability to manage and advance personal career goals and the career goals of others; and the ability to create a coaching culture, and authentizotic organizations – best places to work.

In writing the chapters in this book, I bore in mind that good leadership coaches take leaders where they want to go. Great coaches, however, will take them to undiscovered shores. Throughout, I make a consistent plea that coaches take a reflective stand. Leadership coaches are not sport coaches. Taking a reflective stand – practicing mindfulness – cautions against knee-jerk reactions in leadership coaching. Exceptional coaches have the ability to acquire knowledge and analyze it both logically and emotionally, the true test being the ability to recognize a problem before it becomes an emergency. We should all aim to be exceptional coaches. To paraphrase a German proverb, "Those who coach must hear and be deaf, must see and be blind."

Chapter 1

The Attachment Imperative: The Hedgehog's Kiss

Ich hab' noch einen Koffer in Berlin
– Marlene Dietrich

Home's where you go when you run out of homes
– John le Carré

One does not discover new continents without consenting
to lose sight of the shore for a very long time
– André Gide

Introduction

How do people relate to one another? How much closeness can we tolerate? Let's look at a couple of scenarios.

First, imagine you're a highly successful professional (you may be one, of course). You have always been effective in your work but most of your relationships are superficial and short-lived, both at the office and in your personal life. Is this "normal" or are you different from other people? You know you are uncomfortable being too close to others and have always found it difficult to give them your complete trust. And you hate being dependent on anyone. But although you never feel the need to be close to others, there are times when you ask yourself whether there's something missing from your life. It seems impossible for you to form deep relationships. Perhaps you have shallow relationships because they are the only kind you are comfortable with. Is there something wrong with you?

Now, let's suppose you are a different executive. One of your colleagues in the office is irritatingly clingy. Whatever you do and wherever you go, she's always around. At first you were flattered to be the subject of so much attention but it has started to make you feel suffocated. In the nicest possible way, you have tried to tell her you need some distance but she doesn't appear to want to hear you. Instead, she complains that her relationships with other people are no longer what they used to be, and she is clearly upset that no one apart from herself seems to be bothered about it. This makes you wonder whether her behavior is really so inappropriate. Is she being cold-shouldered? Who has the wrong attitude, she or you? Yet it doesn't feel right to have her hanging around you all the time. It's as if she only feels OK when she has someone she can go through life with. How much clinginess is normal?

These two examples are snapshots of the dynamics of the interpersonal field, the kind of scenarios the German philosopher Arthur Schopenhauer used his famous parable of the hedgehogs to illustrate (see p. 15). Schopenhauer thought his hedgehogs provided a very appropriate symbol of the human condition. How close can you get to others before you start to feel uncomfortable? Some people can get very close; for others, closeness is anathema. To obtain a deeper understanding of what goes on in human encounters, we need to explore attachment behavior – how dependent we are on other people for emotional satisfaction. What is the nature of the ties that bind us to others and endure over time?

Our behavior toward others derives from the kind of attachment pattern we have learned to be comfortable with. The roots of what makes up our comfort and discomfort run very deep. The template for all our relationships is laid down at a very impressionable age, with the early "dance" between mother (caregiver) and child. Early mother-child interaction patterns determine the nature and quality of present and future attachments. New relationships will be affected by the expectations developed at this early stage of development.

"Early mother-child interaction patterns determine the nature and quality of present and future attachments"

In these early years, a blueprint is created that will influence the way we relate to others throughout our life and even across generations.[1] For example, as parents, insecurely attached adults may lack the ability to form a strong attachment to their children. They will be unable to provide the necessary attachment cues required for a child's healthy emotional development, thereby predisposing their children to a lifetime of relationship difficulties. In this way, what was initially a dyadic issue turns into a generational issue. Attachment problems may continue from generation to generation unless an individual breaks the chain. Understanding these developments makes it even more important to know the nature of our relationship patterns.

Attachment disorders in children can usually be traced to the effects of having an emotionally unavailable caregiver, that is, a primary contact who is either withholding, inconsistent, physically absent, or frequently changing.[2] This scenario can be exacerbated by separation from parents, due to death or divorce, or physical or sexual abuse during childhood. Children growing up in this kind of environment will be burdened with problems of self-esteem and identity formation, and be prone to dysfunctional interpersonal relationships.

These difficulties can play themselves out very differently as children grow up. Some children may become overly clingy, always fearful that any relationship they are in will fall apart. Other children (subjected to other kinds of parental dysfunction) will develop feelings of detachment, failing to form long and lasting relationships with anyone and finding it very difficult to trust even those close to them. If not checked in good time, these patterns will continue into adulthood and predispose an individual to a lifetime of relationship difficulties that manifest themselves in the way interpersonal relationships (both at work and at home) unfold.

What is attachment?

In its simplest form, attachment is a deep and enduring emotional bond established between a child and caregiver during the first years of life. The way this relationship unfolds, positively or negatively, will set the tone for all future relationships.[3]

In his seminal work on attachment, the psychoanalyst John Bowlby noted that children's mental representations or working models of relationships lay the foundation for all their future relationships and experiences.[4] According to Bowlby, attachment and separation are elemental forces that drive our behaviors and decisions and the failure to form a secure attachment with a caregiver can be linked to

> "attachment and separation are elemental forces that drive our behaviors and decisions"

several types of problem behavior. The way these attachment patterns resolve themselves influences our self-efficacy (our belief in our ability to complete tasks successfully), self-confidence (our positive perceptions of our general abilities), and self-esteem (our feeling of self-worth and self-satisfaction).

The ability to form attachments is biologically driven and is part of our evolutionary heritage. We are born with a repertoire of preprogrammed, instinctive, biological behaviors that help us survive as infants. Infants who seek the closeness and security of their mother (or other primary caregiver) will have an evolutionary advantage. The children of mothers who are responsive to their needs and provide security are more likely to survive and pass on their genes.[5] Babies' crying, smiling, grasping, and clinging are very purposeful activities. Such behavior will keep them close to their primary caregivers who will protect them from danger, feed and comfort them, and teach them what's good and bad about the world in which they live. This intensive *pas de deux* is facilitated because parents also have instinctive behavior patterns, such as soothing babies when they cry, caressing them, making sounds that appeal to them, and mirroring them (i.e., playfully imitating a baby's facial expressions), all of which enforce caring behavior. The main purpose of these processes is to maintain proximity between infant and caregiver, ensuring the infant's safety and protection, essential factors for the continuity of the species.[6]

Based on the nature and quality of their early attachments, children develop systems of thought, memory, belief, expectation, emotions, and behavior that act as a template for the way they engage in and handle all future relationships. How these attachment patterns work themselves out in our inner theater very much depends on the nature and quality of repeated interactions with our caregivers. Depending on their responsiveness (especially in situations of stress), specific working models of relationships are constructed in our inner theater. These can be positive (i.e., people can be trusted, confided in, helpful in distress) or negative (i.e., no one can be trusted, people are not really caring, we are all alone in the world).

Although Bowlby focused primarily on understanding the nature of the infant-caregiver relationship and its implications for socio-emotional development, he also asserted that the schemas of self and others, created from the parent-child interaction, are present in other kinds of relationships: "Attachment is an important component of human experience from the cradle to the grave."[7] He suggested that the same motivational system that underlies infants' attachments to their caregivers also underlies the emotional bond that develops between people later in life. These early relationship patterns will influence us throughout the course of our life.

As we mature, we transfer attachment relationship patterns from our parents to other people in our life. The quality of attachment established early in life will affect all our adult relationships, including romantic love, friendship, and workplace behavior.[8] The way individuals talk about themselves and their feelings reveals how they have organized their attachment experiences and how they will regulate their behavior toward others. People with a secure working model will be more likely to engage in positive behavior, while the opposite will be the case for people who have an insecure working model.

Attachment scenarios

In their child observation studies, the developmental psychologist Mary Ainsworth and her colleagues (expanding on Bowlby's work) described a number of attachment patterns in infants that become internalized, and have an effect on mature functioning.[9] They singled out three basic attachment styles: secure (positive), anxious-ambivalent, and avoidant (both dysfunctional).

Positive attachment patterns

Secure attachment
Parents of securely attached children react rapidly to their children's needs and are generally responsive. They also tend to play and are involved

with their children. Due to their consistent, appropriate responsiveness, a secure bond will be established between caregiver and child, resulting in the child's openness to emotional experiences and willingness to engage in creative and productive emotional interaction. Such parents have created a "secure base" for their children, which enables them to venture successfully into the world. This secure base contributes to a child's healthy cognitive and social development; it establishes trust and reciprocity, which becomes a pattern for all future emotional relationships.

Securely attached infants are prepared to explore their environment when the caregiver is present. Although they may display some degree of separation anxiety when a parent leaves, they are easily comforted upon their return. Drawing on their basic sense of security, they will perceive other people as dependable, caring, and trustworthy.

As time passes, secure children mature into secure adults, who expect others to be trustworthy and responsive, a *Weltanschauung* that reinforces their sense of inner security. These people regard themselves as wanted, worthwhile, competent, and lovable. They will form a secure sense of self, which includes a sense of competence, self-worth, and a healthy balance between dependence and autonomy. Secure attachment patterns also contribute to the development of empathy, compassion, and conscience.

Dysfunctional attachment

When attachment needs are not met, children feel insecure. They learn as infants that proximity seeking does not elicit satisfactory responses from caregivers. Children subjected to dysfunctional childrearing feel bad, unwanted, worthless, helpless, and unlovable. They perceive others as insensitive, hurtful, and untrustworthy, unresponsive to their needs. And they perceive the world as unsafe and life as painful and burdensome.

These children may resort to desperate strategies to get some kind of response from their caregivers, one of which is hyper-activation, the other deactivation – in other words, activities that focus on moving toward people or moving away from them. These strategies can be interpreted as exaggerations of the primary attachment strategy. The first (anxious-ambivalent) manifests itself through intense protest or energetic efforts to regain proximity; the second (avoidant) is characterized by the suppression or denial of attachment needs and the maintenance of distance in relationships.[10] Some of these children will always be on the lookout for comfort and attention, while others – the avoidant ones – may resort to emotional distancing and greater reliance on themselves than others.

Anxious-ambivalent attached children are more fearful and less confident than infants who are securely attached. Inconsistent support from caregivers during the vulnerable years of early childhood creates feelings of persistent anxiety associated with interpersonal relationships, and exaggerated levels of negative emotions. Having been exposed to an unpredictable combination of responsiveness and rejection, these children become anxious and ambivalent. They demonstrate extreme separation distress when a parent leaves, and ambivalence or anger upon their return. They monitor their caregivers more closely, attempt to stay by their side and respond more dramatically when they are in trouble. In adulthood, a pattern of anxious-ambivalent attachment is characterized by chronic worry and anxiety over the availability and responsiveness of people important to them; this can make them appear clingy and emotionally needy. To elaborate on Schopenhauer's metaphor, they are the hedgehogs that try to come too close.

Avoidant attached children have problems with intimacy – an outcome of the unavailability and non-responsiveness of their caregivers. They are uncomfortable being close to others and proximity makes them nervous. Although they may want emotionally close relationships, they cannot handle them. They demonstrate few signs of needing their caregivers; they do not spend a lot of time trying to get their caregivers' attention; and they do their best to cope with problems on their own. Distancing has become a defensive psychological strategy. They are unlikely to feel (or express) empathy, and may even take pleasure in the misery of others. Their behavior can be deeply infuriating. These are the hedgehogs that keep their distance, fearful of getting hurt.

Adult attachment patterns

In adulthood, the early template of attachment will shape the quality of an individual's subsequent attachment experiences.[11] This doesn't mean, however, that attachment patterns are written in stone. Existing representations can be updated and revised in the light of new experiences. Attachment challenges early in life will not deterministically predispose an individual to a life of insecure attachment. However, early dysfunctional attachment can contribute later in life to repetitive patterns of unhealthy and conflictual relationships. It is highly likely that people with adult attachment disorders will display negative and

"early dysfunctional attachment can contribute later in life to repetitive patterns of unhealthy and conflictual relationships"

provocative behavior patterns and engage in self-destructive behavior. Often, feelings of detachment, anger, and frustration are their constant companions. They don't know how to connect to others, let alone how to create any emotional bonds. Their need for control means that they are more likely to lie, cheat, and be very manipulative. They may have inferior communication and listening skills, and find it difficult to accept any form of guidance.

People with attachment disorders tend to lack empathy. They find it difficult to give and receive affection. They often feel depressed and sad but do not necessarily show their feelings. They find it difficult to compromise and when they find themselves in a healthy relationship, may be tempted to destroy it preemptively. Such behavior can be seen as a form of protective reaction – a way of managing anxiety – as they fear the other party will break up the relationship anyhow. At the core of this self-destructive pattern is often an unconscious fear of success. They are tempted to sabotage themselves when things are going exceptionally well.

Types or dimensions?

More recent works on attachment behavior have proposed four attachment styles[12] and can be seen as an elaboration of the three-group attachment style model originally proposed by Ainsworth and her associates.[13] This alternative model is differentiated by the use of a dimensional as opposed to a stylistic approach to the study of attachment behavior.

According to this model, it is possible to organize reactions between two parties within a two-dimensional space. The *anxiety* dimension corresponds to anxiety and vigilance about rejection and abandonment. The *avoidance* dimension corresponds to the discomfort associated with closeness and dependency – the reluctance to be intimate with others.

These two orthogonal dimensions describe general patterns of thoughts, feelings, and behaviors that occur within the context of relationships.

In this conceptual scheme, people who score high on anxiety tend to worry whether the other person is available, responsive, and attentive. People who score low are more secure in the expected responsiveness of their partners. In the case of avoidance, people at the high end of this dimension prefer not to rely on or open up to others. People at the low end are more comfortable about intimacy with others and more secure about depending on others and having others depend on them.

In this dimensional system, the secure and anxious-ambivalent classifications were retained from the three-category model, but the avoidant category was split into two: *fearful-avoidance* and *dismissing-avoidance*.[14]

The adult relationship "dance"

Secure attachment: Using this framework, a prototypical secure adult would score low on both these dimensions (low anxiety/low avoidance). People who form secure attachments in childhood are likely to have secure attachment patterns in adulthood. Such individuals have a strong sense of self and want close relationships with others. They have a relatively high sense of self-esteem, feel liked by others, and build relationships relatively easily.[15]

"secure attachments in childhood are likely to produce secure attachment patterns in adulthood"

They hold positive representations of the self (e.g., viewing themselves as worthy and lovable) and of others (e.g., viewing them as responsive, attentive). They tend to have trusting, long-term relationships and very few worries about abandonment. Their lives are well-balanced: they are secure in both their independence and their close relationships. They tend to have a positive view of life and know how to manage and express their feelings. They have good social skills. They are comfortable sharing feelings with friends and partners. They are willing to disclose their true thoughts, feelings, wishes, and fears. These people have learned that, when they feel stressed or threatened, seeking proximity (a primary attachment strategy) brings comfort and relief. They are prepared to seek out social support when needed. They enjoy intimate relationships. A secure attachment pattern also provides a defense against stress and trauma, making for resourcefulness and resilience. In addition, these feelings of inner security contribute to the ability to self-regulate, which results in effective management of impulses and emotions. In general, the world feels safe; life is worth living.

Anxious-ambivalent (preoccupied): Adults who have an *anxious-ambivalent* (preoccupied) attachment style (low on avoidance/high on anxiety) are very self-critical and insecure. Their lives are not balanced: their insecurity turns them against themselves and leaves them emotionally desperate in their relationships. In relationships, they can be very clingy or even smothering, appearing anxious, needy, in constant need of comfort, and never satisfied by attention from others. They are very high maintenance, as they constantly want to be heard. This kind of attachment behavior is also characterized by feelings of unworthiness and a constant need for others' approval. As a result, others are reluctant to get as close to them as they would like them to be. Realizing this, they become concerned that others don't like them. The fear of rejection is an ever-present shadow and is the engine that drives them to be overly dependent on others.

But in spite of their continuous search for approval and reassurance from others, nothing anyone else does will ever be enough to alleviate their self-doubt. Their worries about their likeability lead to frequent breakups, often because the relationship feels cold and distant. Given their high level of anxiety, they may want to "merge" completely with another person. Ironically, it's precisely this that scares others even further away.

Furthermore, they may provoke conflict to "test" others. This is their way of finding out whether others will really stick with them in all circumstances, in spite of their negative behavior. But because of their provocative behavior, their relationship founders and their worst fears come true. These are the hedgehogs that struggle to find an appropriate distance.

Using the dimensional approach, the high avoidant dimension presents two options: *dismissing avoidant* (low anxiety/high avoidance) and *fearful avoidant* (high anxiety/high avoidance), which has parallels to the often-described schizoid and avoidant personality types.[16] For example, people who grew up with disorganized, absent parents often develop avoidant patterns of attachment. Since, as children, they detached from their feelings during times of trauma, as adults, they continue to be somewhat detached from themselves. These people's lives are not balanced: they do not have a coherent sense of self nor do they have a clear connection with others. They find relating to others extremely difficult. While fearful avoidant people want human interaction and contact but are afraid of rejection, dismissive avoidant people seem to be completely unable to form personal relationships. They are uncomfortable being and interacting with others. But they don't seem to care. They prefer isolation. The problem for the rest of us is that it is not easy for us to determine what avoidant type we are dealing with.

Fearful avoidant: Fearful avoidant people avoid attachment relationships in order to prevent being hurt or rejected by their partners. Although they would like to have emotionally close relationships, they find it difficult to trust others completely, or to depend on them. They are unable or unwilling to share their thoughts or feelings with others. They often make excuses to avoid intimacy (such as working long hours or the need to travel). They are afraid of being hurt if they allow themselves to become too close to others. They invest little emotion in romantic and social relationships and experience only a modicum of distress when a relationship ends. Other common characteristics include a failure to support partners during stressful times. Empathy does not come naturally to them.

Dismissive avoidant: Dismissive avoidant people are quite comfortable with themselves and experience no need for closeness. They are cerebral individuals with an extremely strong defensive system and have deeply suppressed their emotional side. This is a highly defensive mode of self-reliance. They want to feel independent and self-sufficient, not to depend on others or have others depend on them. The desire for independence often appears to be an attempt to avoid attachment altogether, and remaining invulnerable to feelings associated with close attachment to others. They tend to be loners and regard relationships and emotions as relatively unimportant. Their typical response to conflict and stressful situations is to distance themselves. Their lives are not balanced: they are turned in on themselves, isolated, and emotionally removed from others.

What is your attachment style?

This short questionnaire is based on several different assessment instruments developed and used by attachment researchers.[17] It is designed to measure your attachment style – the way you relate to others. When you have completed it, you will know more about your basic attachment style and how it influences your relationships. While this questionnaire cannot fully describe every aspect of your attachment style, it can provide a quick assessment of how you relate to others. Answer the questions as honestly as you can, rating each item on a scale of 1 to 5.

1 = Strongly disagree
2 = Disagree
3 = Neutral
4 = Agree
5 = Strongly agree

1. I feel people withdraw when I get too close to them.
   1 2 3 4 5

2. I spend a great deal of time worrying about my relationships with others.
   1 2 3 4 5

3. I often expect the worst to happen in a relationship.
   1 2 3 4 5

4. I worry that people will not like me when they know what I am about.
   1 2 3 4 5

5. I find it difficult to assume that other people care about me.
   1 2 3 4 5

6. I always worry that I am not good enough.
   1 2 3 4 5

7. I worry that others care less about me than I care about them.
   1 2 3 4 5

8. I am always yearning for something or someone I feel I cannot have and rarely feel satisfied.
   1 2 3 4 5

9. I need others constantly to show that they like me.
   1 2 3 4 5

10. I often worry that people close to me will leave me.
    1 2 3 4 5

11. I find it difficult to express positive emotions to others.
    1 2 3 4 5

12. I become uncomfortable when other people express emotions.
    1 2 3 4 5

13. I find it difficult to talk to others about my problems and concerns.
    1 2 3 4 5

14. I will never be really intimate in my relationships with others.
    1 2 3 4 5

15. I prefer not to be too close to people.
    1 2 3 4 5

16. I feel uncomfortable in opening up to other people.
    1 2 3 4 5

17. I am uncomfortable going to others in times of need.
    1 2 3 4 5

18. I pull away when other people try to get too close.
    1 2 3 4 5

19. I find it very important to have "alone" time.
    1 2 3 4 5

20. I find it difficult to depend on anybody.
    1 2 3 4 5

Calculate your score on the basis that an answer of 1 equals 1 point, 2 equals 2 points, and so on.

While this questionnaire cannot fully describe every aspect of your attachment style, it can provide a basis for understanding more about the kind of style you prefer. If your total is 40 points or fewer, you appear to have a secure attachment style. People with secure attachments feel more comfortable with themselves and their relationships. They are prepared to share their feelings with others, and are likely to turn to others for support. They tend to have happier, long-lasting relationships, and are less subjected to psychological disorders.

If your score on questions 1 to 10 is 40 or more, you may have an anxious-ambivalent style. People in this category are usually less satisfied with their relationships than securely attached people. Since they feel an excessive desire to be close to others, they can be clingy, suspicious, dependent, jealous, controlling, and even at times domineering.

If your score on questions 11 to 20 is 40 or more, you may have an avoidant style. The higher the score, the more avoidant you tend to be. Avoidant people have difficulties in their interpersonal relationships. They tend to avoid forming attachments to others, and, if they do attempt to do so, the relationship may be characterized by mistrust or a lack of confidence. In this test, however, no effort was made to single out dismissive from fearful avoidants.

Changing dysfunctional attachment patterns

Although there are no quick fixes for people with attachment disorders, which can be quite resistant to change, attachment styles can be modified. Positive life experiences and/or appropriate interventions can be the catalysts to changing relationship patterns. However, making such changes happen is a process, not an event. Modifying dysfunctional relationship patterns represents a real journey.

"modifying dysfunctional relationship patterns represents a real journey"

As for most change processes, this journey of change needs to start by recognizing that there is a problem. There are a number of signs and symptoms that are indicative of dysfunctional attachment patterns,[18] summarized in Exhibit 1.1.

EXHIBIT 1.1 SIGNS AND SYMPTOMS OF ATTACHMENT PROBLEMS

Anxious-ambivalent:

- Problems with self-esteem
- Finding others unpredictable/difficult to understand
- Idealization and devaluation of relationships
- Possessive/needy/clingy behavior
- Impulsiveness
- Failure to take personal responsibility for problem situations
- Feeling underappreciated/wronged
- Perceiving relationships as unbalanced

- Unstable relationships
- Lack of self-control/extreme emotions
- Confusion
- Discomfort with anger
- Sensitivity to rejection
- Jealousy
- Difficulties in dealing with life's adversities
- Addictive behavior

Avoidant:

- Difficulties with genuine trust, intimacy, and affection
- Relationships feel either threatening to one's sense of control, or not worth the effort, or both
- Difficulties with authority figures
- Compulsive self-reliance
- Sensitivity to blame
- Inability to give support to others
- Perceiving others as undependable
- Difficulties in maintaining friendships
- Using work as an excuse to avoid personal relations
- Difficulties in expressing emotions
- Apparent lack of empathy
- Pessimistic view of people and society
- Negative or provocative behavior

Many people with attachment disorders have a deep desire for love and affection but are unable to express this desire effectively. They want to be accepted but do not really have the skills to achieve acceptance. Negative experiences in childhood have directed them toward defensive scenarios (for example, denial and repression) as ways of coping with deeply rooted emotional issues.[19] Typically, they also have a tendency to blame others (projection) for their problems. Negative self-perceptions, however, often cause them to blame themselves as well. These people may engage in very self-destructive activities. If several traumatic losses have occurred, it becomes hard to differentiate between self-sabotage or the roll of the dice of life.

Steps toward change

Homo sapiens has a great capacity for rationalization. We are extremely talented at deluding ourselves. To create preparedness for change, a multi-prong effort will be needed, however, with effective interventions on many different levels. Possible change strategies include psychodynamic understanding, cognitive and emotional restructuring, family and group psychotherapy, paradoxical intervention, motivational interviewing, and the use of psychodrama (role playing) to break through the barriers of the mind and prompt these people to reveal (and actualize) emotional issues. Sometimes a psychiatrist's involvement may be needed if there is evidence of mood disturbances caused by chemical imbalances in the brain. (For example, antidepressant medication can often make people with attachment disorders less sensitive to feelings of rejection.) A combination of medication and talking therapy (psychotherapy) may be more effective than either form of treatment by itself.[20]

If people with attachment disorders have decided to ask for help, the coach or therapist first needs to create a safe environment in which they can face their inner demons. A healing atmosphere or environment must be in place so that people feel able to reveal their vulnerability. The goal is to help these individuals develop the capacity to trust and express emotions in a more appropriate manner than they have done in the past. This is the first step toward living a happier and more productive life.

Depending on the type of attachment disorder that is presented, a coach/therapist needs to vary the intervention technique. For example, a key problem for people with anxious-ambivalent attachment disorders is the inability to self-soothe. Unable to do this for themselves, they look to other people to do it for them. The product of this incapacity is a panic reaction manifested as extreme clingy, needy behavior. They are frightened that the relationship will fall apart and of the emotional devastation that may follow. From a cognitive point of view, it is important to enable these people to reduce their level of anxiety by substituting negative thoughts with positive ones, as negativity fuels anxiety. Many anxious-ambivalent people make unverified, negative assumptions about what others are thinking. Unfortunately, such negative thought processes become self-fulfilling prophecies. Given their talent for cognitive distortion, they tend to blow small issues out of proportion, and as a defensive reaction may break relationships for no real reason at all.

Because of their inability to talk properly about what bothers them, and their lack of interpersonal skills, anxious-ambivalent people often find themselves in impossible situations. They are extremely talented at miscommunication and frequently set traps for themselves. Learning how to communicate effectively will therefore be one of the main goals in coaching/therapeutic interventions. Because these people are highly likely to have grown up in contexts where they were unable to talk about their problems and resolve conflict, learning how to communicate effectively in order to resolve their own issues must be a high priority.

Unraveling the strands of the past will help any journey of personal insight. People with attachment disorders need to come to grips with the issues from the past that are the source of their dysfunctional relationship patterns. Typically, they will have incoherent and partial unconscious memories of their caregivers, due to serious childhood trauma. It will be important for them to sort out how they experienced these childhood difficulties. They have to transcend old, dysfunctional behavior patterns, and find new ones that are more adaptive to their current stage in life. They also need to become aware of the role they themselves play in the creation of interpersonal difficulties. They need to recognize their personal responsibility in creating conflict within relationships.

Learning how to confront unresolved childhood grief, with the help of others, will be a major part of such interventions. They need to realize that what may have been an effective survival strategy when they were young may no longer be effective in adulthood. As trust is difficult for many of these people, trust exercises can form the homework to accompany an intervention program. Essentially, they need to reframe their perceptions of others and become more trusting. They need to confront their self-defeating behaviors and face the difficult issues that help perpetuate them.

While anxious-ambivalent attachment patterns may be difficult to change, it is even more of a challenge to deal with people who have an avoidant attachment style. In the first place, they don't readily volunteer to do something about their problem. They will only ask for help when the disorder starts to interfere with their life very significantly or otherwise impact them in a negative way. This usually happens when an individual's coping resources are stretched too thinly to deal with stress or demanding life events.

Avoidants hold many self-limiting beliefs, as well as an unrealistic view of social standards and of themselves. They tend to be socially inhibited and feel socially inept. Because of feelings of inadequacy and inhibition, individuals with avoidant attachment problems will try to avoid any form of activity that involves socializing or interacting with others. Therefore, to have any form of impact, these people need gradually to face the precise situations that they're most afraid of and typically avoid. Systemic exposure (by creating structured exercises), combined with reframing unrealistic thinking will set their mind and emotions on the right path. Since such individuals avoid social situations as much as possible, their people skills have often atrophied or have never truly developed. Training them in key people skills, including such simple things as how to start a conversation and keep it going, is crucial.

As in any form of intervention, it is essential for the coach/therapist to gain and keep the client's trust. Without it, the client will avoid coaching or therapy. The primary purpose for such interventions for people with avoidant attachment problems is to begin challenging their exaggerated negative beliefs about themselves – which may be even more difficult if these thoughts have never reached consciousness.

From a psychodynamic perspective, in coaching or therapy it is important to identify early losses. In almost all types of attachment interventions, emotional recovery from past experiences of loss is going to be key. Individuals need to work through grief and loss issues, which implies some form of education about the origin of their feelings. **"emotional recovery from past experiences of loss is going to be key"**

In this archeological dig for origins, the identification and validation of feelings is important. People need help to understand the cause of their attachment patterns. They need to be encouraged to express their feelings safely, to figure out where specific feelings stem from, and acknowledge, recognize, and accept early childhood traumas by reliving them. Healing can only take place by revisiting and reframing the client's past traumatic experiences.

Whatever these might have been, these experiences need to be mourned, otherwise there will be no resolution. Mourning may necessitate cognitive restructuring of faulty thinking patterns, attitudes, and perceptions. There has to be insight about the origins of these behavior patterns in order to arrive at closure. Usually, closure implies dealing with unresolved relationship longings associated with parental attachment figures. Belief systems and physiological reactions to attachment relationships will need to be reorganized to enhance self-esteem. This includes stimulating an individual's mood state moderation system – helping people to accept responsibility for their own behavior and to pursue happiness.

The role of the change agent

People with attachment disorders like these may experience the coach/therapist in a variety of different ways, depending on the nature of the early experiences that interrupted the normal attachment bond. These transference relationships can take many different forms.[21] They may perceive the coach/therapist as not being there, of not caring, of caring too much, of trying to hurt them, of pulling away from them, of being disgusted with them, and so on. These feelings are important as in some ways they reflect the person's earliest experiences – the things that prevented secure attachment in the first place. Such reactions provide openings for interventions and insight.

Closing the circle

Attachment theory has provided us with the framework to understand better the process and influence of our interpersonal history on new relationships. It enables us to realize that internal representations, developed during the primary relationship, continue to be influential throughout our life.[22]

But given the important role these behavior patterns play in enabling some form of psychological survival, they will be highly resistant to change. We are more likely to assimilate new relational information, even at the cost of distorting it, than accommodate information that is at odds with our existing expectations. However, this resistance to change doesn't mean that change is impossible. On the contrary, the scripts in people's inner theater may change as they encounter new private and public relationships and gain new understanding about previous experiences, especially those related to attachment.[23]

Whenever we undertake a journey toward personal change, understanding our attachment patterns will be important. Schopenhauer's dramatization of the hedgehogs' dilemma – finding a comfortable distance – still rings true. Our attachment script affects the nature of our interpersonal relationships, our emotional management, and our outlook on life. Understanding attachment patterns will help us understand and guide relationships. How we deal with attachment issues will influence how we deal with problems at work and at home and determine the roles we play in a group setting. Every action we take, every time we talk to others, provides more insight into how we have organized our attachment experiences.

Overcoming attachment dysfunction is never easy. As I have indicated, it takes a lot of work and effort. It implies moderating our distancing or closing behaviors – finding a satisfactory solution to the hedgehogs' dilemma. It means learning to have more relaxed control over our mind through understanding the real causes of happiness and unhappiness. It implies learning to have more satisfactory relationships and searching for a more enjoyable life.

True recovery from attachment disorders only occurs, however, when we can look at ourselves squarely and face our attachments and inner demons, free from false perceptions. Healing can only take place when we are prepared to face the things that have troubled us, and find new resolutions. It implies being able to accept the many conundrums of life. As the Zen saying goes, "The tighter you squeeze, the less you have." We have to learn that once we stop clinging and let things be, we will be freer. At the same time, we can't have relationships with no strings attached, as it is the strings that hold a real relationship together. To avoid attachments for fear of loss is to avoid life.

The Art of Forgiveness: Differentiating Transformational Leaders

"He insulted me, he hurt me, he defeated me, and he deprived me." Those who do not harbor such thoughts will be free from hatred.

– Buddha, The Dhammapada

Show no pity. Life for life, eye for eye, tooth for tooth, hand for hand, foot for foot.

– Deuteronomy 19:21

Forgiveness allows us to let go of the pain in the memory and if we let go of the pain in the memory we can have the memory but it does not control us. When memory controls us we are then the puppets of the past.

– Alexandra Asseily

An-eye-for-an-eye-for-an-eye-for-an-eye… ends in making everybody blind.

– Mahatma Gandhi

Introduction

Individuals, teams, organizations, institutions, and societies can only move forward when people aren't preoccupied by past hurts. Therefore, one of the factors that differentiate truly transformational from more run-of-the mill leaders is the ability to turn feelings of resentment, bitterness, and blame into something constructive and reparative. When leaders forgive, they dissipate built-up anger, bitterness, and animosity, releasing an enormous amount of pent-up energy that can be used in much more constructive ways. Forgiveness offers people the chance to take risks, to be creative, to learn and to grow their own leadership capabilities. Through forgiveness, truly transformational leaders instill a sense of pride, respect, and trust, creating heightened levels of commitment, self-sacrifice, motivation, and performance in followers.

Forgiving means accepting the fallibility of the human condition. It demonstrates courage, vulnerability, integrity, and trust, all constructive ways to build collaboration and connections. Forgiveness fosters healing, restitution, and restoration in both giver and receiver. It facilitates excellence and improvement. But it does not mean forgetting – forgiveness does not mean condoning the hurt that has been caused. On the contrary, remembrance is important because without it, there is always the likelihood that past hurts will be repeated. Forgiving means taking the sting out of a memory that otherwise threatens to poison our existence.

Forgiveness sets us free

The case of Nelson Mandela, the former president of South Africa, provides a remarkable illustration of forgiveness. This transformational political leader captured the imagination of people around the world. His dignity, humility, and courage have made him a role model to billions. Who can forget seeing Mandela standing on the balcony of Cape Town's city hall on February 11, 1990, his arms outstretched, greeting the thousands of people eager to see him after his long imprisonment on Robben Island? As he said in a speech broadcast around the globe, "I greet you all in the name of peace, democracy, and freedom for all."

In Clint Eastwood's 2009 film, *Invictus* (a Latin word meaning unconquerable, invincible, or undefeated) Nelson Mandela's philosophy of leadership is brought to life. The film is based on John Carlin's book, *Playing the Enemy: Nelson Mandela and the Game that Changed a Nation* (2008), and examines the relationship between Mandela (played by Morgan Freeman) and François Pienaar, the captain of the Springboks, South Africa's national rugby team (played by Matt Damon). At the time, rugby represented the game of the oppressors.

The 1995 World Rugby Cup was going to be held in South Africa, a time when the political situation in the country was explosive. Many blacks, having been humiliated and mistreated by years of apartheid, were demanding revenge, while the white minority was extremely anxious about how South Africa was going to look under Mandela's leadership. Was it going to be a rainbow nation, or a nation divided? Mandela saw what could have been a very violent situation as an opportunity for healing. He recognized that rugby had a deeper meaning off the field, and that the World Cup had the potential to become a great symbolic opportunity for reconciliation and forgiveness. Shortly before the championships began, Mandela invited Pienaar to his official residence for tea.

Mandela knew that the Springboks were expected to lose in the first rounds of the game, but he had other ideas. The meeting with Pienaar gave Mandela the opportunity to discuss leadership strategy – to explain to him how important it was to have the team help him to heal the nation – and to ask Pienaar to inspire and lead his team of underdogs to victory. Later, he gave Pienaar a copy of the William Ernest Henley poem "Invictus," saying that it had helped him when the future looked very bleak. (This poem famously ends: "I am the master of my fate / I am the captain of my soul.")

Here it is important to remember that, in spite of fierce opposition by most members of the African National Congress, Mandela was reaching out to his former enemies. For President Mandela, the past was past; the future was what mattered. He had come to realize that a life lived without forgiveness would put him (and others) in another kind of prison. Even though most members of his party thought Mandela was going too far, he was prepared to prove them wrong. He lectured his party members on the strength in forgiveness. To use his words: "Forgiveness liberates the soul, it removes fear. That's why it's such a powerful weapon." He made very clear that only through forgiveness would they be able to build a unified nation, and create a shared future; the alternative would be continued strife and chaos.

The symbolic image of Mandela striding onto the rugby field at Ellis Park Stadium wearing the shirt of the team captain became a catalyst for reconciliation, restoring dignity to the black majority while reassuring white South Africans that they need not expect hatred and revenge. By concentrating on forgiveness, Mandela became the most admired and revered political leader of his time. In forgiving, he showed how different he was. He demonstrated to the world that it takes more courage, more stamina, and more humanity to forgive than to take revenge. His act was a profound lesson in leadership, demonstrating that forgiveness is a power that breaks the chains of bitterness and hatred.

It is quite an eye-opener to compare Nelson Mandela's philosophy of leadership and forgiveness with that of Robert Mugabe, the president of Zimbabwe. Mugabe seems to have a completely different *Weltanschauung*. Instead of generosity, restraint, and forgiveness, Mugabe opted for bitterness, vindictiveness, anger, and hatred. He decided to be vindictive not only to the country's whites, but also toward huge segments of his black compatriots who held opposing views. In 2000, Mugabe encouraged his most militant supporters (many of them veterans of the civil war of the 1970s), with the help of armed gangs and, frequently, Zimbabwe African National Union Patriotic Front officials, to begin forcibly occupying the country's 5,000 white-owned commercial farms. People who were not on his side were the next objects of his wrath, resulting in stolen elections, and even more violence. Subsequently, Zimbabwe became a land with a ruined economy, populated by citizens living miserable and fearful lives under the threat of terrible human rights abuses.

What about you?

How do you react when someone hurts you? Do you have a strong urge to get even – to inflict hurt on the other person in return? Are you unable to turn the other cheek? Will you hold a grudge against that person for the rest of your life? When you take a long, hard look at yourself, are you more like a Mandela or a Mugabe? If all your answers to these questions are affirmative, you are not alone; most people are reluctant to turn the other cheek. While forgiveness is never easy, bitterness seems to be easier – as is hatred. But what about the people who are prepared to forgive?

The forgiving leader

We all know that lives are not calm, flowing rivers. Relating to others, whether friends, strangers, or family members, is always accompanied by the risk of being hurt, and such hurts happen all the time. Our parents may have been too tough on us; our teachers at school or university may have been unpleasant, a colleague may have sabotaged a project we were working on, or our life partner might have had an affair. Getting hurt is part and parcel of the human condition. The most logical reaction to being hurt is to get angry, to want to get back at the transgressor(s). We want to hurt them the way they've hurt us. We want them to feel our pain. Unfortunately, many of us have been in this dark place.

As a leader, the vicissitudes of the human condition become even more magnified. Leadership never takes place in a vacuum. Leading people and organizations means dealing with a maelstrom of relationships, which implies an enormous amount of emotional management. Leaders operate in settings in which strife is rife, and if left unresolved, will become a festering drag on effectiveness. Such conflicts need to be dealt with to allow organizations to move forward.

Truly transformational leaders are acutely aware of the cost of bearing grudges. They recognize the havoc that can be created by an unforgiving attitude. Exceptional, transformational leaders recognize that holding grudges is a form of arrested development; it holds people back. Like Mugabe, they will get stuck – along with everybody else; in the case of Mugabe, a whole country has become stuck. In contrast, as Mandela has demonstrated, forgiveness by a leader is not a sign of weakness but a sign of strength. "Forgiveness," according to the former president of India, Indira Gandhi, "is a virtue of the brave."

Leaders are responsible for creating a culture of forgiveness,[1] and creating such a culture has many advantages. To begin with, forgiveness builds loyalty and good corporate citizenship. In organizations with a forgiveness culture, people are more likely to make an extra effort, which has important consequences for the bottom line. If people feel that they will not be forgiven for the mistakes they make, they are not going to be at their most productive; they will not take risks and will waste energy worrying about past transgressions. Forgiveness also helps transgressors to have a more positive outlook on the future. People are more likely to be open, and less likely to hide mistakes, transgressions, and wrongdoings when they operate in a forgiving environment. They will be more likely to create a coaching culture, a way of interacting that will have a positive effect on the bottom line. Forgiveness helps create authentizotic organizations, places of work where people feel at their best.[2]

To energize their people, truly effective leaders need to be at peace with themselves and past and present events in their life, which includes forgiving others for transgressions, and not bearing grudges. When we let go of our grudges, we build collaboration, reduce conflict, and release a lot of pent-up energy that can be used to move countries, institutions, organizations, teams, and individuals forward. True forgiveness supports the retention of valued employees, allows greater creativity and innovation, leads to increased profitability, and generates greater openness to change.

"To energize their people, truly effective leaders need to be at peace with themselves and past and present events in their life"

An eye for an eye

Unfortunately, the default model of too many people in leadership positions, when they feel wronged, is righteous indignation, the urge for revenge and/or avoidance behavior toward the transgressor. This behavior is a legacy of our prehistoric past; vengeance warns the boundary violator to stay away and not cross the boundary again, or risk escalation and more negative consequences.

From an evolutionary point of view, this response may have served a critical purpose in the genesis of social and cooperative systems. A strong reaction to fairness or unfairness may have been programmed into our brain, making us "hard-wired" to retaliate when other people do us harm.[3] Vengeance or a preference for negative reciprocity has always been an important part of Homo sapiens' (and our predecessors') emotional repertoire.[4] It is our way of protecting ourselves – keeping offenders at bay.

Anyone who has ever been victimized – and that includes survivors of crime, accidents, childhood abuse, political imprisonment, and warfare, as well as lesser evils – must decide whether or not to forgive the perpetrator. There can be no middle ground in this decision: either we decide to forgive the person who has hurt us, or we hold on to bitterness and anger. Unfortunately, holding on to grudges (in spite of a temporary feeling of satisfaction) can be very costly to our mental and physical health.

The law of "an eye for an eye" has existed under many different names for a very long time, as the law of retribution, the *Lex Talionis*, or the law of equivalency. The first written record of this law can be found in the Babylonian Code of Hammurabi (named after the King of Babylon who ruled *c.*1792–1750 BCE). The Code of Hammurabi subscribed to the "eye for an eye" theory of punishment, but was intended to be humanitarian, in that the punishment had to fit the crime. To enable societies to function smoothly, boundaries had to be established concerning types and severity of retribution. Over time, the *Lex Talionis* became a powerful weapon for motivating, creating, sustaining, and regulating the cooperative behavior required of humankind, and, as we have found out for ourselves, it doesn't come easily to respond otherwise.

Although taking revenge can be viewed as part of our evolutionary inheritance as *Homo sapiens*, we are not completely on automatic pilot when we are wronged. If we choose to do so, we can act differently. Humankind could not have survived without the option of a different kind of behavior. We have a choice in how we deal with people who hurt us. Granted, taking revenge may make us feel righteous, but at the same time, it is one of the more primitive reactions in our emotional repertoire. It also, dangerously, leads to counter-reaction: revenge tends to invite more revenge, and so on, leading to a further deterioration in relationships. This is the major reason why most societies warn their citizens not to take justice into their own hands, insisting that the state alone has the duty and the right to punish wrongdoers.

"revenge tends to invite more revenge"

In spite of the danger of entering a downward spiral, humankind seems to find it easier to hate than to forgive. To absolve someone who has wronged us appears to be difficult, since it may appear that the transgressor isn't suffering any consequences for his or her hurtful behavior, and others may interpret the apparent non-reaction as a sign of weakness. What makes such a situation even messier is that there are some people who may be attracted to the victim role, and continuing to feel angry and resentful reinforces the feeling of being the victim. Given all these opposing forces, it makes forgiving an activity that requires a lot of effort and courage.

Revenge is neither sweet nor satisfying

Being stuck in a non-forgiving mindset is not a very happy position. Revenge is neither sweet nor gratifying. When we are preoccupied by anger, there is very little room for other emotions. It takes an enormous amount of energy to hate, and maintain hatred. When we cannot forgive the people who have hurt us, these feelings can become a mental poison, an insidious drug that only hurts ourselves. Ironically, the people who have hurt us – the people we would prefer to forget – keep on haunting us. And instead of being able to move on, these people remain part of our lives. When we let go of our hatred, however, we feel much better. We should remind ourselves that forgiving is not something we do for other people; it is something we do for ourselves. Forgiving is about letting go and moving on with our lives, creating greater freedom.

Feelings of hatred, spite, bitterness, and vindictiveness are demanding taskmasters: revenge is a multi-headed monster that is never satisfied. As soon as one head is cut off, another pops up in its place. Revenge is so consuming

"revenge is a multi-headed monster that is never satisfied"

that pretty soon hatred takes over from all other emotions, creating a life governed by endless cycles of resentment and retaliation – not exactly a prescription for peace of mind. Numerous studies have shown that bitterness and hate create a fertile ground for stress disorders, causing a range of symptoms that negatively affect the immune system.[5] In addition, an unforgiving attitude is positively correlated with depression, anxiety, hostility, and neuroticism,[6] and also with premature death.[7]

In comparison, taking the high road of forgiveness contributes to greater spiritual and psychological well-being, lower anxiety levels, less stress, fewer hostile feelings, lower blood pressure, fewer symptoms of depression, and reduced risk of alcohol and substance abuse. People who forgive more readily also tend to have fewer coronary health problems.[8] Consequently, we can look at the willingness to forgive as a sign of spiritual and emotional maturity.[9]

Forgiving, not forgetting

But forgiveness is very different from condoning a transgression. It is not a matter of excusing whatever unacceptable behavior has occurred – realistic forgiveness is about healing the memory of the harm, not erasing it. Forgiving means no longer being a prisoner of the past, but creating a new way of remembering. Truly transformational leaders such as Mahatma Gandhi, Nelson Mandela, and Aung San Suu Kyi seem to have figured this out. They refused to rehearse past hurts; instead, they chose serenity and happiness over righteous anger, realizing that holding on to resentment, bitterness, and spite is not what transformational leadership is all about. When we forgive, we do not change the past, but we can change the future.

What is forgiveness all about?

The *Oxford English Dictionary* defines forgiveness as "to grant free pardon and to give up all claim on account of an offense or debt." In other words, forgiveness is the renunciation or cessation of resentment, indignation, or anger due to a perceived offense, disagreement, or mistake. It means ceasing to demand punishment or restitution; it concerns the re-establishment of an interpersonal relationship that has been disrupted through some kind of transgression.

Forgiveness can be perceived in many ways, however. It can be described as an emotion, a decision, a behavior, or an attitude change.[10] It can also be seen as a motivational phenomenon that has affective, cognitive, and behavioral components. In particular, however, forgiving can be viewed as an interactive *process* that includes the person who forgives (and who must in the process forgive themselves), the person forgiven, and the relationship between the two. Forgiving means acting constructively in response to the hurtful actions of someone with whom we have some kind of relationship, and controlling the impulse to act destructively.[11] In most contexts, this kind of forgiveness must be granted without any expectation of restorative justice, and without necessarily expecting a response by the offender (who may even be dead). It helps, however, if the transgressor can and does offer some form of acknowledgment, some kind of apology, or even just asks for forgiveness.

Generally speaking, forgiving is a process whereby negative emotions are transformed into positive ones for the purpose of bringing emotional normalcy back to a relationship. In order to achieve such a transformation, the offended person must forgo retribution, but this is not the same as excusing or condoning. Forgiveness doesn't mean that what happened was OK, and it doesn't mean that the person who caused the hurt is necessarily still welcome in our life. It just means that we have made peace with the pain, and we are ready to let it go.

Forgiveness is also a concept with deep religious roots. Most religious traditions include teachings on the nature of forgiveness.[12] Many of these have provided a basis for a variety of contemporary practices of forgiveness. Some religious doctrines or philosophies emphasize the need for people to seek divine forgiveness for their own shortcomings; others emphasize the need for people to practice forgiveness of one another; still others make little or no distinction between human and divine forgiveness.

The forgiving individual

Are some people more likely to forgive than others? Is there something that differentiates them from those who remain vindictive, vengeful, and bitter? In short, what makes leaders behave like a Mandela?

Research on personality traits has shown that people high on the forgiveness scale tend to be more emotionally stable, thrive in the interpersonal realm, and experience fewer interpersonal conflicts.[13] Forgiving people are also more open to cooperation, compassion, and social harmony. Such people welcome a transgressor's repentance, as well as any excuse that may plausibly reduce the severity of the transgression. Because of this *Weltanschauung*, they are more prepared to take the road of reconciliation.[14]

The relationship between forgiveness and personality has generally been explored within the taxonomy of the five-factor trait models of personality.[15] Taking this conceptual model as a base, the most consistent, and often most statistically significant finding across a number of these studies is that higher levels of forgiveness are predicted by lower levels of "neuroticism." People scoring high on "neuroticism" – more specifically, hostile anger – are more likely to engage in revenge and avoidance motivation. Higher levels of "extraversion" and "conscientiousness" have sometimes been found to correlate significantly with higher levels of forgiveness, and people scoring higher on the "agreeableness" dimension of the Big Five personality traits are likely to be more forgiving. No statistically significant relationship has been reported, however, between forgiveness and the "openness to change" personality factor.[16]

Chronological age also correlates positively with forgiveness: it appears with age, we tend to become more forgiving.[17] Those who forgive more also tend to be more religious or spiritual.[18]

A psychodynamic lens

Helpful as the five-factor theory may be in understanding the forgiving personality, this framework can be expanded by applying a psychodynamic lens, assessing how factors such as reality testing, affect management, defensive structure, sense of identity, and the nature of object relations play a role in the forgiveness equation.[19] Taking these psychodynamics factors into consideration in my work with leaders, I have found that certain dynamics appear to differentiate the more forgiving from the less forgiving leaders.

Degree of obsessional (shameful) rumination: A major component of the ability (or inability) to forgive is the degree and intensity of obsessional rumination. Rumination means "chewing something over" in our mind. It alludes to those endless internal dialogues and fearful obsessive thoughts that spin around, clogging our mind, making day-to-day living frightening, intolerable, and emotionally draining.

These persistent, irrepressible memories are one of the reasons some people get stuck – why they cannot move on in their life. In most instances, such obsessive worries have to do with the security of a current relationship (at work or at home) – worries disconnected from the demands placed on the individual by the environment. As is to be expected, the common trigger for such obsessional rumination is a personal transgression, and the more offensive the transgression, the angrier the emotional reaction will be, and the stronger the vengeful thoughts will be in the rumination process. People who exhibit this kind of behavior seem to go around in circles. They remain stuck on the transgression, trapped in a regressive way of looking at things that becomes overarching and overwhelming.

When applied to emotions, shameful rumination usually involves the belief that, somehow, if we think about something long enough, if we try to understand the emotions involved, we might be able to control these internal processes. Although this may very well be true, finding the root cause is not easy. For some people, this kind of self-talk becomes so all-consuming, and takes on such a self-destructive bent, that normal functioning becomes extremely difficult. Naturally, the content of rumination (determined by the scope of the transgression and individual differences in emotional reactions) will be an important factor in shaping subsequent affects, motivations, and behavior following the transgression. But whatever the case, the intensity of rumination (and its content) becomes important in predicting the intensity of vengeful behavior.[20]

Individuals characterized by obsessive or shameful rumination respond to injustice quite differently from individuals who do not have this characteristic. If rumination is broadly understood to mean increased effortful mental work following a negative event, forgiving individuals tend to engage in a very different form of rumination following transgressions, compared to unforgiving individuals. In the more forgiving, the rumination is not centered on revenge imagery, but more aimed at thwarting the development of hostile and cold attitudes, and also at trying to reestablish or maintain positive and loving attitudes toward the transgressor(s).

The inner voices that make up these rumination processes are not necessarily under the control of an individual's conscious mind. They operate under a very different set of rules. Therefore, to overcome obsessive rumination, the individual needs to explore what these internalized rules are – a process that requires a considerable degree of self-awareness. Although acquiring the necessary self-awareness is difficult, it is only by understanding our inner landscape that it is possible to take back control and stop this destructive rumination process.

To deconstruct the destructive rumination process, we need to look at the scripts of our inner theater and how these are formed by events that take place during our childhood and schooling. Some of us may have internalized very harsh rules set by our parents and other authority figures; others may have been more fortunate in acquiring a more benign, forgiving inner landscape or superego. The superego comprises the organized part of our personality structure – mainly but not entirely unconscious – that provides the moral, ethical standards by which we deal with life.

The superego's criticisms, prohibitions, and inhibitions become internalized in our brain, and form our conscience, and its positive aspirations and ideals represent our idealized self-image, or ego idea.[21] Failures in healthy development may lead to a failure to construct a personal system of justice that is fair, meaningful, and satisfying. Children who have suffered developmentally destructive experiences in their early years may be more predisposed to react violently when provoked, because such experiences prevent the development of healthy notions of reciprocal behavior, and can contribute to psychopathological behavior and destructive relationships. The experiences affect the way these children (and, later, adults) deal with shame, empathy, rage, and aggression. In particular, people who have been subjected to rigid, autocratic, and unfair standards of child rearing, or to childhood abuse, seem to be more likely to seek to exact revenge for past injuries and injustices. Shame seems to play a vital role – the more individuals feel shame, the more likely they are to become angry, hold malevolent intentions, and incline towards revenge.[22]

Degree of empathy: Empathy can be defined as a vicarious emotion that is congruent with, but not necessarily identical to, the emotion of another person.[23] According to some evolutionary psychologists, empathy is the evolutionary mechanism that motivates altruistic and pro-social behaviors.[24] Empathy has both emotional and cognitive components – emotionally it means the vicarious experiencing of another's emotional state, while cognitively it concerns the ability to imagine another person's experience accurately.

Empathy also pertains to the internalization of rules about the protection of others. It is the mechanism that motivates the desire to help others, even at a cost to ourselves. Consequently, it plays an important role in how individuals become socially competent people with meaningful social relationships. Imagining and feeling what another individual experiences makes empathy one of the most important determinants of our ability to forgive.[25] A variety of pro-social phenomena, such as conflict resolution, cooperation, altruism, and the inhibition of aggression, become easier where there is empathy for the other person.

In the case of forgiveness, being empathic involves considering all the other factors that may have influenced the behavior of the transgressor, as well as considering the transgressor's humanity. For example, the offended individual may imagine how the transgressor experiences guilt and distress over the way his or her actions have caused hurt and damaged the relationship. Empathy may cause the offended party to worry that the transgressor feels isolated or lonely because of their estranged relationship. Finally, and perhaps most directly, empathy for the transgressor may simply prompt the offended party to make efforts to restore the relationship. In other words, empathy may lead to a yearning for restored positive contact with the transgressor. In this way, experiencing empathic reactions toward the transgressor reduces the damage done by the transgressor's hurtful actions, and by extension reduces the desire for revenge or continuing estrangement. The hurt person will be more likely to pursue conciliatory courses of action toward the transgressor to relieve the latter's distress, and perhaps to contribute to the restoration of the relationship.

Transgressors who experience empathy toward the person they have hurt are more likely to apologize out of a sense of guilt, or perhaps due to their own concerns about the loss of a valued relationship.[26] Victims are more likely to develop empathy for transgressors when their relationship has been close, committed, and satisfactory; thus, pre-offense closeness, apology, empathy, and forgiveness are highly interrelated. The wish to forgive can be viewed as a sign that the person who has transgressed means more to the offended person than the wrong they have committed. Often, we forgive people because we still want them in our lives.

Empathy is a skill that we learn in early childhood. Naturally, the most effective teachers of that skill are our parents.

"Empathy is a skill that we learn in early childhood"

Mother-infant synchrony, as expressed in the interactions in the first years of life, is directly associated with levels of empathy in childhood and beyond.[27] Attachment security facilitates the development of empathy, so parents who provide a warm, positive environment for their children, and demonstrate sensitivity to their needs and emotions through synchronous interactions (and talking about emotions with their children), are likely to have more empathic children.[28] This is due to the nature of their parent-child interchanges, which help the child's brain to develop the necessary inhibitory mechanisms for self-regulation of aggressive and impulsive behavior.[29] The outcome becomes self-evident: children who are more empathic tend to do better at school, in social situations, and in their adult careers. They are also more likely to assume leadership positions. In contrast, children who are raised in situations of disrupted attachment relationships and exposed to aggressive (and even abusive) models of parenting will not develop the proper intrapsychic structures necessary to adequately modulate affective arousal, which includes feelings of shame, vindictiveness, and revenge. For these people, the default model is not going to be a forgiving nature.

Although empathic leaders can become quite angry with people who have hurt them, they will still care deeply about their relationships with such individuals. Generally, they are moved by the suffering and repentance of those who offend. They are eager to know what mitigates their offenses; and they are keenly aware of their own moral failings. In contrast, a mark of deeply unforgiving people (and leaders) is that being angry about what happened makes them willing to abandon the relationship – to start thinking the transgressor is not worth having as a colleague, subordinate, or friend, or to start talking about divorce, or to seriously consider disowning a son or a daughter.

Degree of emotional self-control

Forgiving leaders are not so caught up in the perceived injustices in their life that they can't find a way past them. Unforgiving leaders tend to become caught up in negative emotional spirals and are more inclined to focus on what they do not have, and how they may have failed. Unsurprisingly, power motivation, authority issues, and the desire for status are more important to them.[30] Given the dynamics of power, such leaders are also more likely to have a distorted idea of how others perceive them. They waste time and effort in comparing themselves to others, comparisons that do nothing for their sense of self-worth. These people are haunted by feelings of envy, bitterness, vindictiveness, and spitefulness toward others' achievements. Their dark thoughts immobilize them and prevent them from moving forward in their own life. Much of their energy is channeled toward undermining people for whom they have negative feelings.

These dark thoughts can result in an extremely emotionally debilitating condition that, when unresolved, can have a range of negative consequences. Outbursts of rage are frequently a feature of their behavior. Such leaders will be touchy and edgy when thinking about the person they resent, yet may deny their anger or hatred for that person. When these negative feelings gain the upper hand, the more long-term consequences can be a hostile, cynical, sarcastic *Weltanschauung* that becomes a barrier to healthy relationships and prevents personal and emotional growth. This will contribute to difficulties in self-disclosure, trouble in trusting others, and very precarious self-confidence. Such feelings often turn into in a downward spiral, cutting off communication or creating miscommunication.

Generally, this type of negative emotional spiral is brought on by the realization of some lack, deficiency, or inadequacy, and envy becomes a "dark" emotion that motivates the individual to spoil things for others. Truly envious people falsely assume that self-worth can be only be attained through possessions or achievements. Such leaders feel the pain of deprivation even when they are not actually deprived. Inevitably, they always compare themselves unfavorably to others: to their success, their reputation, their possessions, their luck, or their qualities. As they believe that they don't have these characteristics themselves, they experience a loss of self-worth, and a wish that the envied person loses the things they desire in the delusionary hope that it will restore their own self-esteem. Due to their conflicts with self-esteem or self-limitations, they enter a vicious, negative cycle; and their unhappiness causes them to further envy those who are happy. When people are haunted by such feelings, they create a self-imposed purgatory.

The saying, "You can choose your friends, but you can't choose your family," rings very true for people who are victims of this kind of emotional turmoil. Negative feelings may **"You can choose your friends, but you can't choose your family"** start early in life; when sibling rivalry rules, and parents are unable (or unwilling) to modify such behavior, envy will rear its ugly head. These people (as children and later adults) have been unable to develop adequate impulse control, making the acting out of revengeful actions more likely. Thus the people we envy and the possessions or advantages for which they are envied tell us much about ourselves, about our values, our aspirations, and our negative self-concept.

How forgiving are you?

The questionnaire that follows is designed to help you to make a quick assessment of the role of forgiveness in your life and your capacity to forgive. In addition, the questionnaire will provide insights into the nature of your interpersonal relationships. Answer the questions as honestly as you can, rating each item on a scale of 1 to 5.

1 = Strongly disagree
2 = Disagree
3 = Neutral
4 = Agree
5 = Strongly agree

1. I continue to behave negatively toward a person who has done something that I think is wrong.
   1 2 3 4 5

2. If someone does something bad to me, I will retaliate.
   1 2 3 4 5

3. I continue to be unpleasant toward others who have hurt me.
   1 2 3 4 5

4. I find it very difficult to overcome bad situations in my life.
   1 2 3 4 5

5. If others mistreat me, I think poorly of them.
   1 2 3 4 5

6. I hold on to grudges and negative feelings over perceived wrongdoings.
   1 2 3 4 5

7. I don't need much provocation to retaliate against another person.
   1 2 3 4 5

8. I continue to feel resentful even if the offender has asked my forgiveness.
   1 2 3 4 5

9. I am not really the forgiving type.
   1 2 3 4 5

10. I find it difficult to accept any remorse and sorrow expressed by others for their actions or words that have hurt or disappointed me.
    1 2 3 4 5

11. I often feel that I have had a rough deal in life.
    1 2 3 4 5

12. I strongly believe that if someone makes mistakes, or acts wrongly, there should be consequences.
    1 2 3 4 5

13. I seem to get into arguments more often than other people.
     1 2 3 4 5

14. I often feel very resentful about things.
     1 2 3 4 5

15. I find it very hard to let go of grievances.
     1 2 3 4 5

16. I am always on my guard against people who might hurt me.
     1 2 3 4 5

17. It would be very difficult for me to forgive my partner if I thought
     that he/she had betrayed me.
     1 2 3 4 5

18. I would find it hard to forgive a colleague if he/she took advantage of me.
     1 2 3 4 5

19. I find it very difficult to let go of anger and hatred.
     1 2 3 4 5

20. I don't have the kind of worldview that welcomes forgiveness.
     1 2 3 4 5

Calculate your score on the basis that an answer of 1 equals 1 point, 2 equals 2 points, and so on.

Look at your ratings and add up the points. If you arrive at a score of 40 or less, you belong to the group of people who are truly forgiving. If you score 80 or more, forgiving doesn't come naturally to you. You will be a happier person, however, if you work on the forgiveness equation. If you score between 40 and 80, you belong to the group of people who are able to forgive, but not without difficulty.

The art of forgiving

Mahatma Gandhi warned that, "The weak can never forgive. Forgiveness is the attribute of the strong." We cannot change what has already happened to us; there is no delete button for the past. **"there is no delete button for the past"** Whatever transgression we have experienced, it is going to be with us forever, so the crucial issues are how we choose to deal with transgressions and how we metabolize our feelings. For some people, the memories of being hurt become like permanent videos implanted in their heads, and every time they play them, they feel the pain all over again. Others may have better coping mechanisms – they find ways to hit to the stop button. What determines an "ending" is whether the hurt party is prepared to look for a forgiving resolution. Individuals need to ask themselves whether they want to spend the rest of their lives with a pain for which they were not responsible. The alternative is to do something about it.

The case of John

A CEO in one of my leadership programs, let's call him John, presented a problem he had with his chairman. John also mentioned as an aside that he often had debilitating headaches that became so painful that he was unable to function. Despite a battery of tests, doctors had been unable to find anything the matter with him and he was at a loss why he had them. I asked John whether he could recall any specific situations when these headaches occurred. After some thought, he said that there might be a pattern. The headaches would start suddenly every time he found himself in conflict with an authority figure. I asked whether the headaches were recent, or whether they had a much longer history. He replied that he had had them for as long as he could remember, and that they had started when he was quite young. In response to further prompting, John revealed that as a child he had frequent disagreements with his father, a man with an explosive character who would sometimes beat him. John recalled how he deeply resented his father's actions, but felt totally helpless. He told me that he was not on speaking terms with his father – something that upset the other members of his family, particularly his mother. As might be expected, family gatherings were extremely difficult, if not impossible, and John had not seen his parents for a very long time. I asked John if he was ready to forgive his father, since these incidents had happened so long ago. But when I asked this question, his body language made it quite clear that forgiving was something he had never considered.

When I saw John again at the next module in the program, three months later, he appeared much more at peace with himself, much less tense. I asked him whether anything significant had happened during the interval. It turned out that, after mulling over the idea of forgiving, he had taken the initiative and sent a "forgiveness email" to his father. The latter had immediately responded in, to John, a surprisingly receptive way. Given the response, John decided to visit his parents to have a talk with his father. This talk became the beginning of a series of conversations that helped him see his father in a very different light. John said that he was not condoning his father's behavior toward him when he was growing up – it was not the way to rear children – but he had become more aware of how irritating some of his actions must have been to the whole family and that his parents, at times, must have been at their wits' end. More important to him, however, was that by reaching out, he had become part of the family again. Apart from his joy at rebuilding the family connection, there had been a remarkable decline in his headaches, and he realized that dealing with authority issues at work had become less conflict-ridden. He had become less prickly, more understanding – and more forgiving.

A journey, not an event

In deconstructing what forgiveness is about, we need to realize that it is not a one-off event or decision, it is a process. Just saying sorry will not suffice. Forgiving is a journey – an undertaking that takes time, determination, and persistence. Whatever is needed for healing, it is a learning process that takes place at the boundaries of the conscious and unconscious regions of our inner theater. Like separation and other forms of mourning, it has a specific pattern. The work of Bowlby and Parkes,[31] based on child observation studies, is very helpful in understanding the kind of grieving process that forgiving is all about.

When a transgression occurs, there will initially be an experience of numbness, shock, and denial, mental states that may cause an individual to feel a sense of unreality. This will be followed by a phase of yearning and protest in which grief may come in waves of crying and diffuse anxiety. The third phase may be a state of disorganization, a low mood, and a sense of hopelessness. Finally, in the case of forgiveness, the individual engages in a form of reorganization, involving letting go of the attachment, and looking at future possibilities.

This stage model is not necessarily linear. While we go through the forgiving process, our reactions may move backwards and forwards, and what happens doesn't necessarily follow a consciously planned scenario – forgiveness occurs during the journey, while we are walking, playing, sleeping, and dreaming.

The link between reconciliation and forgiveness also involves exploring two dimensions of forgiveness at the boundaries between conscious and unconscious behavior: the intrapsychic and the interpersonal. The intrapsychic dimension relates to the cognitive and affective processes and interpretations associated with a transgression (i.e. internal state), whereas interpersonal forgiveness addresses the ongoing relationships between the people involved in a transgression. Complete forgiveness will only be possible if these two components are in sync; otherwise, we may only be dealing with forms of pseudo-forgiveness.

Self-reflection, self-understanding, and self-expression

The first step on the forgiveness journey is to remind ourselves how the energy required keeping a grudge alive will ultimately drain our strength; how a desire for revenge may defile us, and may even unconsciously make us as hurtful as the person who has hurt us. We need to acknowledge that forgiveness is a much better option for our mental and physical health than carrying old wounds, which become a burden that steals pleasure from the life we have now. Thus the capability of *self-reflection* is important for promoting positive behaviors toward others and facilitating social interactions and relationships.

Second, while going through this self-reflection process, it is important to understand why the transgression happened in the first place. Again, for reasons of mental health, we need to find explanations. Here the capacity to be truly empathic comes into play. The ability to put ourselves in the transgressor's shoes is a *sine qua non* to understanding what has really happened. While we will probably not agree with the rationale, we need some kind of *self-understanding* that explains why whatever happened occurred.

Third, it will be necessary to *express the emotions* attached to the hurt. Without doing this, it will be very difficult to let go. If the transgression elicits anger or sadness or hurt, these feelings need to be deeply felt and expressed. Naturally, the best option is to express these feelings toward our transgressors, particularly as they may not even be aware of the hurt they have caused. If we want to maintain a relationship with the person we are trying to forgive, we need to find ways to communicate why we are angry and what needs to be done to find a resolution. Whatever the transgression may have been, the forgiver needs to fully express how it made him or her feel. It is not enough simply to try to forget, because merely bypassing the emotion doesn't make for true forgiveness.

Fourth, for true forgiveness to occur, the forgiver needs to feel a reasonable amount of assurance that the transgression will not happen again. Whether it comes in the form of a sincere apology from the transgressor or another form of explanation, a modicum of trust needs to be re-established. But such trust may only go so far, as it is questionable whether the person who has been hurt will ever feel truly safe.

Finally, the step that ends the forgiveness cycle is letting go, and this may be the most difficult step to take. It is never easy to promise not to hold a grudge – letting go of a grudge means ending the rumination process, stopping oneself from dwelling on the injustice, and affirming that the transgression will not be referred to in the future. Being able to do this, however, also means letting go of a position of power; only when forgivers surrender the dominant role can they and their transgressors relate to one other again on an equal basis. For many people, this final step is what makes forgiveness such a challenge.

The road to forgiveness is not easy. Too many get stuck on the journey, finding it hard to let go of bitterness and negative brooding. But these people should be reminded that they have a choice. They can choose to carry on regretting things, or consider that things have happened for a reason; that they may benefit from learning from the experience. Such understanding will tell them what they could have done differently to prevent the transgression in the first place. They also need to realize that the process isn't just about learning to forgive those who have hurt us. It's also about the recognition that we all make mistakes. It is essential to realize that forgiveness is ultimately a gift we make to ourselves. Only through forgiveness can wounds heal. And as we let go of grudges, we no longer define our life by how we have been hurt.

> **"forgiveness is ultimately a gift we make to ourselves"**

Pseudo-forgiveness

While true forgiveness is hard, pretending to forgive is easy. Saying "sorry" is merely a temporary measure that never really erases the permanent scar underneath. Unfortunately, too many people get caught up in pseudo-forgiveness because it means they don't have to cope with unpleasant emotions. Such people refuse to deal with the fact that unconscious resentments do not respond to traditional logic and reason. In spite of expressions of forgiveness, whatever happened continues to cause discomfort although, on the surface at least, everything seems to be all right.

For example, we may refuse to admit that we are angry with someone close to us, which results in our unconsciously hiding our anger from ourselves in a desperate attempt to "protect" our relationship with that person. But this self-deception means we keep the resentment alive; we are not really protecting the relationship, we are slowly chipping away at it. And as long as the hurt is left to brew secretly in the unconscious, genuine forgiveness remains impossible. When something is merely repressed, it lingers in the dark shadows of the unconscious along with all the emotions associated with it.

Although forgetting through repression of the problem is not the answer, the process of forgetting may have a function. Thus there is a paradox: we should not forget, but we have to forget. On both an emotional and a spiritual level, forgetting is a natural part of the human experience and a natural function of the human brain.[32] Part of the function of memory is to forget in order to prevent unhelpful information from being encoded, as it can distract our focus from what really matters. Forgetting is necessary to prevent our brains from becoming jammed with trivial information. Thus the relationship between forgiving and forgetting becomes clouded by the idea that it is part of our evolutionary development for time to quell the longings of vengeance and hush the promptings of rage and aversion. Thus even when it may be hard for us to forgive, because of the way our brain is programmed, paradoxically without conscious awareness, we may be on a subliminal forgiveness journey.

Professional help

If the road to forgiveness appears to be halted, however, or if the transgression has had such a devastating effect that it is impossible to move on, the time has come to seek professional help.[33] Arriving at forgiveness has always been an integral part of the psychotherapy process, as we need to deal with aspects of our inner theater with which we are unhappy. The "scripts" in that inner theater have to do with people, and we may have to come to terms with some self-destructive elements of our personality. We may come face-to-face with the unforgiving parts of ourselves. Since the pain of not forgiving someone or oneself may take an emotional and physical toll on us, various forms of psychotherapy may help in treating the symptoms of not forgiving, and facilitating the forgiveness process. Psychotherapy may need to be complemented by medication, such as antidepressants or anti-anxiety treatments, if there are associated somatic problems.

From a therapeutic perspective, forgiving is made more difficult by the various defense mechanisms (denial, repression, displacement, and particularly projection) that come into play, hampering a deeper under-standing of the problem and blocking a resolution. For example, the projection of "sins" onto others is a common, human process, because this frees us from having to confront and deal with these issues ourselves.

While in therapy, we need to keep in mind that we have no control over the thoughts and feelings of the people who have done us wrong. It is not helpful to say that these people need to change. Focusing all the attention of the forgiveness journey on the other, who may admit no wrong and seek no forgiveness, diminishes our personal, internal power. If we strug-gle with the question of forgiveness, it is only by acquiring an attitude of compassion for others' weaknesses, realizing our human limitations, and being aware that true power only comes from within, that we can be helped. But to arrive at such a place requires an intense journey into our inner world. It requires letting go of negative thoughts of vengeance or victimization, and refocusing on the positive attributes we find in ourselves and others. People struggling with forgiveness need to accept that life is a series of learning experiences and that all life's encounters can make us wiser. Letting go of anger, spite, vindictiveness, and resentment is what personal growth is all about.

Homo homini lupus

In other words, man is a wolf to his fellow man. Few looking at our human history would doubt the truth of this famous observation. We all have a darker side. Few of us are candidates for sainthood. In many instances, sainthood may be a cover for rigidity, inflexibility, harshness, and doctrinarian behavior. Someone who looks for growth and personal development cannot be defined by a spotless life of constant kindness, smiles, and an even temperament. People who are prepared to learn from their mistakes, who know how to make amends, and choose not to repeat errors are much more realistic. These are the kinds of people who move society, institutions, organizations, and individuals forward.

Retaliatory and conciliatory behavior appears to be a fundamental part of our social and evolutionary makeup as *Homo sapiens*. Our tit-for-tat mindset implies that human relationships require balance and reciprocity. A built-in sense of fair play is part of the human condition, and we are easily outraged when the rules of fair play are broken. We go to great lengths to maintain a balance between the carrot of forgiveness and the stick of retaliation. Faced with transgressions, revenge appears to be our default position, but vengeful acting out is not the way to effective institution building.

However, the history of *Homo sapiens* has taught us that vengeance breeds more vengeance, creating endless vendettas and escalation of conflicts. History has also taught us that we have always needed various forms of social control in the form of restorative justice to manage the expression of revenge. Individual and social healing, not punishment, may be what is more needed in society.

Forgiveness can change the way society, institutions, organizations, teams, and individuals operate. Forgiveness is what brings transformational change, a quality recognized by truly transformational leaders. Such leaders appreciate what the human condition is all about – they recognize its frailty and vulnerability. Because error is human, forgiveness enables mistakes, failures, flaws, and breakdowns to become opportunities to awaken greater wisdom, compassion, and capability toward the people we deal with and ourselves. Without a context of forgiveness, life in any setting (society, institution, or organization) will become difficult.

Truly transformational leaders can create greater internal harmony and a sense of reparation by practicing the art of forgiveness, by using failures and unwanted situations to develop a culture of compassion and understanding, where people feel safe to express themselves. Forgiveness enables the creation of authentizotic organizations, because it offers people the chance to take risks, learn, and grow their own leadership abilities within the organization. And forgiveness is not only for others, but also for ourselves – leaders, too, must have the hope of forgiveness.

The psychiatrist Thomas Szasz once said, "The stupid neither forgive nor forget; the naïve forgive and forget; the wise forgive but do not forget." As I have indicated, forgiveness is a rebirth of hope. Once forgiving begins, dreams can be rebuilt because forgiveness is the key to freedom, the way out of an endless cycle of resentment and retaliation. Although forgiving doesn't change the past, it permits the building of a new future.

CHAPTER 3

Are You a Victim of the Victim Syndrome?

Self-pity is easily the most destructive of the non-pharmaceutical narcotics; it is addictive, gives momentary pleasure, and separates the victim from reality.

– John Gardner

If it's never our fault, we can't take responsibility for it. If we can't take responsibility for it, we'll always be its victim.

– Richard Bach

Take your life in your own hands, and what happens? A terrible thing: no one to blame.

– Erica Jong

Introduction

Do you know people who always behave like victims? People who blame others when bad things happen to them? And do they blame their family, partner, people at work, or any number of things that they perceive to be victimizing them? The world these people live in appears to be peopled by victims, victimizers, and occasional rescuers. And if you have ever tried helping them, have you discovered that "rescuing" them from the trouble they are in can be an excruciating process? Do you resent the way every bit of advice you offer is brushed aside or rejected, often contemptuously?

If any of these observations apply, you may be dealing with people who suffer from the victim syndrome.[1] These are people who always complain about the "bad things that happen" in their lives, due to circumstances beyond their control. Trouble seems to follow them wherever they go.

This is not to suggest that they are making it up. On the contrary, there is always truth in their stories. Bad things happen to all of us; that's life. It's not a rose garden. But there are many different ways of dealing with the difficulties that come our way. Most of us, when faced with life's obstacles, do something about them and get on with it. But people with a victim mentality are incapable of doing so. Their negative outlook on life transforms every setback into a major catastrophe. Even their way of absorbing information causes chaos and stress. To complicate this already difficult equation, people suffering from the victim syndrome are prone to aggravate the mess in which they find themselves. Strange as it may sound, they are often victims by choice. And ironically, they are frequently successful in finding willing victimizers.

Worse, people with a victim mentality are very difficult to handle. They have an extremely fatalistic outlook on life. Because they believe they have no control over the way events unfold, they have a poor sense of responsibility. Every negative outcome in their life is attributed to people or circumstances beyond their control. Every effort made to help them, or to present a solution to their predicament, is met by a huge arsenal of reasons why it will not work, some of them quite ingenious. Their problems are apparently unique and therefore insoluble. They appear always to be trying to prove the helper wrong. Anyone prepared to help them is left with a sense of utter frustration.

Personality styles

People with a victim mentality are passive-aggressive in their interactions with others. The passive-aggressive style is a very subtle, indirect, or behind-the-scenes way of getting what they want and expressing anger without openly acknowledging it, or directly confronting the source of it.[2] People who feel powerless usually resort to the passive-aggressive mode. Because they have difficulty acknowledging their anger directly (given the way they feel about themselves), they seem superficially compliant to others' needs, but are experts in passive resistance.

The blame game is part of victims' repertoire. Although their own actions are responsible for whatever situation they find themselves in, they are very talented at finding excuses why things don't work out. A common means of getting their way is to lay guilt trips on others through various kinds of emotional blackmail.[3] They will sulk, pout, withdraw, bungle, make excuses, and lie. Their talent at sending mixed messages catches others off guard. With these people we can never be entirely sure what was said or what is expected.

This behavior has a self-defeating, almost masochistic, quality. It is as if people in the grip of the victim syndrome welcome the process of getting hurt and are attracted to problematic situations or relationships. They fail to accomplish tasks crucial to their wellbeing. They set themselves up to fail, associating with people and situations that end in disappointment, failure, or mistreatment, even when better options are clearly available. They reject opportunities for pleasure, or are reluctant to acknowledge that they are enjoying themselves. Self-sacrifice is more their thing, even if unsolicited by the intended recipients of the sacrifice.[4] They have a persistent and detrimental pattern of behavior that, in its extreme expression, includes playing Russian roulette, drunk driving, excessive smoking, drug abuse, obsessive gambling, risky sex addictions, self-mutilation, and suicide.

The victim, victimizer, rescuer cycle

"The world is a dangerous place for people with a victim mentality" The world is a dangerous place for people with a victim mentality. They have always to be prepared for the worst, as it is full of people who are out to hurt them. It is a harsh environment of victims, victimizers, and occasional rescuers. Their locus of control is likely to be external, that is, they believe that what happens to people is contingent on events outside their control. Powerful others, fate, or chance primarily determine the events in their lives.[5] This kind of belief system is highly congenial to a victim mentality.

To compound the negativity of this outlook, people with a victim mentality know how to inflame others, although this may not be a conscious process. They have a knack for dragging others into the emotional maelstrom they create, keeping them off-balance with their talent for shape shifting. One moment, they present themselves dramatically as victims; the next they are morphing into victimizers, hurting the people who are trying to help them. Victim, victimizer, rescuer: it is a very messy and very fluid process.[6]

People prone to the victim syndrome are also masters of manipulation, which can make interactions with them infuriating. It is almost as if they invite people to help them, only to prove subsequently that their rescue attempts are futile. To add insult to injury, they are very good at turning things upside down, claiming that their would-be rescuers' efforts to help are actually damaging them. This can affect their behavior in such a manner that it actually causes these expectations to be fulfilled.[7]

When asked why they behave in this way, they will say that they "have their reasons." If pressed for an explanation, the "reasons" for their (at least superficially) non-sensible behavior often appear muddled and incomprehensible. People suffering from the victim syndrome are not clear why they do what they do. They have only a limited insight into the reasons for their self-destructive behavior. And even when the reasons are clear – and the means of improvement obvious – they don't want to hear what is being said. They seem to prefer being stuck in their muddle. This is what makes their behavior so puzzling and irritating.

Victims' talent for high drama draws people to them like moths to a flame. Their permanent dire state brings out the altruistic motives in others. It is hard to ignore constant cries for help. In most instances, however, the help given is of short duration. Like moths in a flame, helpers quickly get burned; nothing seems to work to alleviate the victims' miserable situation; there is no movement for the better. Any efforts rescuers make are ignored, belittled, or met with hostility. No wonder that the rescuers become increasingly frustrated, and walk away.[8]

"Victims' talent for high drama draws people to them like moths to a flame"

Of course, the essential question is why these "victims" are asking for help in the first place. Do they really want to be helped? Given the endless holes they keep on digging for themselves, they may just be looking for attention. And even negative attention is better than no attention at all. We notice how the victim style becomes a relational mode – a life-affirming activity: I am miserable therefore I am. This is a common scenario for people prone to the victim syndrome. Let's look at an example.

> Viktor, the CEO of a sustainable energy company, was wondering about the best way to deal with Amelia, one of his vice presidents. Although she had many positive qualities, Amelia was very high maintenance. She took up more of his time than any of his other direct reports and managing her was far from being a pleasure – she was such a drama queen, making scenes if things didn't go her way. And it didn't take much to make her feel wronged.

> Viktor was puzzled why such a highly competent professional always needed to play the role of victim. How was it possible for someone so bright and so talented to be so blind about her inappropriate behavior? It grated on Viktor, who had been the great advocate of gender diversity in the firm, that whenever Amelia got herself into trouble, she always blamed the "old boy" network. Viktor knew that was a poor argument. None of the other women in the company had ever mentioned it. He had bent over backward to increase the ratio of women at senior management level in the company. The idea that there was such a thing as an old boys' network in the company that was holding back women was ridiculous.

> Meetings with Amelia were like walking on eggshells. Going through her bi-annual feedback report with her was the worst. You never knew how she was going to react. John genuinely dreaded these sessions. Telling her how she could have handled a specific situation more effectively was an exercise in master diplomacy.

> And now it was time for Amelia's next appraisal. Viktor was having sleepless nights. He still had vivid memories of Amelia's overblown reactions the last time when he gave her what he thought was constructive feedback. When he talked about how a specific situation could have been handled more effectively, she went into overdrive, starting a heated argument about his input, and denying any responsibility for the way things had gotten out of hand. Couldn't she see how remarkable it was that every time something went wrong, it was always somebody else's fault? When Viktor persisted, and tried to show her that she had not just

been an innocent bystander in the example he had given, Amelia lashed out at him, again presenting herself as a victim. After these exchanges, Viktor would feel thoroughly miserable, wondering why he had bothered to go through the exercise in the first place. He felt as if he had victimized her. A typical feature of their particular *pas de deux* was that he would end up feeling sorry for her and try to calm her down. Viktor wondered how effective this approach really was, as the same scenario kept on repeating itself.

There are many Amelias – professional "victims" who act out a great variety of "scripts" in both the private and public sphere. Let's take another example.

In an hour's time, Donald, the CEO of a global bank, was due to meet Adam, one of his key people in the retail side of the business. He guessed Adam would probably want to talk about the new regional vice president position that had become available, as the present incumbent was retiring. Donald didn't think Adam was ready for the job and he was wondering how he could handle the issue if it arose.

Donald thought Adam was psychologically immature and lacked the emotional intelligence he'd need to handle the various stakeholders with whom he would have to interact. There were numerous reasons for his doubts. Adam would never take personal responsibility when things went wrong. He was always making excuses, and blaming others. He tried to weasel out of mistakes that were made on his watch. And he was vindictive. People who had "done him wrong" were never forgotten. Adam could reel off a list of them – a list that never got shorter.

On a previous occasion when Adam hadn't received a promotion he was expecting, he had stormed into Donald's office and asked him point blank whether it was because a colleague had badmouthed him. Donald denied it and explained that Adam hadn't been given the promotion because of a recent foul-up – but Adam didn't want to hear what he was saying. He refused to recognize that it was his own mistake that had "put him on ice," as he termed it, for a period.

It was not the first time that Adam had handicapped himself. With his knack for putting himself in situations that inhibited his capacity to succeed, he could be his own worst enemy. On that occasion, Donald had managed to calm him down a little by convincing him that the setback was only temporary. But he was at a loss to know what could be done to get Adam out of this conspiracy mindset and prevent him getting involved in situations that led to difficult consequences.

Adam's volatile moods were a real problem and inappropriate for a banker. Emotionally, he had a lot to learn, as their most recent interaction had proved. Adam had mailed Donald, asking to have lunch with him. Donald had responded immediately, explaining that it was too short notice; he had to be abroad all week taking care of some personal matters. He assumed that would be the end of it, but he was much mistaken. On his return, his assistant told him that his refusal to see Adam had created high drama. Apparently, Adam had blamed him for not being there for him, convinced (despite all assurances to the contrary) that Donald didn't really care for him when it mattered.

Adam had his qualities, but Donald was frankly tired of his dramatics. Why were things always exaggerated? Why was he being subjected to this emotional blackmail? He felt trapped. Adam had a victim mentality; he radiated negativity. Could his mood state be contagious, and affect the other members of his team?

The world is full of genuine victims. But without negating the reality of victimization, being a victim is also a state of mind. We can reframe difficult life situations positively or regress to a victim mindset. There is always the option to make difficult situations look like things have been "done to" us. However, whenever we refuse to take responsibility for our behavior and actions, we unconsciously choose to act as a victim. We have a lingering sense of betrayal, of being taken advantage of by others. Although the positive aspect of this position is the sense of being absolved from responsibility, the negative aspects – feelings of anger, fear, guilt, or inadequacy – far outweigh it.

Are you suffering from the victim syndrome?

Most of us dislike seeing others in trouble and want to help. But when our desire to help goes unanswered or meets with contempt, no matter what efforts we make, we should be on our guard. If you work in a role that involves helping or mentoring people who are struggling with personal or professional issues you should remain vigilant for the warning signs of the victim syndrome. Use the following checklist to see where the person you are trying to help fits on the victim syndrome scale. The more affirmative answers you can give to these questions, the more likely that person is to have a victim mindset.

- Are you dealing with people for whom always something goes wrong?
- Does every conversation end up centered on their problems?
- Do they have a tendency to play the "poor me" card?
- Do they engage in negative talk about themselves?
- Do they always expect the worst?
- Do they tend to act like a martyr?
- Do they feel that the world is "doing it" to them and that there is nothing they can do about it?
- Do they believe that everyone else has an easier life?
- Do they focus solely on negative events and disappointments?
- Do they never feel responsible for their negative behavior?
- Is their misery contagious, affecting the mood state of others?
- Do they seem to be addicted to misery, chaos, and drama?
- Do they feel that the world is out to get them?
- Does blaming others seem to improve their state of mind?
- Do they have a tendency to make others take responsibility for them?
- Do they have a knack for finding rescuers and victimizers?

What's so attractive about being a victim?

How does the victim mindset benefit the "victim"? What is the advantage of playing the victim role? And what makes these people keep doing it, despite the misery involved?

To answer these questions, we have to look beyond the obvious. A considerable amount of this behavior is beyond conscious awareness. But just as every cloud has a silver lining, every problem has its upside somewhere. To understand what is going on, we need to consider the positive aspects of being a victim. The apparent pure misery notwithstanding, there are benefits attached to playing the victim role.

Secondary gain

With victimhood, there is always the question of "secondary gain," a phenomenon with which people in the helping professions are very familiar. Secondary gains are the external and incidental advantages derived from a victim's misery, even though the person in question may not consciously be aware of them.[9] Secondary gains are the "benefits" people get from not overcoming a problem. They occur when an individual's problems persist because of the advantageous impact of the attention, affection, remuneration, access to medication, and other incentives that accompany them. Sometimes people are aware of these sources of secondary gain, but more often they lack the insight that this psychological process is taking place. They need to be shown the ways in which they are gaining from their injury.

People resort to secondary gain to get some benefit out of something that otherwise appears completely irrational. Although, objectively, secondary gain doesn't advance a life situation, subjectively it may do so, because of the benefits that accrue. Secondary gain is an important mechanism in explaining why people remain stuck in dysfunctional behavior patterns, why they persist in their misery and do not change things for

"Secondary gain is an important mechanism in explaining why people remain stuck in dysfunctional behavior patterns"

the better. Some people get a perverse pleasure from their emotional dysfunction.

However, people are not usually aware of secondary gain. These "victims" are not being consciously manipulative or faking their distress. Their misery feels very real and their reasons for holding onto it are hidden from them. The pull of the unconscious is very strong and prevents them from realizing that the cost of holding onto the condition is far greater than the gain.

Secondary gain may be a significant perpetuating factor in victimhood. Unfortunately, it is a process that is poorly understood and can be confused with malingering. Psychology 101 tells us that when people repeat specific behavior patterns, we can be sure that they are getting some kind of payoff from them.

The benefits

Playing the victim can satisfy a variety of unconscious needs. The "poor me" card elicits others' pity, sympathy, and offers of help. It's nice to be noticed and validated; it feels good when others pay us attention; and it's pleasant to have our dependency needs gratified. Being a victim is a great excuse for not questioning

"playing the victim can satisfy a variety of unconscious needs"

difficult life issues. We can remain passive and not take responsibility for our actions. We can take refuge in victimhood to accuse others of the behavior for which we are really responsible. This is particularly tempting because blaming others for life's wrongs can have a cathartic effect. We should never underestimate the sense of relief that comes with shifting the responsibility for our misery onto someone or something else. Resorting to this tactic is a relatively low-risk proposition. We don't have to take any chances.

Assuming martyrdom is also a highly effective cover for our own aggressive inclinations. The blame game combines helplessness with self-protection – passivity and activity. As the world is perceived as a dangerous place where nasty things can happen, people suffering from the victim syndrome strike out in this surreptitious way in order to defend themselves against the inevitable aggression of others.

There are other advantages to treading water in a sea of misery. Misery loves company, meaning that people who are miserable find solace in others who share their feelings. People with a victim mindset attract others. The feeling we are not alone creates a sense of solidarity, support, and interconnectedness. Perhaps we are also nurturing a secret desire for a "white knight" to materialize, and help us out of our misery – at least temporarily – until the victim, victimizer, rescuer cycle repeats itself.

So playing the victim can be a combination of coping strategy, a form of manipulation, and an attention-seeking device. Of course, there are limits to how far others will go in their support of a "victim." Constant complaining can be very tiresome. Victims will eventually lose out if a situation continues to be insoluble whatever solution is provided and otherwise willing helpers fail to get a handle on victims' behavior.

Where does the victim mindset come from?

Personality development can be as diverse as grains of sand on a beach. Each life experience is unique, although as we are all human, there are patterns in personality development that largely remain the same. Character development is always an outcome of the interface between nature and nurture. Within the context of our genetic matrix, our personality evolves through developmental processes. Much of what creates a victim mindset finds its foundation within the family of origin. Victimhood, however, is not the natural state of things. It is taught.[10] If bad things happen to people while they grow up, they will have a pessimistic outlook on life.

Depending on their own sense of victimhood, parents can either create a supportive, trustful environment for their children, or do exactly the opposite and perpetuate a bad situation. Thus they create a generational problem of victimhood, in which secondary gain gets the upper hand. For children growing up in these family situations, suffering is a way of soliciting attention and forestalling parental criticism and indifference. It makes for a paradoxical relational style in which life seems to improve when it is going badly. The parents become kinder when the child feels bad. Presenting a suffering exterior gives the child respite from an otherwise hostile and neglectful family environment.

Unfortunately, this is a very dysfunctional form of relating. Parents in these families do not recognize the harm they are doing to their children, just as their parents were unaware of what they were doing to them. But that is no excuse for bad parenting. The continuation of a dysfunctional developmental cycle is not a given. Parenthood comes with certain obligations. We can't ignore the basic needs and rights of our children. We expect adults to take a stand against abuse and create a different developmental cycle.

What gives this issue urgency is that many people with a victim mentality have been physically, sexually, and/or emotionally abused. But children do not have the emotional or cognitive capability to see abuse for what it is, and get out of an abusive system. They are forced to remain in their one-down position and may even come to see these dysfunctional forms of relating as the norm, perpetuating such self-defeating pathological behavior. Their family background may prompt them actively and repeatedly to look for situations that preserve their suffering. The script in their head runs, "See how much I am suffering? You *must* love me." This pathological way of relating is preferable to their fear of abandonment.

A common "solution" to this dysfunctional equation is that these people may feel loved only if they are punished. They may even feel insecure if punishment is withheld for any length of time. Their background may make them gravitate toward the kind of people who are prepared to inflict some form of punishment, as it is the only kind of intimacy they understand. They learn to seek out situations that re-create their early experiences.

However it is reinterpreted, child abuse always evokes feelings of hurt and insult. Because children are essentially **"child abuse always evokes feelings of hurt and insult"** powerless to stop the abuse or to convince anyone to help, they begin to perceive the whole world as "unfair" and have to find ways to cope with it. One logical human reaction is retaliation, doing to others what has been done to them. Although they may find it hard to metabolize these unacceptable feelings, the remnants of these hurts contribute to feelings of hate and desire for revenge. The experience of feeling wronged may also lead to problems of anger management. At the core, however, is the vindictive drive to get even with their parents. If violent, abusive behavior was the norm, they may join the abusers, and behave similarly.

Many of these children harbor such deep anger toward their parents that they unconsciously desire to remain dysfunctional, as a way of getting back at them. Dysfunction is their way of showing their parents how they have messed up. It's a self-destructive way of dealing with the issue but they have no conscious awareness of the defense mechanism at work. These unconscious feelings of revenge permeate all their behavior. While they deny that things are not well, they fail to acknowledge their unconscious bitterness about their fate, refusing to see how much they have been hurt.

Children who find themselves in destructive situations may wonder why this is happening to them. As they learn that blaming the world does not provide any immediate gratification, some of them learn to blame themselves for not being "good enough." Blaming, and punishing, the self can provide an immediate, controlled, but convoluted form of satisfaction. These children cannot see, let alone consciously accept, that they are now causing most of their own pain. They hope that by acting in this way they will hurt others. However, the bad feelings about being wronged are still there, pushed into the unconscious, and continue to have an effect. Consequently, these people create filters through which they interpret their situations and circumstances in life, each time reaffirming their sense of powerlessness.[11] These unconscious feelings, no matter how much they are denied, will continue to color all their interpersonal relationships.

So the abused child grows into an adult embittered by the unfairness of the world (represented by its caregivers). Powerless as they feel, at every disappointment, they find some convenient, secret means of (unconscious) self-sabotage – and will then say triumphantly, "See, they did it again. Life is unfair." This is a self-destructive way of coping. In showing the world the wrongs it can do, they mobilize a self-fulfilling prophecy.

"Self-saboteurs are masters at snatching defeat out of the jaws of victory" Self-saboteurs are masters at snatching defeat out of the jaws of victory, provoking the failure, humiliation, or punishment they feel they deserve, and undoing any good luck that comes their way. Their only sense of worth comes from self-sacrifice.

Another person's suffering evokes strong natural responses of wanting to help, or be supportive (at least initially). People suffering from the victim syndrome are likely to exaggerate or dramatize their misfortunes, to make the need for rescue even more compelling. Unfortunately, satisfying this need does not bring a "cure." Others' sympathy is precisely the reason for remaining stuck in this victim mentality. Worse, as I suggested earlier, it may even turn into a self-fulfilling prophecy, as people with this mindset will eventually begin to sabotage their own success and happiness – after all, things will always turn out badly for them, so why try? This self-sabotage becomes a form of protective reaction and brings with it the unconscious satisfaction of inflicting guilt on others – that is, they secretly hope their self-inflicted suffering will make others realize the damage they have done to them. This is a convoluted way of inflicting harm on the people who have harmed them. Whether it's expressed as overt social aggression or silent self-sabotage, revenge – a dark and cruel wish to inflict harm on the people who have been hurting them – is at the core of these processes. Let's look at another sample case.

As a child, Cal was forever in trouble of one sort or another. Some of his problems seemed inevitable, given his inauspicious family circumstances.

His mother had a hard time holding on to the men in her life. His father, a hard-drinking, abusive man, left his mother, moved to another country and remarried. Cal and his older brother, who had borne the brunt of their father's abuse, were glad to see him go.

Cal's mother was famously a drama queen, blowing things way out of proportion whenever she had the chance. Chaos and drama followed her wherever she went, and if there was a lack of drama, she knew how to create it. She was often the author of her own misery, good at playing the victim. Most of the people who dealt with her ended up emotionally exhausted. Unsurprisingly, she found it difficult to hold down a job and the financial situation at home was always precarious.

Men drifted in and out of her life, leaving Cal and his brother with a half-brother and half-sister. Looking back, Cal was subliminally aware that it had been tough growing up in his mother's household. However, some of his friends had commented on how like his mother he was.

Early on, Cal had serious difficulties at school. He was dyslexic, had poor concentration, and was easily distracted. He often skipped class, claiming he didn't feel well. His mother's gullibility was a great truancy aid, and she colluded with him. Helping him find excuses for his absence fed into her own sense of victimhood. Whenever Cal found himself in trouble, his mother would do what was necessary to bail him out. Although she might castigate him for what he had (or had not) done, she would eventually rescue him. But by constantly alleviating the natural consequences of his choices, his mother deprived him of the opportunity to learn from his mistakes.

This dysfunctional way of dealing with life made Cal increasingly dependent on others. His mother's well-intentioned rescuing sent a disempowering message, creating the foundation of a victim mentality. And as time went on, things got worse. As a teenager, Cal discovered drugs and his school record worsened with his new dependency. Apart from mathematics, which he was good at, he couldn't see the point of school. But at least there was math. Helped by his teacher, who was supportive, he managed to pull himself together enough to graduate from high school and get into a local college.

During his college years, Cal discovered women. Initially, he seemed to seek out women who let him down but eventually he moved in with a woman who seemed really to care for him. They both came from dysfunctional families and like their parents before them, their relationship quickly became very difficult, characterized by constant shape shifting: victim, victimizer, and rescuer. Looking back, Cal understood that they were both unconsciously validating their respective childhood dramas by projecting their painful beliefs and judgments onto each other. He would blame her, and she him, to help each other out of their predicament. Fighting seemed to be their default form of relating, even though it was a strange kind of intimacy. Later, Cal came to see that he tended to reject people who treated him well – making the help others provided ineffective.

Growing up with this victim mentality, Cal found himself becoming angrier as time went by. At home, he expressed his anger self-destructively toward his own children. He also acted it out at work. For example, when he was promoted to a more senior position in the company, he became extremely anxious and his poor functioning drew others' attention. He seemed to have a talent for self-handicapping and creating impediments that sabotaged a good performance. When things went wrong, it was always other people's fault, not his. When he lost his job, and his wife asked for a divorce, he realized that something needed to be done. Things couldn't go on like this.

With his family background, Cal had grown up expecting to be victimized. To fulfill these expectations, he re-created the dysfunctional patterns and feelings of helplessness he had experienced early in life. That was how he thought relationships were supposed to be. He anticipated future disappointments, and sabotaged things when they were going well. He encouraged others to take advantage of him, almost as if he enjoyed being exploited. At the same time, he rendered ineffective all attempts to help him. When he was promoted, he went into self-sabotage overdrive. After he was fired from the job, and took a less visible position, he felt much better.

Victims of childhood abuse may become victimizers, victims, or both. The pain and rage from the abuse and betrayal may turn inward, becoming self-destructive, or turn outward toward others, manifested in passive-aggressive behavior. Blaming everyone and everything for their predicament is a common pattern. Furthermore, victims are drawn to one another, programmed to be attracted to abusive relationships. There is an element of learned helplessness in their behavior. The psychological profile of victimization includes a pervasive sense of passivity, loss of control, pessimism, negative thinking, and strong feelings of guilt, shame, self-blame, and depression. All these can lead to hopelessness and despair.

Cal's story shows that some people with a victim mindset may have inherited (as I mentioned earlier) a chain of dysfunction passed down from generation to generation. Some parents unconsciously give their children the same damaging treatment they received themselves.

Living by design

Can people stuck with a victim mentality break out of this self-destructive cycle? Are there ways to stop them sabotaging themselves? Can they start living by design? People who like to play the victim must challenge their ingrained beliefs, and learn to assume responsibility and care for themselves, rather than look elsewhere for a savior.

In helping people susceptible to the victim syndrome to live by their own design, it may be useful to ask them whether they derive any benefits from retaining an apparently insoluble problem. What would they lose if they solved it? It may strike them as a strange question but as they try to answer it, they may realize that suffering has become an essential part of their identity. If they would give up this way of relating to others, what would their life look like?

Acknowledging the secondary gains attached to their present state could be the first step on a journey of greater self-awareness. People who suffer from the victim mindset need to understand that they own their misery. They are rarely aware of the extent to which they contribute to it. Have they ever thought why they naturally assume the victim role, seek out abusers, or invite abuse? Very often, when victims recognize secondary gain for what it is, it loses its value.

Helping people to overcome their victim mentality necessitates a careful analysis of the nature and quality of their interpersonal relations.[12] Once victims have learned to understand and be upfront about the secondary gain mechanisms at work, they may find it easier to come to grips with the fact that those unconscious mechanisms have been at the core of their problems. Closer scrutiny will enable them to realize that secondary gain was all that was keeping these self-defeating patterns in place. This will be the beginning of a journey in which they learn about alternative ways of coping and finding other paths through life, rather than remaining stuck in self-destructive cycles.

However, what helps victims best is the development of a healthier self-concept. They need to become cognizant of their victimized self-image and exchange it for something more constructive. This kind of transformation necessitates cognitive and emotional reorientation, new ways of thinking about themselves. They must ditch their self-projection as a martyr, because an identity based on helplessness is no longer acceptable. They need to learn to feel good about themselves. However, building a new **"building a new identity and** identity and attitudes will take time. **attitudes will take time"**

Victims also need to learn how to stop attracting people who cause them grief. They need to recognize how their passive-aggressive, manipulative behavior evokes hostile reactions in others. They have to stop the kind of behavior that perpetuates victimization and find new ways of interacting that include space for their self-respect. They need to learn that relational experiences do not have to be exercises in victimization.

People dealing with individuals with a victim mindset should recognize that there is a difference between rescuing and helping. With rescuing there is no progress, and the victim remains stuck in a dependent state. Rescuing perpetuates their tendency to hand over control and responsibility for their condition to others, even though outsourcing their life to others creates this sense of powerlessness in the first place. It is not difficult to understand why they behave in this manner. For example, Cal had been exposed to so many unhealthy injunctions – such as don't trust, don't feel, don't talk about anything meaningful – that he questioned his own competence. He was caught up in a vicious circle of helplessness and hopelessness. If people are haunted by these feelings it is hard for them to be truly authentic. Anxiety, fear, and lack of self-belief all contrive to make them feel like victims until they take control of their feelings.

In all situations of change, including change for the better, adopting a different outlook on life is hard. Many people prefer to remain victims because they find it difficult to work toward healing and living a proactive life. If victimhood has been a major life theme, it will not be easy to put aside. It might feel more comfortable to carry on blaming external or uncontrollable factors for things that go wrong. This is an effective way of channeling their anger about their fate in life and absolves them from personal responsibility. But this just perpetuates the mindset that nothing can be done to control their lives.

To tackle this, people susceptible to the victim syndrome need to practice other forms of dialogue but this requires a solid dose of awareness about their predicament. If they are unable to think differently about themselves, they will fall deeper and deeper in a downward spiral of despair and unworthiness. They must give up the benefits of using victimhood as an excuse for their conscious or unconscious blame game and take responsibility for their own actions. They need to own their own life, which means being honest about how they manipulate others, put themselves in the victim role, and use self-deprecating stories about their own ineptitude to evoke sympathy.

These people need to realize that they are no longer as helpless as they were as children. They must learn that it is preferable to make conscious choices rather than let their unconscious decide for them. However, this means breaking the downward spiral of helplessness and low self-esteem and being completely honest with themselves. They need to do away with learned helplessness,[13] take charge of their lives and stop being dependent on other people for their security.

When people have a greater sense of empowerment, they begin to accept that they can be the masters of their own destiny. With the self-esteem and confidence that empowerment brings comes the courage to face the vicissitudes of life head-on, and search for their own "cure." They will be able to move beyond the victim mentality and out of their funk of sadness and self-pity. There will no longer be any need for self-sabotage or blame.

We should not underestimate the challenge of letting go of such a fundamental part of their identity. Their history of hurt and trauma has defined who they are and they have been playing the victim over and over again in their mind. The bitterness of a grudge works like a mental poison that harms no one but themselves. The desire for revenge can be exhausting and in its worst case transform people into victimizers themselves. But it can be equally hard work getting to a place where they can let go of their feelings of resentment and thoughts of revenge and develop a sense of forgiveness. Even if they can forgive hurts and insults, it doesn't mean they will be reconciled with the person who inflicted them. Reconciliation requires that others recognize the injury inflicted, repent, and find a form of reparation.

Emotional sense-making is an essential element of overcoming the victim mentality. However, many people have a very limited knowledge of their emotional life and may need help from others to become more emotionally astute. Professional help from psychotherapists, psychoanalysts, or coaches can help people deal with the hurts that are the source of their victim mentality. While seeking in every possible way to take responsibility for their lives, they will begin to see that even if they cannot control what happens to them, they can always control their responses. When they accept this, life's circumstances will no longer control them, because they have been freed to choose their response. Taking responsibility for our own life can be hard work, and implies making difficult decisions. But if we exercise control, we can get on with life. We need to remind ourselves that we are not only responsible for what we do, but for what we don't do. As the novelist Joan Didion once said, "The willingness to accept responsibility for one's own life is the source from which self-respect springs." Taking personal responsibility is a must. We cannot change the circumstances, the seasons, or the weather, but we can change ourselves.

"We need to remind ourselves that we are not only responsible for what we do, but for what we don't do"

Chapter 4

Are You in the Rescuing Business?

Non omnia possumus omnes. (We can't all do everything.)
– Virgil

Act as if what you do makes a difference. It does.
– William James

We make a living by what we get, but we make a life by what we give.
– Winston Churchill

The need to please

Do you get a kick out of helping other people? Or do you seem to attract people in desperate need of rescuing?

As some of us may have learned from hard experience, letting our own psychological and emotional hang-ups creep into our professional interactions can spell disaster. Take for example, the following business scenario.

> Thomas had been with the company for over 20 years, the past five as CEO, and was proud of his track record. He really believed in developing his staff – he saw himself as a "people person," eager to help others make the most of themselves. He'd made the company what it was today: a

happy, effective, and successful place to work staffed by a contented workforce. Ironically, however, Thomas was probably the least contented of them all.

Miranda had worked hard to get where she was now – Vice-President Finance – and she relished the challenge that came with it. She liked the people she worked with and she especially liked Thomas, who had taken a keen interest in her progress. Indeed, Thomas was anxious to coach her in the skills she'd need in her relatively new and highly pressurized role. And he felt that he was the best person to do so.

A few weeks into her new job, Miranda and Thomas had had their first informal meeting to check on progress. Miranda felt happy with the way things were going, but confessed to feeling daunted by some of the challenges that lay ahead. Thomas reminded her that she had his full support at all times.

That would have been enough for Miranda. She appreciated a helping hand in these early days and weeks of her new position. But before long she wondered whether the feedback sessions were more for Thomas's benefit than her own. Instead of allowing her to get on with the job – and to make her own mistakes, if necessary – Thomas seemed intent on continual intervention on a micro level.

The effect was debilitating. Miranda's emerging confidence was stifled by a sense that Thomas actually lacked faith in her. As far as she could see, he seemed preoccupied with her weaknesses and blind to what she had always thought were her strengths. As their relationship unfolded, she decided that she needed to take greater control over her life. To start that process, she compiled a report enumerating her achievements to date and presented it to Thomas at their next meeting. She thanked him for his support but stated firmly that she no longer needed any special help.

At first Thomas felt hurt and rejected. He didn't like the distant stand Miranda had suddenly taken. It felt like a slap in the face. Shocked by the power of his own emotional response he suddenly felt very foolish.

What role had he taken on vis-à-vis Miranda? Had he been using their meetings to feed his own ego and satisfy possibly inappropriate feelings? In short, whom had he really been helping?

Thomas thanked Miranda for the report – he never read it, there was no need – and assured her that he had every confidence in her abilities.

Chastened, and ashamed of his own silliness, he resolved never again to let his own emotional neediness interfere with professional relationships.

Successful executives seldom get to the top alone. Even the most talented, charismatic, and self-sufficient people need the help and cooperation of other people if they are to realize their true potential. Business – as so many business leaders are wont to remind us – is fundamentally about people. And of course people need mutual support, help, and leadership.

Being prepared to help your colleagues and staff aspire to ever-higher levels of achievement is one of the fundamental roles of any leader, and some are naturally better at it than others. It is to our mutual benefit to help work colleagues and the urge to do so is both natural and laudable. Compassion, service, and dedication – these are all noble virtues and highly prized in a society where, ideally, we all help each other. From an evolutionary psychology perspective, it can be argued that we may be hard-wired to behave in ways conducive to the sociability of the species. Without the intention to cooperate, it would have been very difficult to survive as a species. Thus, we can even argue that human behavior is oriented not only toward the "survival of the fittest" but also the "survival of the nicest."[1]

But the desire to help is not always driven by such selfless, altruistic motives. Some people are motivated less by a desire to benefit others and contribute to the common good, and more by a deeper emotional need within themselves. These people are "rescuers" for whom the need to help is like an addiction. They suffer **"rescuers suffer from the disease to please"** from the disease to please; they are unable to differentiate between their own needs and those of the people they purport to help.[2] At best they make very ineffective helpers; at worst, they harm others by attempting to co-opt the people they should be helping in an attempt to resolve their own problems. This specific modus operandi comes at a cost to themselves and the people who work with them, possibly even fostering unnecessary, unhealthy, and inappropriate dependency relationships. Ironically, as time goes by, these "helpers" may begin to feel helpless, powerless, resentful, and irritated. Instead of generating exhilarating highs, helping turns into a debilitating energy drain.

So how do you spot somebody suffering from rescuer syndrome? How do you know if you are a rescuer yourself? And how can the problem of rescuer syndrome be solved?

Are you a rescuer?

When the natural urge to help other people becomes contaminated with unresolved emotional or psychological issues, it can quickly morph into a rescuer pattern without our being aware of any change in our behavior. Anybody whose role involves helping or mentoring people who are struggling with personal or professional issues should remain vigilant and look out for the warning signs of rescuer behavior. The following questions provide a useful checklist.

- Do you find it difficult to make time for yourself?
- Do you find it hard to stop thinking about other people's problems?
- Do you take a personal interest in the problems of those you are helping?
- Do your colleagues and co-workers sometimes feel like family members?
- Do you ever take responsibility for people who are in trouble?
- Are you inclined to make decisions on behalf of somebody who has asked for your help?
- Do you make excuses – explicitly or implicitly – for a person you are helping?
- Do you ever offer help to people who appear not to realize that they have a problem?
- Do you feel uncomfortable receiving help from other people?
- Do you often worry about what other people think of you?
- Do you feel guilty when you are unable to solve another person's problems?
- Does helping other people make you feel more worthy as a human being?
- Do you feel unfulfilled or anxious when there is no crisis to solve?
- Do you find it difficult or impossible to say "no" when people ask favors of you?
- Do you find it difficult to set boundaries when people put demands on you?
- Do you ever feel that your efforts to help somebody are unappreciated?
- Do you sometimes feel anger and/or resentment to be giving all the time?

- Do you feel resentful when those you are helping show no gratitude for your efforts?
- Do you ever feel mentally or physically exhausted with the effort of helping other people?
- During your childhood or adolescence were you ever made to feel responsible for the security or stability of the family?

The more often you answer "yes" to the questions above, the more likely it is that you are prone to the rescuer syndrome. Being aware of your susceptibility is the first step in countering what can be a debilitating and destructive pattern of behavior.

The rescuer trap

What we call the "rescuer syndrome" is common in all walks of life but in a professional context it can prove debilitating to individuals and damaging to businesses. It can undermine the natural balance in working relationships, interfere with productive teamwork, and reduce individuals' effectiveness.

Rescuer syndrome manifests itself when helping turns into a compulsion based on one central, but very flawed, conviction: that the only way to be appreciated is to do what other people want. These helpers don't help others out of choice; on the contrary, they seem impelled to enter into and prolong a kind of rescuer-victim relationship. It is probably fair to say that people suffering from rescuer syndrome are suffering from an addiction, much as eating, smoking, drugs, alcohol, or sex can become addictive. To outsiders, rescuing behavior can resemble some kind of heroic martyrdom. However, there is an upside to it. A closer look at its underlying dynamics may reveal that acting in this way gives rescuers an excuse to avoid dealing with their own problems.

> "people suffering from rescuer syndrome are suffering from an addiction"

However, rescuers are seldom aware of their underlying motivations and most genuinely believe that their interventions are for the better. Bearing in mind that rescuers are also very often in a senior executive position in relation to those they purport to be helping, it is often very difficult to rein them in and make them aware of the harm they are doing.

Practitioners in the helping professions – psychoanalysts, psychiatrists, social workers, counselors, coaches, and other qualified clinical professionals – are trained to differentiate their own emotional and psychological needs from those of their patient or client. They are not immune from rescuer syndrome, however. Many will have heard the story of the social worker driving along a treacherous mountain road: as he hits a patch of ice and his car plummets over the precipice, one of his clients' lives flashes before his eyes.

Helping professionals have a huge responsibility to look out for their clients' or patients' welfare. But they too are only human, and experience the same conflicting interests and needs as any other person. To be effective in their role, helping professionals must be able either to address their own needs outside the relationship or to suspend them. If they are unable or unwilling to examine their own behavior, a desire to help can go too far, turning helpers into "rescuers" unable to differentiate between their own needs and those of their clients.

Legal and ethical standards are in place to safeguard against inappropriate and potentially harmful transference in the clinical context. In clinical training, psychotherapists, psychiatrists, and psychoanalysts pay a great deal of attention to transference.[3] They go to great lengths to point out to their clients that certain behavior patterns, appropriate at an earlier stage of life, are no longer effective in the present. Their clients seem to be engaged in a "false connection." They are confusing the therapist with an important person from their past. But there are no such safeguards to regulate interpersonal relationships in a more traditional sense like a business situation. In such situations, there will not be the kind of pushback provided by the psychotherapist. Thus, those afflicted with the rescuer syndrome can often use their relationships with other people to re-enact and resolve their own emotional and psychological problems.[4] The outcome can be extremely damaging for the other person who, without being aware of what's happening, has been handed a whole new set of issues to work through – those of their "helper."

Rescuer syndrome, while not an officially recognized disorder, is a widely acknowledged phenomenon and is especially prevalent in the context of interpersonal relationships. Rescuers are sometimes characterized as "white knights," "Florence Nightingales," or "Mother Teresas" and are prone to the so-called "hero or heroine complex," which drives them to seek out people in need. Many don't realize their behavior is compulsive and dysfunctional, and many genuinely believe that their efforts are entirely for the benefit of those they are trying to rescue. The challenge is to enable people to recognize the signs that they might be suffering from rescuer syndrome; only then can they address their own problems and become effective, constructive helpers.

Real helping is a joint effort – it should never be a one-way street. Taking control of somebody else's affairs robs them of their ability to help themselves. The ultimate aim of helping, especially in the business context, is to make the helper's continuing intervention unnecessary – but rescuers cannot accept the inevitable redundancy this entails. Instead (because they need to be needed) they will try to engineer the relationship into one of co-dependency in which the person they are helping cannot cut free from the helper. When this happens, the person being helped often has no choice but to go with the flow; any initiative they take is stifled or undervalued.

But both parties inevitably suffer. The person being helped actually receives no help – and quite often the reverse – while the rescuer becomes overloaded and overwhelmed as the relationship becomes increasingly one-sided and unfulfilling. Eventually the rescuer may become helpless, powerless, resentful, and irritated. Instead of generating the exhilarating highs they aspire to, their behavior becomes a debilitating energy drain.

Some people are serial rescuers, always on the lookout for somebody who needs their help. Others become rescuers because of the specific circumstances that arise in their relationship with a particular individual. In the example I began with, Thomas felt especially protective of Miranda because of her relative youth in relation to the senior role she had been given. Instead of seeing her as somebody endowed with above-average capabilities, Thomas saw a young, vulnerable girl being thrown in at the deep end. He assumed that she needed rescuing, even in spite of the fact that he had taken a leading role in appointing Miranda to the Board.

In this case, Thomas's behavior towards Miranda was driven by strong paternal feelings (he had two sons of about Miranda's age, but no daughter), which were complicated and heightened by a suppressed sexual attraction to her; Miranda was a very attractive young woman. Thomas therefore felt highly protective of Miranda while at the same time he needed her to want his attention.

For people like Thomas, falling victim to rescuer syndrome brings about a crisis followed by a period of recovery and, in most cases, a return to normal interpersonal relationships. Serial rescuers, on the other hand, usually fail to reach crisis point and so never confront the problem. For these people, rescuing follows a cyclic pattern: they find somebody who needs help and then proceed to attempt a rescue that usually fails. The rescuer then goes in search of another person to "help." Serial rescuers often have several "projects" running simultaneously because they are incapable of ignoring someone whom they believe needs their help and because their disease to please makes them incapable of saying "no" to anyone who comes to them for help.

Very often, when "helping" becomes "rescuing," the person being helped will respond to the rescuer's ministrations by backing away. Indeed, the unwelcome attentions of a rescuer can sometimes inspire someone to take a proactive role and deal single-handedly with whatever issues they had struggled with previously. Although this is a good outcome for the person being rescued, it has the paradoxical effect of demonstrating to the rescuer that their intervention was instrumental in achieving success. A more common outcome is that the relationship deteriorates with the subject of the rescue attempt becoming dispirited and confused while the rescuer becomes increasingly frustrated. Eventually, the rescuer simply gives up and abandons the rescue attempt to go in search of the next victim.

People who successfully work their way out of an entanglement with a rescuer are usually those who, like Miranda in our example, are fully functional executives who require no more than arm's-length mentoring. In many instances they soon realize that the rescuer is not helping and they take steps to extricate themselves. But some people who ask for help operate on a very different basis: lacking initiative, they work on the assumption that the world owes them a living and that they are entitled to load their problems onto a helper. These are the people least likely to find a resolution to their problems because rescuers give them the excuse not to rise to the occasion. The result is usually a stalemate that can persist for as long as the rescuer is getting something out of the relationship.

All relationships entail an element of co-dependency if only in the sense that each party wants, and usually gets, something from the other. In most instances it is a mutual reciprocity and is not dysfunctional; but when the relationship becomes one-sided and a rescuer is partnered with a passive or emotionally detached personality, both can suffer. In this sort of relationship the rescuer can soon become frustrated by repeated but unsuccessful attempts to extract positive feedback from the rescue and will eventually become both mentally and physically exhausted by the experience.

I remember working with an executive coach who would call the office of one of her clients to tell them that he was sick, when in fact her client was a chronic alcoholic who was prone to frequent bouts of heavy drinking which rendered him incapable for days at a stretch. This is the kind of "help" that goes above and beyond normal care-taking behavior and is entirely counterproductive. The coach's behavior gave positive feedback to her client's self-destructive lifestyle and made his alcoholism sustainable. When I asked the coach why she did this she explained that her client had repeatedly told her that he couldn't manage without her and that he always felt much better after she took control for him.

The coach also said that this man was one of her best clients – and it's not difficult to understand why: he gave her the kind of positive feedback that made her feel good and created for her the illusion that she was actually helping him. The reality, of course, is that the coach was simply satisfying her need to be needed while the client was encouraged to sink deeper into his self-destructive cycle of binge drinking. Coaches with co-dependent tendencies are drawn to highly needy people and although (at least initially) their interaction with these people may be gratifying for both parties, it will not last. Rescuing never results in permanent solutions for dependent people.

> **"rescuing never results in permanent solutions for dependent people"**

Although an extreme example, this situation amply demonstrates how somebody with rescuer syndrome can feed off a vulnerable and dependent colleague. Most rescuers feel uncomfortable in equal relationships and feel most satisfied when able to elicit gratitude and appreciation from somebody who has effectively become dependent on their "help." Many rescuers need this fix on a regular basis and typically become anxious when the people they are supposed to be helping get their act together and no longer want their help.

In order to avoid the disappointment and rejection experienced when somebody decides they no longer need rescuing, some rescuers operate from a distance – interfering behind the scenes and without the cooperation (or indeed the knowledge) of those they believe they are helping. We have all experienced instances when somebody has pre-empted our actions and made decisions for us in an attempt to help us on our way: our parents did this for us as young children.

The difference, of course, is that young children are learning. Observing the actions of their parents and other adults is part of such a learning process. When an eight-year-old girl announces that she wants to dance like her favorite pop star, her mother is not acting dysfunctionally when she unilaterally enrolls her daughter in Saturday morning dance classes. Such a response is natural and constructive. However, the mother has acted in a way that imposes an obligation on her daughter – in this case an obligation to give up her Saturday mornings. But for an adult to act unilaterally on behalf of another adult (even a close relative), and especially in a way that imposes an obligation on the second adult, is to undermine the basis of the relationship and create a dysfunctional imbalance. This is true even if the person being rescued would have made the same decision or taken the same action if left to his or her own devices.

An example of "behind the scenes" rescuing is illustrated in the case of Sue, which I elaborate below. This story shows how the actions of a compulsive rescuer can harm the interests of those supposedly being "helped" without them even knowing that the rescuer has been at work. In this case there is the added component of separation, concealing the activities of the rescuer, which makes it all the more difficult for others to identify and address the problem. The outcome in this case was harmful only to the rescuer – those she was trying to rescue remained (and still remain) entirely unaware of her activities.

> Sue was the director of a corporate university in a global organization. Although efficient and helpful, she was fired after it was discovered that she had been protecting a number of the weaker participants in the company's flagship program (without their knowledge), giving them

unwarranted recommendations – while their contribution, compared to the other participants', was really below par.

In each case there was little, if any, doubt that these participants were very unlikely to get the plum assignments they desired.

So why did Sue intervene in this way? She hoped that by taking a very different perspective vis-à-vis other faculty members of the corporate university, she would create doubt in the minds of her collaborators, giving these poor-performing participants a second chance. Given their showing in the program, however, there was a high probability that they would fail – a talent strategy that could turn out very costly for the corporation.

There was nothing in this for Sue personally other than to satisfy her rescuer compulsion. She had no close working relationship with any of the participants in the program and they knew nothing of her actions. However, Sue had put herself in an untenable position and the organization had no choice but to dismiss her for gross misconduct.

A disproportionate need to be liked – a common trait in rescuers – is usually associated with a shaky self-image. Rescuers fear that putting their own interests first will be perceived by others as unkind, uncaring, and selfish (and rescuers care deeply about what others think of them). For many rescuers, saying "no" to someone who has asked a favor is letting them down and possibly even a repudiation of their relationship. Of course there are often very good reasons for declining a request for help: lack of time, resources, or expertise for example, or simply a belief that the person asking for help doesn't really need it. But a rescuer only has to see a person in need and – however inconvenient, inappropriate, or burdensome the task – they will feel an obligation to add that person's request to their list of projects. It is not surprising that rescuers often get overloaded with an unmanageable amount of emotional baggage.

As Sue's story shows, rescuers are just as much at risk of harm from their actions as those on whom they prey. This is hardly surprising, since what drives them to seek people to rescue is their own emotional or psychological insecurity, which they choose to manage by projecting onto one or more unwitting "victims" instead of confronting and tackling it head-on. Rescuer burnout is common if, as is often the case, the attempted interventions end in failure. Rescuers become fatigued and lose their sense of idealism and purpose.[5]

Rescuer burnout

Struggling under the weight of too much self-imposed responsibility rapidly takes its toll, as the helper is faced with diminishing returns. And things can get out of hand if the rescuer does not see quick results. Rescuers need the immediate gratification of seeing the results of their efforts, otherwise their stress levels quickly escalate. Even if there are no instant solutions to the problems presented to them, rescuers can feel inadequate if they don't soon provide concrete results. In their haste to be helpful they can compound problems or create new ones and they then suffer for having failed to accomplish the unrealistic goals they have set themselves. Their unhappiness is compounded by their feelings of frustration and disillusionment when they don't receive the gratitude they believe they deserve. It may cross their mind that the people they are trying to help don't really appreciate what they are offering, or worse, don't seem to want to be helped. Eventually, rescuers begin to fear they are no longer doing anyone any good and become cynical, tired, apathetic, and resentful.

In many situations, all that people who ask for help really want is to be listened to. They do not want to be told what to do. Rescuers who leap in feet first to find a "solution" presuppose a "problem" that might not actually exist. Instead of providing the passive sounding board the other person needs, they take control of the situation and start planning a course of action that is often inappropriate and totally unnecessary. Rescuers have forgotten that the purpose of helping is to allow others to discover their own course of action.

"Rescuers have forgotten that the purpose of helping is to allow others to discover their own course of action"

What feeds the need to please?

Professionals such as psychoanalysts, clinical psychologists, and psychiatrists who help people overcome emotional or psychological problems for a living know that they have to recognize the inner forces that motivate them to help others and remain constantly aware of their own emotional needs.[6] The same applies to anybody who adopts a helping role within the working environment: they must acknowledge that their own state of mind will affect the relationship they have with others. This doesn't mean, however, that we all have to be perfectly well adjusted and free from any form of dysfunctional behavior before helping somebody overcome a personal or professional difficulty – if that were true, very few people in the helping professions would ever qualify. But it does mean that, having acknowledged our own psychological situation, we must learn to separate our needs from those we aim to help.

To understand why people are prone to the rescuer syndrome we need to look into the unconscious part of their lives to make sense of the interrelationship between the "self" and the "other."[7] Children who have received consistently warm, sensitive, and responsive care from their primary carers will grow up securely attached to those close to them; they will have formed an internal working model of the "other." They become secure and confident adults with a healthy sense of self-esteem. But for children whose caregivers are needy or frequently absent, the outcome can be very different.

The dysfunctional family background of the typical rescuer can range from one in which ineffective parents or carers leave their children with no choice but to take on the parenting role themselves (and in the process lose touch with their own needs) to families that may look loving and stable from the outside but in which the parents' obsession with trying to make their children achieve perfection has created an oppressive and stifling environment.

In the first type of family, it is the parents who need parenting and the children are left to fend for themselves emotionally. Without the warmth and responsiveness they should be getting, the children grow up feeling that their needs and feelings are unimportant; they become premature caregivers. People from this kind of background find it very difficult to ask for help from others, feeling that to do so is a very selfish act. Their unsatisfactory early attachments lead to a tendency in later life to try and repair their damaged sense of self by working through painful childhood experiences that have never been resolved.

In the second type of family, the love of the parent or carer must be earned. Children growing up in this kind of environment are always striving for approval by meeting their parents' unrealistic expectations. The rigid conscious and unconscious rules laid down within the family leave little room for the child to express his or her individuality: they don't feel loved for what they are but for what they do. This early experience of conditional parental love turns the developing child into an approval addict in adulthood.

These people have an intense desire to put right the perceived wrongs of the past and their striving for perfection conceals a very real need to be accepted and recognized by their peers. Whatever they do, however, it never seems good enough and they continue to feel inadequate, flawed, and inferior. People from these two family types learn to believe that the only way they can enter a relationship is through self-denial, suffering, and sacrifice. They continually suppress and deny their own legitimate needs and replace them with the compulsive need to be useful or helpful to others.

As adults, some are still troubled by these difficult early life experiences, which create distorted assumptions about themselves and others. Cast in the role of helper in childhood, and with few emotional resources, they may be left with feelings of guilt for not having helped the ghosts from their past – meaning their dysfunctional childhood experiences – adequately.

Faulty assumptions

In addition, rescuers often operate on the basis of a number of faulty assumptions, for example: "I should always be helpful and try and please others. If not, bad things may happen"; "I should always be happy, and never show any negative feelings toward others"; "My self-worth depends on what other people think of me"; "Unless I do what other people want, I will be rejected." Frequently, this compulsion to help – to please others – is maintained by the many "musts" and "shoulds" that linger from childhood and become terrible drivers. These helpers become addicted to other people's approval, but to no avail. They never feel pleased with themselves; they never reach their self-imposed standards; and although

"striving for perfection sets people up for failure"

there is a lot to be said for setting high standards, striving for perfection is another matter altogether. It sets people up for failure. And so people suffering from rescuer syndrome enter a self-perpetuating stress cycle.

Focusing on the needs and concerns of others means rescuers can avoid having to confront their own emotional issues. They are seldom in touch with their own emotions. This attunement to others' needs may go so far that they no longer know what they really want or need themselves. Sometimes, they don't even know what to think or feel. Worse, some rescuers experience intense stress, feelings of inadequacy, and low self-regard because they persist in looking for "redemption" by helping others – the old script they follow tells them that doing things for other people will guarantee their love and respect. Instead, they may be setting themselves up for use and abuse.

By helping and caring for others, at their own expense, rescuers risk becoming a caricature of themselves. When rescuing others becomes the main driver, there can be unhealthy consequences for the giver, the receiver, and relationship as a whole. Trying to meet others' expectations only contributes to self-destructive or unduly self-sacrificial behavior. These rescuers may do more harm than good and prevent people who are looking for help discovering salient issues on their own.

Managing the rescuer syndrome

The only way to address the problem of rescuer syndrome is to face it squarely, although this will not be easy. Rescuers can only change their behavior if they learn to recognize the flaws in their reasoning and examine some of the assumptions they have about themselves. For example, they need to take stock of the kind of people they are attracted to and learn to detach from the toxic people in their lives – people who are emotionally and physically draining. They should take a serious look at the reasons why they feel compelled to want to help someone[8] and if they decide that they are doing it for the wrong reasons, walk away from the relationship. When rescuers realize that they no longer have to heal the whole world as they were encouraged to do in childhood – a time when they were least capable of doing it – they will be not only more effective, but also much happier.

Tackling rescuer syndrome does not mean having to give up helping others. The urge to help others is a force for good, so long as it is not allowed to mutate into the dysfunctional behavior of rescuer syndrome. Constructive rescuers can be catalysts in the process of helping people solve their own problems and their role is to encourage others to make difficult decisions for themselves. But to be constructive helpers, people need to be able to think rationally, objectively, and dispassionately about other people's problems. And to be able to do that, they must have sufficient self-knowledge to know how to prevent their own emotional health affecting those they aim to help.

Being a constructive rescuer

There is a role for constructive rescuers in an organizational context, and, ideally, any effective executive with a solid dose of social and emotional intelligence will have the psychological and interpersonal skills needed to play the part. Constructive rescuers are sensitive to the needs of others – within reason. They don't engage with others' problems at the cost of their own health and happiness; they don't let others use them as a dump for their emotional baggage; and they make it clear to the people they work with that they should recognize and accept the consequences of their own troubled behavior. Their role is to be a catalyst in the problem-solving process, rather than put others in their debt (see Exhibit 4.1).

They are also prepared to face difficult questions and ready to tell the truth, even if it is not what people would like to hear. But they time their inventions well, striking when the iron is cold: too soon and their support will be unappreciated; too late and the opportunity will be lost. Their openness and frankness, and their ability to recognize and express their own feelings in the interface with the people they work with, makes these exchanges extremely valuable. And rescuers can be even more constructive if they can do all this with a sense of humor.

EXHIBIT 4.1 CONSTRUCTIVE RESCUERS – A PROFILE

- Emotionally receptive to their own and others' thoughts, feelings, physiological responses, and behavior.
- Respectful of others' autonomy and ways of functioning.
- Good at asking questions that make others feel challenged and supported rather than criticized.
- Empathetic listeners – their ability to make people feel understood enables them to build effective relationships.

- Emotionally sensitive – able to share others' emotions without losing their sense of boundaries.

- Tolerant of ambiguity – they value the cognitive complexity of the human condition and do not strive for closure.

- Self-disciplined – knowing where to draw the line.

- Self-aware – conscious that their emotional health affects the quality of their work.

We all have our unique combination of strengths and weaknesses; we all have a darker side; and we all need help at times, including those who do the helping. But it is imperative that helpers help themselves before they start to help others. Executives can raise the quality of their relationships with the people they work with by becoming aware of their own unique attachments and aversions. By knowing their own limitations, and ensuring that they have their own support system, they will ensure that they don't fall victim to rescuer syndrome.

"But it is imperative that helpers help themselves before they start to help others"

CHAPTER 5

The Psycho-Path to Disaster: Coping with SOB Executives

The more he talked of his honor the faster we counted our spoons.

– Ralph Waldo Emerson

The psychopaths are always around. In calm times we study them, but in times of upheaval, they rule over us.

– Ernst Kretschmer

The world is a dangerous place. Not because of the people who are evil; but because of the people who don't do anything about it.

– Albert Einstein

The fast track illusion

Richard typified the enigma of upward failure. To people who knew him superficially, he seemed successful but people closer to him were less convinced. Those who had only a passing acquaintance with him thought him an obvious candidate for a senior position in the company. However, others who knew more about his track record came to a very different conclusion. None of the assignments for which Richard had been responsible had been truly successful. In fact, his career had been a moving disaster – but thanks to his seductiveness, charm, and talent at manipulating others, he had got away with it. Richard was like the proverbial cat with nine lives. Disaster frequently struck due to his incompetence or laxness, yet he had an uncanny ability to limit negative fallout. His mental agility when faced with such moments of truth, and the speed with which he moved on to another assignment, and then another, were remarkable. It was always left to his successor to clean up the mess he had made.

As a leader in the organization, Richard could be best described as "the great unfinished" – completing projects was not one of his strengths. He left such mundane activities to others. And if his bait-and-switch strategy (misleading his superiors and co-workers) failed to work, he had a knack of pinning the blame on whoever suited him. He had never been any good at taking responsibility for his actions. To him, his self-serving way of doing things was the most natural thing in the world. Even his most recent assignment (the role of senior VP of a small media company) he had left without controversy, having been headhunted to join a much larger organization – but only just in time. Once he was no longer there, the results of his disastrous tenure became apparent.

Yet, on first impression, Richard had a lot going for him. Good-looking and gregarious, he had the gift of the gab and was an expert at sweet-talking everyone he met. Most people watching or listening to his webcasts, podcasts, interviews, or presentations would consider him eloquent and socially adept. Fortunately for him, only a very few could see through his glibness and superficiality. His apparent "can-do" attitude toward whatever obstacles came his way didn't hurt his career prospects, either. He came across as a very decisive, action-oriented, gifted executive. His talent for impression management also made him remarkably effective in dealing with his superiors: he always told them what they wanted to hear. Small wonder that most people who met Richard saw him as fast-track material; however, an astute observer of his behavior would be tempted to see him as a con artist.

For example, most of the promises Richard made turned out to be vacuous – and he was a habitual liar. He could lie point-blank to someone's face while appearing honest and candid, only to stab them in the back as soon as they turned away. A number of people who had worked closely with Richard suggested his lying was compulsive. Whenever there was a risk he would be caught out in one of his lies or half-lies, he was able to change the subject quickly. Mysteriously, he had got away with this very dysfunctional leadership behavior, seemingly forever. In that respect, he was a true Machiavellian, a real survivor. Manipulation came as naturally to him as breathing. His ability to make friends in high places and home in on people willing to protect him also helped him in his climb to the top. He easily won over the main decision makers, for example, by taking an interest in their family and hobbies, participating in their vices, offering to do their dirty work, and promising them great results if given free rein.

People who had worked for Richard – and quit – described him as exploitative and deceitful, shamelessly ready to take credit for other people's work. They also complained about his ruthlessness and "instrumentalism," the way he used others purely as means to an end. For the yet unconvinced, they would list a whole lineup of victims who had crossed his path.

Richard was so manipulative that most people didn't notice what had hit them until they were victimized. Incompetent though he was in many areas, Richard had a remarkably good insight into the needs and weaknesses of other people. Good liars are often good judges of people. Power-driven himself, he knew exactly how to take advantage of other people's vulnerabilities, directing his energy toward insecure people in particular. He operated like a spider, weaving a web of lies and deceit, catching his victims unawares, sucking the life force out of them, discarding the empty husk, and moving on to the next victim. He was extremely effective in taking away people's belief in themselves and their abilities, and their trust in others, leaving some of them cynical, bitter, and almost unable to function. Because he was prone to boredom, Richard seemed to need a constant supply of new victims to re-energize himself.

What really puzzled those who had the measure of Richard was that the people caught in his web usually described their initial encounter with him as like finding a soul mate, typically claiming, "We have so much in common," "We're so much alike." They seemed to delude themselves into thinking that they had initiated an instant friendship. They failed to recognize that Richard had really been engaging in an exercise in mimicry, reflecting their own persona back on the person he was talking to, a talent that is sure to be endearing – it's nice and easy to fall in love with yourself.

Richard could also be compared to a canny trapeze artist, always able to regain his balance due to his talent for getting others to cover for him whenever he got himself into trouble. And according to some who had not been conned by him, one of Richard's most recent victims was the company's head of communications. Those in the know felt that he was taking advantage of her naivety; given the way she talked about him, some wondered whether their relationship, which seemed to be a one-way street, went beyond work. She might be emotionally involved, but was he? She was always at his beck and call and always prepared to cover for him. People who had figured out what Richard was really like doubted whether he had an empathic bone in his body; when it came to emotional sensitivity, he was color-blind. It was true that he seemed able to say the right thing at the right time but where was the real feeling? It seemed that he only knew how to pantomime feelings, rather than experience them. Short-term self-gratification seemed the only thing that counted.

Apart from these significant character flaws, Richard also demonstrated poor behavioral control. His emotional state could be very volatile, shifting between anger, happiness, and misery. People were recounted incidents when he had lost his temper, dressing people down in public. Witnesses to these outbursts reported that they didn't last very long and seemed to be instantly forgotten.

Finally, a serious concern for some people in the office was the confusion about Richard's background. Some began to question whether he was an imposter, citing impressive but fictitious credentials. Suspicion circulated about his previous activities and the opacity of his career time line. Some whispered that there were some gaping holes. What was Richard trying to hide?

Driving people crazy

Imagine being completely free of internal restraints and doing whatever you please. Imagine a mental state that entails no conscience. Imagine having no feelings of remorse or guilt, whatever unpleasant things you may be doing. Imagine caring only for number one, and having absolutely no concern for the well-being of others. Imagine responsibility being an empty term, having no conceptual meaning. Imagine giving no second thought to the shameful, harmful, or immoral actions you have taken.

"Imagine caring only for number one, and having absolutely no concern for the well-being of others"

Wouldn't such an emotional deficit be a great blessing? Wouldn't life be much simpler and more pleasurable without inhibitions? A conscience is a nuisance; empathy is a drag. Without the usual pangs of shame and guilt, you would be able to do anything. Nothing would hold you back.

We tend to assume that a conscience is a universal human feature, which makes it hard (for most of us) to imagine that there are people with this kind of personality makeup. And because we can't imagine that such people exist, they become to all intents and purposes invisible to us. We are unprepared for encounters with these individuals. We don't recognize them. The presence or absence of conscience creates a deep divide between people.

For the purpose of maintaining our own sanity, we had better accept that a small portion of the population has a psychological makeup and mind-set very different from the rest of us. Alien though they are, they blend in with the general population. They assume a kind of stealth position within organizations and society. Not only are they conveniently invisible, they may not even realize that they *are* different – they are equally invisible to themselves. Their lack of conscience means that the usual tools for societal control don't work and are irrelevant to them. The implications of this can be severe. These people can bring havoc to the lives of others and are often described as psychopaths.[1]

Alien though psychopaths may seem to most of us, they have always been around. Many of the historical figures who committed crimes against humanity fall within this category. Under traumatic social situations, like war, poverty, economic breakdown, epidemics, or political strife, for example, psychopaths may even acquire the status of leaders and saviors. We only have to think of Adolf Hitler, Josef Stalin, Mao Zedong, Kim Jong-il, Serbia's Slobodan Milošević and Radovan Karadžić, or Syria's Bashar al-Assad for some real-life examples. But we probably come across psychopaths more often in popular fiction and films, like the highly decorated renegade Colonel Kurtz in *Apocalypse Now*; Hannibal Lecter in *Silence of the Lambs*, turning cannibalism into gastronomy; the investment banker and serial killer Patrick Bateman in *American Psycho*; or Martin Vanger, another serial killer and a successful CEO in *The Girl with the Dragon Tattoo*. These morally depraved individuals represent the "monsters" in our society. They are portrayed as unstoppable and incorrigible predators whose violence is planned, purposeful, and emotionless.

But only a small subset of psychopaths becomes the violent criminals so often fictionalized in films and novels. There are many less extreme forms of psychopathy, quite different from what we usually associate with the kinds of character disorder found among criminal types. Not all psychopaths are destined for prison; some may even be in top executive positions. Wherever power, status, or money is at stake, such individuals will be around. The power games that typify organizational life come naturally to them. Compared to the monstrous historical and fictional characters mentioned here, these people are not overly violent or antisocial; their disturbing behavior is not so in your face. Instead, they are likely to channel their energies in less obvious, less violent ways. They know how to blend in and conceal their difference in order to manipulate others more effectively. Thus if we create a spectrum of pathology, fictional psychopaths like Kurtz, Lecter, Bateman, and Vanger would represent the extreme end of the spectrum while the successful psychopathic executive would sit at the other.

The major differentiator between psychopaths and the rest of the population is their lack of conscience. These people are unable to experience "normal" feelings of shame, guilt, or remorse. And although their stealth behavior makes them hard to recognize, there are plenty of them out there. According to Robert Hare, a major specialist in psychopathy, approximately one percent of the population falls within the psychopath category – and a much larger number can be found in executive positions. Estimates vary, but approximately 3.9 percent of corporate professionals can be described as having psychopathic tendencies, a figure considerably higher than is found in the general population.[2] From these observations we can deduce that many people working in organizations have a fair chance of experiencing a pathological boss.

To increase our understanding of this kind of behavior in an organizational setting, in this chapter I introduce the *Seductive Operational Bully*, or SOB executive – an individual who could also be described as psychopath "lite" – and differentiate SOBs from more traditional psychopathic types. (I will say more about this later.) Compared to "heavy" psychopaths, most of whom can be found in prisons or mental hospitals, SOBs are much better at keeping up a consistent outward appearance of normality. Their behavior may even be so adapted to certain organizations that some of them will reach top executive positions.

Unburdened as SOBs are by a conscience, they can be quite effective – at least for a while. Many global corporations have become highly attractive to people who are eager to advance themselves at the expense of others and the companies they work for. Financial institutions in particular have turned out to be playing fields where SOB executives can really flourish. People like Richard Fuld, former CEO of the now bankrupt Lehman Brothers, or Bob Diamond, former CEO of Barclays have not exactly been role models of exemplary business leaders. Only recently have we woken up to the fact that trusting our money to "banksters" can be a highly risky proposition. Because financial institutions need a high level of trust in order to function effectively, we make the false assumption that the people who run these institutions are honorable. But SOB executives, of whom trustworthiness is not a feature, flock to these financial institutions. They feed on the trust placed in them by others to their own advantage. Such "feeding" frequently is of a very pathogenic nature.[3]

Given the difficulties in identifying these people (due to their stealth characteristics), how many individuals have psychopathic tendencies will remain guesswork. To classify a person as a "psychopath lite" can be an uphill challenge. But within this category we can find many seductive politicians, investment bankers, and other snake oil salesmen such as cult and religious leaders – people not necessarily included in a superficial count. Furthermore, many white-collar criminals may turn out to be psychopaths. It should also be noted, however, that full-blown psychopaths are extremely rare in top management positions, as such people tend to self-destruct.

It's difficult to recognize SOBs as most people working for them lack the knowledge and skills to respond effectively and deal with them. Either they don't understand the cause of their problems, or they don't know how to fight back. To make matters worse, SOB executives usually have the dedication, focus, and business acumen to create the appearance of success. Their weapons include emotional blackmail, dishonest yet persuasive language, discrediting others around them, deflecting the issue at hand when confronted, concealed threats, and lies or distortion of the facts. SOBs have

"SOBs have mastered the art of manipulation disguised as helpfulness, good intentions, or working 'for the good of the company.'"

mastered the art of manipulation disguised as helpfulness, good intentions, or working "for the good of the company." They are very talented at hiding their true motives, while making others look incompetent, uncooperative, or self-serving. Moreover, they are highly skilled at making others lose their job, do their job for them, or even getting others to apologize when confronted about their own manipulative behavior. The only thing that counts for SOBs is winning. Winning means getting their way, and maintaining a position of power and control over others. They can undermine their opponents with subtle innuendo, making sure the slander reaches the major power-holders in the organization. Most remain oblivious to their underhand methods – to such an extent that SOBs are often held up as examples of leaders on the fast track. But while SOBs are being rewarded for undeserved success, frustration builds up among the people in their immediate surroundings for whom life in the organization has become a nightmare. And organizations of all sizes can be duped, charmed, and ultimately destroyed by SOBs, if they are given enough power.[4]

As I have suggested, SOB executives are adept at climbing the corporate ladder because they can cover up their weaknesses by subtly charming superiors and subordinates. Some may even be so stealth capable that nobody ever recognizes the psychopathic quality of their behavior. Their effectiveness in using others as scapegoats helps in hiding their own incompetence. When we put their activities under the microscope, many of them are really terrible performers. And their toxic influence can be dramatic. As their concerns with their own advancement and enrichment in terms of power and money take precedence over any concerns over the continued success of the business or organization they work for, disaster may loom. They can wreak more havoc on organizations than most other dysfunctional executives do, as they drag other people into their destructive web. Ironically, as these people are unable to comprehend the meaning and significance of their behavior for other people, and to judge their probable reactions to their behavior, they are often astounded to find that others are upset by their exploits.

An essential point to keep in mind, however, is that "tough" or "demanding" bosses are not necessarily SOBs as long as they are respectful and fair, and their primary motivation is to obtain the best performance from their people by setting high, yet reasonable expectations for working effectively.

What makes for an SOB executive?

To understand SOB executives better, we need to take an excursion into the field of psychiatry and neuropathology, and have a closer look at psychopathological behavior.[5] This peculiar condition has been recognized for centuries, described as "madness without delirium" and "moral insanity." In 1835, the physician James Cowles Prichard portrayed "moral imbecility" as a mental derangement, not of intellect but of perverted feelings and depraved behavior patterns.[6] Emil Kraepelin, one of the founders of modern psychiatry, used many terms to describe psychopathy, including antisocial, morbid liar or swindler, impulsive, self-serving, glib, and charming but lacking inner morality.[7] In the late 1800s a German psychiatrist coined the term "psychopath."[8] However, it was Hervey Cleckley, in his classic discourse on psychopathy *The Mask of Sanity*, who broadened the definition to include behavioral patterns such as manipulativeness, insincerity, egocentricity, and lack of guilt – characteristics of criminal behavior that are also found in less manifestly disturbed individuals, including executives.[9] Psychopaths were described as predators who control and intimidate others to satisfy their own selfish needs, always looking out for number one.[10] Lacking in conscience and empathy, they are prepared to take what they want, and do as they please, violating social norms and expectations without any feelings of guilt or remorse.

Descriptions of psychopathy, sociopathy, and antisocial personality disorders[11] can be quite confusing. Looking at the literature, we will discover that many of these classifications are repetitive, overlap, and are used interchangeably. As a matter of fact, the term psychopath (and its later 1930s synonym, sociopath) has always been a sort of "wastebasket" category, originally widely and loosely applied to violent and unstable criminals.[12] To emphasize this point, the American Psychiatric Association's Diagnostic and Statistical Manual for the Mental Disorders tends to view the terms psychopathy and sociopathy as misnomers, preferring to remain with observable behavior. According to them, the identification of variables such as remorse and guilt gives clinicians too much room for subjective interpretations.[13] The World Health Organization, however, has taken a different stance in its International Classification of Diseases (ICD-10) by referring to psychopathy, antisocial personality, asocial personality, and amoral personality as synonyms for dissocial personality disorder.

It becomes apparent, as we wade through this nosological mess, that the use of these different terms depends largely on the background of the people using them. For example, the term sociopathy is preferred by psychologists and sociologists, who see personality disorders as social factors, produced by childhood trauma and abuse. In contrast, neuroscientists, biologists, and geneticists view psychopathy as a consequence of physiological defects that result in the underdevelopment of the part of the brain that is responsible for impulse control and emotions.

An etiological diversion

But where does psychopathy come from? What causes it? First, psychopathy does not spring into existence unannounced in adulthood. From early on, children with a psychopathic disposition behave differently from other children in indeterminate ways. They are said to be more "difficult," "willful," "troublesome," or "hard to relate to." But whatever the early indications of psychopathy may be, the etiology of psychopathic behavior is complicated by the intricate interplay of biological and environmental variables. Mental health professionals spend an inordinate amount of effort trying to figure out whether nature or nurture contributes to this condition. For example, children can manifest a psychological problem called conduct disorder.[14] This presents itself through a repetitive and persistent pattern of behavior whereby the basic rights of others, or major age-appropriate norms, are violated. Such behavior is often the precursor of antisocial personality disorder. However, while these childhood signs have been found in a significantly higher proportion of psychopaths than in the general population, not all the subjects of such childhood diagnoses turn out to be psychopaths as adults, or are even dysfunctional. Again, we are faced with the nature-nurture conundrum. There are no early life experiences that are consistently found to be directly associated with a subsequent diagnosis of psychopathy. Many people who experience a difficult childhood grow up, succeed in overcoming their past, and turn out to be upstanding citizens. Decades of research and clinical observation have failed to produce consistent findings about negative experiences in the background of psychopaths. Most people who are maltreated in childhood do not become psychopaths or criminals (although, in many cases, serious problems may ensue).

"The origin of a central feature of the psychopathic mind continues to mystify mental health professionals"

Because of the paucity of direct causal relationships, the etiology of psychopathy has remained rather obscure. The origin of a central feature of the psychopathic mind – lack of conscience and lack of empathy – continues to mystify mental health professionals.[15] No wonder, then, that there has been a trend within forensic psychology to discount possible adverse childhood experiences as precursors of adult criminality. Many criminologists hold the view that true psychopaths are born, not made. They point out that children's ability or inability to bond readily, and their problems with attachment behavior, are largely the result, rather than the cause, of psychopathy. From this perspective, the causality of abuse has not been popular. Psychopaths' talent for preying on others' sympathy is legendary. No wonder that diagnosis of the condition has overshadowed etiology.

The question remains: what can be viewed as developmental and what as genetic in the creation of psychopathy? Given the lack of consistency about causality, most research about psychopaths has taken a genetic or neurological direction. The biological relationship between the brain and psychopathy is at the center of most of these studies. For example, many intriguing, consistent correlates of psychopathy (affective, semantic, and physiological differences) have been established in the laboratory. Usually, these tests suggest that psychopaths are prone to neurological (probably genetic) anomalies – that is, faulty wiring can be blamed for their condition.[16] According to some of these studies, biogenetic deficiencies (neurological abnormalities, mainly in the frontal lobe of the brain) prevent psychopaths from processing complex emotional experiences. The cause of the non-typical anatomy or chemical activity within this area of the brain may be abnormal growth (possibly genetic), brain disease, or injury.

Psychopathy has also been associated with a reduced response rate in the amygdala, two small regions buried near the base of the brain that are associated with emotional reactions and emotional learning, affecting aggression, sexuality, and recklessness. Dysfunction of the prefrontal cortex, which is responsible for impulse control, decision making, emotional learning, and behavioral adaptation, is also associated with psychopathy.[17] It appears that in psychopathic individuals, only the more primitive affective reactions from the reptilian brain (for example, fight-flight) come through, unmodified by the functions of the cerebral cortex. Because of this specific deficit, psychopaths are unable to "recognize" emotions in others.

This line of research has been supported by studies using positron emission tomography (PET), a nuclear medicine imaging technique that produces a three-dimensional image or picture of functional processes in the body. PET provides a visual demonstration of the reduced metabolic activity of neurons within the brains of psychopaths.[18] Hormonal functioning has also been assessed in attempts to identify physiological differences between psychopaths and "normal" people. For example, a few studies have found psychopathy to be linked to low cortisol levels.[19]

In spite of this considerable body of research evidence depicting physiological differences between psychopaths and the general population, the nature proposition for psychopathy does not necessarily rule out the influence of nurture. In most instances of complex personality dynamics, both nature and nurture play a role. For example, some people may have a genetic predisposition to a disorder, but the environment in which they are brought up very much determines how these dysfunctionalities will be expressed. As 35–50 percent of personality characteristics are inherited, a considerable percentage of what makes people behave the way they do is left unexplained.[20]

Thus in spite of the biogenetic predominance in research concerning the behavior of psychopaths, a substantial number of mental health practitioners continue to address the role of unstable, unhappy childhood environments in the genesis of criminality and antisocial behavior. Psychopathy, parental rejection, and lack of affection seem to be close cousins. Difficult nurture can accentuate psychopathic behavior patterns.[21] The many biogenetic findings notwithstanding, there remains a substantial body of research that points out that inconsistent discipline and disruptions to family life (e.g., divorce, separation, and rejecting, physically abusive parents) can be predictors of adult criminal activity.[22] Most psychopaths begin to exhibit serious behavioral problems – for instance, persistent lying, cheating, theft, arson, truancy, substance abuse, vandalism, and precocious sexuality – at an early age.

Given these inconsistent findings, my earlier suggestion to differentiate between two kinds of psychopaths (the fundamental "heavy,"
positioned at one extreme of the spectrum, and the psychopath "lite" –
the SOBs – at the other end) becomes more comprehensible. Unlike
fundamental psychopaths, born without the capacity to form emotional
bonds (due to serious genetic abnormalities), psychopaths "lite"
experience a deactivation of the development of basic affective patterns
(due to the interplay of nature-nurture). In their case, developmental
forces may have played a more significant role. The repair of faulty
"wiring" was not an option. Their capacity for empathetic response
has been impaired due to repeated disillusionment in their childhood,
caused by physical or sexual abuse or other forms of maltreatment.
Over time, these negative environmental experiences may have led to
the deactivation or poor repair of normal human emotion, resulting
in psychopathic behavior patterns. In later life, affective inhibition can
have serious consequences, particularly if psychopaths function on a
larger stage – like organizations or society.

Fit between individual and organization

For example, the behavior of SOB executives also raises the question of
the nature of the interchange between individual and organization. How
do organizations affect people, and vice versa? How does this interplay
work itself out? Is the modern corporation a heaven for psychopaths? To
illustrate, take Joel Bakan's popular documentary film *The Corporation*,
based on his book of the same title.[23] Bakan's film maintains that modern
corporations are driven by shareholder value, regardless of how this
affects the interests of workers, society, or the environment. And this
simple motivation is seriously worrying. It can easily become a liability,
and dangerous to societal well-being. In their unimpeded pursuit of
profit, many companies pollute the environment, exploit workers, and
commit accounting fraud. Maximizing shareholder value contributes to a
list of pathologies that includes "disregard for the well-being of others,"
"inability to form lasting relationships," and "deceitfulness," adversely
affecting the mental health of the people who work for such institutions.
The film suggests that corporations, driven by self-interest and financial
greed, are themselves psychopathic.

In Bakan's view, corporations motivated to create wealth for their shareholders conveniently ignore the social burdens that accompany their activities. They put others at risk in order to satisfy their profit-maximizing goals, and in the process harm employees and customers, and damage the environment. Instances of serious social damage include child labor, exploitative low wages, manipulative advertising, unhealthy foods, and unsustainable environmental destruction. They can be two-faced and opaque – exercising selective disclosure, they may not reveal information indicating that their products can cause harm; they can be amoral, rationalizing their decisions; they are conscience-free, yet able to mimic caring and altruism, helped by deceptive advertising campaigns. Corporations relate to others only superficially, via make-believe versions of themselves created by media companies. What's more, through their relentless pursuit of profit, a number of these companies get good people to do bad things. This begs the question, from an adult development point of view, of whether it is the corporation that reinforces (and accentuates) people's SOB characteristics, or whether SOB executives create this type of corporation.

Perhaps the outcomes – positive or negative – are an issue of fit. We can construct a simple individual-organization matrix with dimensions such as "health" and "neurosis" and identify the worst of all scenarios: perfect fit between the neurotic organization and the neurotic individual.[24] This combination creates a highly toxic, Darwinian organizational culture. To survive in it, executives need to be ruthless, incessantly looking out for number one. At the opposite end of the matrix, we find a more constructive situation in which both organization and individual are relatively healthy. This is the best fit, but it is also a rare one. I have called these authentizotic organizations, places where people operate at their best.[25] The more problematic quadrants represent situations where there is a misfit between organization and individual. One of these contains a healthy individual in a neurotic organization, which makes the individual sick. It is not easy to remain sane in insane situations. Another quadrant contains a sick individual – an SOB executive, for example – who is responsible for creating a toxic corporate culture in an otherwise healthy organization. See Exhibit 5.1 for a review of the various options.

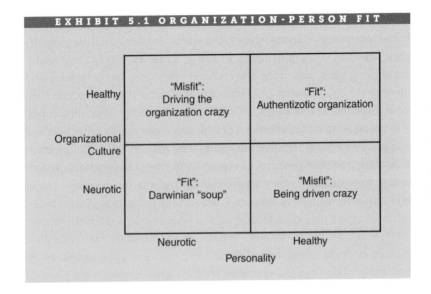

EXHIBIT 5.1 ORGANIZATION-PERSON FIT

		Neurotic	Healthy
Organizational Culture	Healthy	"Misfit": Driving the organization crazy	"Fit": Authentizotic organization
	Neurotic	"Fit": Darwinian "soup"	"Misfit": Being driven crazy
		Personality	

How to identify SOB executives

As I have suggested, SOB executives are difficult to spot – at least initially.

"SOB executives are difficult to spot – at least initially"

Many of us will fail to recognize their Machiavellian disposition, and would even deny or attempt to rationalize their improper, unethical behavior. This is not helped by the reluctance of people who are in the know to admit that they have been betrayed and duped. For senior management, identifying and neutralizing SOBs may require the ability "to listen with the third ear" – to be able to pick up subtle signals in the organization.

So are you dealing with an SOB executive? It's worthwhile to think about the following questions when referring to people with SOB tendencies in your organization:

■ Does s/he come across as too glib and too charming?
■ Is s/he very self-centered?
■ Does s/he have a sense of grandiosity?
■ Does s/he have a constant need for stimulation?

- Is s/he prone to boredom?
- Is s/he a chronic liar, even about minor issues?
- Is s/he cunning and manipulative?
- Does his/her behavior demonstrate a complete lack of remorse, shame, or guilt?
- Is s/he characterized by shallow emotional experiences?
- Is s/he callous?
- Does s/he lack empathy?
- Is s/he extremely self-serving?
- Does s/he have a parasitic lifestyle?
- Does s/he see others as targets and opportunities?
- Does s/he have poor behavioral controls?
- Can s/he act extremely irresponsibly?
- Is s/he very impulsive?
- Does s/he bend organizational systems and rules to their own advantage?
- Does the end always justify the means for him/her?
- Is s/he good at blaming others for their own mistakes?
- Does s/he have a strong sense of entitlement?
- Does s/he construct complex webs of lies?
- Does s/he have difficulty distinguishing fact from fiction?
- Does s/he like to exploit, abuse, and exert power?
- Does s/he act as though "winning" is all that counts?
- Is s/he sexually promiscuous?
- Did s/he have early behavioral problems?

If the majority of these questions are answered in the affirmative, you may be dealing with an SOB executive. The typical executive would rate a "yes" on only a few of these questions.[26]

Unfortunately, being exposed to SOB executives can take its toll on people's health and well-being. Paradoxically, in spite of this, many excuses can be heard for their unacceptable behavior, ranging from "It's just her robust management style" to "He's only trying to stretch that person." In addition, other commonly overheard reactions are that the victims of SOB behavior "must be weak," "must be incompetent"

"being exposed to SOB executives can take its toll on people's health and well-being"

or they would not allow themselves to be dealt with in such a way. Many of the victims of SOBs are so intimidated that they fear losing their job if they speak out against inappropriate behavior. They prefer to remain silent, to take stress-induced sick leave, or worse, decide to leave. Unchallenged, a large percentage of SOBs get away with their tyrannical and destructive behavior. Generally, people prefer to leave an organization rather than take the tenuous path of building a formal case or filing a complaint against them.

Dealing with the SOB executive

Given the power and influence that these individuals wield, can anything be done to make them accountable? What can individuals and organizations do to prevent SOB behavior running wild? What can be done to stop SOBs within an organization?

To respond to these questions, it's important to keep in mind that SOB-like behavior is not just the incidental bad behavior of one individual. SOB executives thrive when others in the organization condone or tolerate this kind of behavior. Thus, this kind of dysfunctional behavior can also be seen as a process whereby the SOB, victims, and bystanders all have an important role to play in creating toxic power dynamics. And in dealing with these kinds of people, we can take both an individual and organizational perspective. To illustrate this process, I will first give an example of an executive who was faced with this challenge.

What can an individual do about it?

Jane Howard was at her wits' end. She felt close to a nervous breakdown. How quickly her life had changed, from extreme fulfillment to deep misery. Initially, she had been very pleased about how well her job had unfolded at the medical instrumentation company for which she had been working. She had been thoroughly successful, moving up from the position of research associate (just after her graduation from engineering school) to being the head of new product development. But now all that seemed to be in the remote past. The tune changed when her boss retired and was replaced by John Preston, an executive who had previously worked for an engineering company. On paper, John looked like a real find. The reality, however, proved quite different. Granted, he seemed to get along well with the people who counted in the company, but the way he dealt with his subordinates was very different. John's way of trying to get better results was management by intimidation. He was tyrannical, particularly when under pressure. He would scream at people, and publicly berate and criticize them. When unhappy or dissatisfied, he was prone to attacks of rage and temper tantrums. This behavior only manifested itself in front of a select audience, never when his superiors or clients were around. And Jane, in particular, was singled out. John blamed her for things with no factual justification, made her the target of practical jokes, and policed her continuously. To take a recent example, before the visit from members of the corporate board, John literally ran around the department for days hollering at Jane to "move faster." After the visit, they heard through the grapevine that the board members had been very pleased with what they had seen. But John took all the credit. He didn't even share the board's comments with any of his employees, let alone express thanks to Jane for her contribution. This was not what she had signed up for; it had been going on for too long and showed no sign of stopping. John's treatment of her had begun to affect her physical and psychological health. She had difficulty sleeping and experienced panic attacks.

An additional provocation was John's habit of constantly changing work responsibilities, deadlines, or priorities. This turned everything Jane did into mission impossible. Was he trying to undermine her self-esteem and self-confidence? Some of her best people had asked for a transfer. Others had quit. While her department had had almost no attrition before John arrived, it now had the highest employee turnover in the company.

Jane's attempts to talk to John and let him know how his behavior had been affecting her and her team got nowhere. He simply wouldn't listen. Worse, her comments seemed to have had a contrary effect; John only redoubled his efforts to make her life miserable. But Jane had nowhere to turn within the organization: no one else managed to get along well with the top brass as well as John did. Any criticism of his behavior would be met with incredulity, in light of his good relations and apparently strong performance. Clearly, John's total lack of respect or care for others, his intimidation, backstabbing, and manipulation were paying off. He was set to meet his self-serving goals.

As I am suggesting, when this kind of behavior occurs in an organization, top management is often the last to know. SOBs' toxic behavior often takes place behind closed doors with no witnesses and little evidence (in the traditional sense). When called to account, SOB executives use their charm and their Jekyll-and-Hyde nature to equivocate. As tangible proof is often lacking, it becomes very difficult to build a strong case against these people. But this doesn't mean that the situation is totally hopeless.

What can Jane do to deal with her SOB boss? Clearly, the first step is to recognize what is happening. She should not take the negative things John tells her at face value and believe them. She needs to be able to decipher the underlying dynamics and remind herself that this may not be about her but about him. It is important that Jane does not lose confidence in herself, or start to believe that she is incapable or incompetent. If she took an in-depth look, she might realize that John is the one with the problem, and has issues that he is trying to project onto her. In many instances, criticisms and allegations toward others are a reflection of the SOB's own insecurities, shortcomings, failings, and incompetence.

That said, it is not going to be easy for Jane to understand and metabolize what John is doing to her. Here an executive coach, a therapist, an experienced friend, and even a legal advisor (who specializes in inappropriate, bullying behavior in the workplace) can be of some assistance in deciphering the SOB's unsettling behavior, and help her deal with the stress John is causing her. Whatever is happening, it's very important that Jane learns how to protect herself. It is also essential for her to recognize the disordered personality behind the SOB's mask. What's more, in light of her bewilderment, Jane needs to accept that SOB executives think very differently from her and have a mindset that is extremely hard to change.

The next question Jane should ask herself is whether she is prepared to report John's transgressions, even when she is not the main victim. For example, if other people in her department are the target of the SOB's manipulations, would she be willing to support them, or become a silent bystander, looking the other way when abuse take place?

One useful way to build a case against an SOB is to start a diary in which the person under duress writes not only what has occurred but also how these incidents felt. A detailed record of what happened after each incident is needed (place, date, time, people involved) and what was said or done. It will be important to ensure that the diary is accurate. This information may be useful later, particularly if more formal steps are taken. Although it will not be easy, Jane should be methodical in how she behaves and performs, and write down what is happening. Furthermore, in itself, the writing of a diary can be a very cathartic experience. It could help Jane understand that she (the victim) isn't the problem but that John (the perpetrator) is. To arrive at a deeper insight into what is happening, it is important to remember that frequency, regularity, and patterns can be the keys to unraveling abusive behavior. Although SOBs are masters at explaining individual incidents, it will be much more difficult for them to explain away consistent patterns of behavior.

Apart from starting a diary, Jane should record everything that is happening to her. Teasing counts. So do sarcasm, cold-shouldering, criticism, and the silent treatment. When John makes criticisms or allegations, she should ask him to substantiate them in writing, providing substantive and quantifiable evidence. If the destructive behavior occurs in email or other forms of correspondence, she should maintain a hard copy of the trail and create a file of messages. It is equally important to record whether the SOB behaves in the same way with her co-workers. If so, she should ask them, too, to document the SOB's behavior and any scenes they witnessed when he was out to get someone. Instead of allowing John to force her into retreat, isolation, and helplessness, Jane should work proactively on building a support network with her co-workers. But she should be aware of the fact that the SOB is likely to be manipulating her colleagues into distancing themselves from her, either by sweet-talking them, or by playing on their vulnerabilities.

If Jane is building a case – and if she decides to take that case up to senior management (presuming the SOB is not part of the top management team) – she should make sure the case is not just about herself. It's always more effective to go beyond the personal, and frame a business case. She should state that she believes it's her duty to the organization to speak up and to not let things continue. She should make clear that she is not the only person affected, but that the SOB is endangering the mental state of other employees. She should explain how costly it is to keep the SOB (i.e., how many people have left because of John, how many days out of office it has cost, disruption at work, loss of productivity, and so on). When referring to the SOB, she should always refer to a pattern of incidents rather than the incidents themselves, which individually may look unimportant.

Jane should be wise to tread lightly, however, when approaching the company's HR department. She should be careful about what she reports, as SOB executives like John frequently have friends in high places. She should be aware that managing an SOB out of an organization can be uphill work. She should anticipate that HR will not believe her, and even deny the reality of the situation. SOB executives are often very successful in winning HR allegiance. People in that department may even have joined John in a plan to get rid of Jane. The same diplomacy and acumen will be needed when approaching HR as when approaching people at the top of the organization.

Jane should be ready to face the consequences of blowing the whistle on John, such as being managed out or made redundant. She should also be prepared for John to deny everything, and expect senior management to disbelieve her. Never underestimate an SOB's deviousness, ruthlessness, cunning, and vindictiveness. He has got away with it before, and he will expect to get away with it again. If her employer refuses to get involved, however, or backs the SOB's attempt to get rid of her, Jane might consider asking a lawyer to write to the CEO of the company outlining the way the SOB has treated her, and stating that she is preparing a legal case on the grounds of his unacceptable behavior. She should also make it clear that if the behavior continues, the company (especially senior management) will become legally liable to the victim for damages.

"never underestimate an SOB's deviousness, ruthlessness, cunning, and vindictiveness"

If Jane is successful, and manages to convince senior management of the seriousness of the matter, she could add that they may have seen only the tip of the iceberg – there may be further revelations about John's SOB behavior. Financial misappropriation or incompetence, breaches of regulations and codes of conduct, safety issues, poor morale, civil action, and similar matters often come to light when SOBs are exposed. Attempts to rationalize what has happened should be checked: SOB behavior is not an incidental or contextual occurrence; it is systematic. It is likely that an investigation of John's career history would uncover a long litany of similar dysfunctional behavior.

Jane should be aware that any idealistic attempt on her part to change John's behavior tends to be doomed. Not only is real behavioral change very difficult, it also takes a lot of time. With SOBs, we are up against formidable adversaries, particularly when they occupy a senior position in the company. We have very little or no control over an SOB's willingness to accept that he or she has a problem and to work on it. SOBs are masters of denial, projection, and rationalization. If things come to a head, Jane must be ready for a long, hard fight with the SOB and her employer.

If Jane is really up against overwhelming odds, she should get out while the going's good, especially if the SOB is the CEO. In that situation, her best option would be to take her career in her own hands, cut her losses, preserve her self-esteem, and move on to another, healthier, organization. Remember, we have only one life.

Organizational preventive measures

Before entry

The best way to prevent SOB-like behavior as exemplified in the case of Jane's boss is to detect these SOBs before they enter the organization. Once they are entrenched, it will be much harder to get rid of them, however. The obvious starting point is the application process. Résumés must be screened for lies and distortions, and references followed up and cross-checked very carefully, including reading between the lines of what others say about the applicant. Structured behavioral interviews, in which interviewees are asked the same questions by different interviewers, can be very useful. SOBs have a tendency to tell interviewers exactly what they want to hear, so as many stories may emerge as there are interviewers. When the various stories don't add up, a closer look is warranted.

It is important to keep in mind that SOBs are notorious for not answering questions put to them. If an honest answer to a question doesn't suit them, they will either lie or answer in such a way that the question is never directly addressed. Lying is preferable to displaying their shallow and superficial knowledge about the job they are applying for. Bullshitting in this way can help them get ahead even if they lack a deep knowledge of the business. A candidate who flatters a senior interviewer but is condescending toward a junior interviewer should be on the watch list: he or she is exactly the kind of person that has psychopathic tendencies.

When conducting these interviews, it is important "to use yourself as an instrument" and pay attention to your more intuitive reactions – in other words, how a specific person makes you feel, and what kind of thought patterns he or she elicits.[27] For example, if something does not "feel" right, it probably isn't right. If you think you are being flattered, look out. If the interviewee tries a game of one-upmanship, be careful not to be drawn into the game – you are likely to lose your bearings. If someone makes you feel uncomfortable, or wary, you may have picked up on his or her scary undertow. If the candidate overwhelms you with hard luck stories, resist your feelings of pity. Empathy can sometimes prevent you from recognizing what is really going on. Above all, retain a healthy amount of skepticism, whatever the person is telling you. Don't wear blinkers.

Using yourself as an instrument, a therapeutic skill, is not for everyone but other tools can be used. For example, from an organizational perspective, psychometric testing may reduce the possibility that one of these individuals enters the fold, particularly into a position of power and influence. Although these tests are not foolproof – and SOB executives may have learned how to outsmart them – they can help single out these people.

Many of these screening procedures will be too cumbersome for most organizations. A better solution to eliminate SOB executives is to create the kind of leadership style, organizational structures, systems, and culture that promote diversity, reflectivity, and openness at all levels, as it will be more difficult for an SOB executive to thrive in such an environment.[28] The leadership of an organization, and the culture that is created, very much determine whether SOB executives have a chance to thrive as the following example illustrates.

The role of organizational culture and leadership

Jim had always felt that he was part of a fantastic company, an organization with great values and a valuable mission. Profit with purpose was a leitmotif in the organization and it wasn't just lip service. It was expected that the company's leadership, at all levels, would behave according to its cultural values. But this all changed a year ago with the arrival of Neil, the new Group Vice President for the region. Gradually, what had once been a very supportive, caring culture, changed into a "Darwinian soup." A one-time team-oriented organization was transformed into a place of work where everyone was out for him- or herself. A workplace that had been driven by integrity and compassion had become a self-serving hell. Employee morale plummeted; nobody seemed happy and nobody smiled. People started to spy on each other, rat each other out, point fingers when things went wrong, and take dangerous shortcuts just to make the required targets. Those who couldn't handle the situation asked for a transfer to another region, or left. Many, however, kept their noses down, and accepted the abusive atmosphere. A difficult job market and the need for a paycheck kept them from leaving. HR, once a powerful support function in the company, was emasculated and no longer had a real role. The signals from Neil were quite clear: no complaints – take it or leave it. Soon enough, most of the people working for him realized that questioning the wisdom of Neil's decisions and practices came at a high price. People who protested were either ignored or silenced. The only thing that counted was financial results – to make profits for the region.

Neil's gospel consisted of emphasizing the values of risk-taking, aggressive growth, and entrepreneurial creativity. On paper, these values looked great, but the way Neil went about it led to a disconnect, destroying previously existing relationships of openness and trust. It was clear that Neil cared more about self-enrichment than the needs of the employees or what was good for the company. Most people realized that Neil showed little regard for meaning and ethics beyond the bottom line. And gradually, the behavior of Neil and his confidants led to an intricate system of deviance that cascaded deep into the organization.

Jim couldn't understand why the company's top executive team tolerated this behavior. The only explanation he could give was that Neil's financial results (at least in the short term) silenced them. But what once had been a great place to work had been transformed into a home for extreme risk-takers and thrill-seekers. It made him wonder to what extent Neil and his top team engaged in unethical, dangerous practices to obtain the kinds of profits they boasted about. Jim wrestled with what he should do. Should he just accept what was happening? Or should he try to use his contacts at head office to signal that the impressive short-term profitability in the region could, in the long term, turn out to be very risky?

I like to emphasize that the culture of an organization very much determines what is viewed as acceptable or unacceptable behavior. Unfortunately, some organizations have a culture that encourages inappropriate behaviors and attitudes; unethical ways of doing things are condoned or even perpetuated by senior management. In such work environments, many people in the organization may view SOB-like behavior as normal or acceptable. Some people (especially those in leadership positions) may turn a blind eye to inappropriate behavior or regard it simply as a personality clash between executives. From an organizational culture perspective, behavior or language that frightens, humiliates, belittles, or degrades can become embedded as a normal mode of communication, increasing dysfunctional organizational behavior. Other negative behavior includes spreading gossip, rumors, and innuendos of a malicious nature, unjustified criticism, belittling opinions, and the isolation of some people. Inappropriate ways of managing may include setting time lines that are difficult to achieve, constantly changing deadlines, denying people access to information and resources, or unfair allocation of workplace entitlements. Such cultural attitudes and practices will create an atmosphere of fear and intimidation and prevent people from speaking up. Unfortunately, these are exactly the types of culture in which SOBs like Neil thrive – and which allow them to get away with unacceptable behavior.

As a preventive measure, like any workplace issue, fostering a culture that is free from SOB behavior needs to come from the top down. Top management need to act as good role models and should not ignore transgressions – rather, they should make it clear that they view such behavior as gross misconduct that carries sanctions. It is also essential that organizations foster a culture of openness and mutual respect, where people can speak their mind.

An organization's leadership should ensure that having a culture of mutual respect is not merely a ritualistic exercise. It's the task of top management to commit themselves to building a working environment that values each organizational participant. Making high-minded statements in annual reports isn't worth much. What's important is what happens on the ground. Values must be internalized. The dos and the don'ts of appropriate behavior should be very clearly stated and enforced. There should be an ongoing discussion of what constitutes acceptable leadership style. It should be clear to everyone in the organization that all allegations of unacceptable behavior will be taken seriously.

"Making high-minded statements in annual reports isn't worth much"

Often, organizations that have robust team processes in place – and effective team leaders who make sure that a team culture prevails – will create a degree of immunity to SOBs. Teamwork is antithetical to SOBs and this kind of collaborative culture can be helpful in keeping them away. Organizations would also do well to put key performance indicators in place, clearly tied to outcomes, to hold people accountable for their actions. This will ensure that SOBs cannot use their bait-and-switch tactics to avoid accountability. Clear organizational policies about what constitutes bullying behavior – including anti-bullying training programs – will not only deter SOBs but will also equip employees with the means to identify and deal with them. Training programs should include a discussion of the traits and characteristics of organizational psychopaths; how they manipulate employees and organizational control systems; and why their behavior is so often confused with good or creative leadership. Exit interviews, if done well, can also supply important information. Many talented employees leave because of SOB behavior; the exit interview is an opportunity to bring these issues to light.

To weed out any SOB who has managed to gain entry to the organization, a culture needs to be in place where it is easy for rank-and-file employees to express concerns about their colleagues and bosses. Because many SOBs don't act up in front of their bosses, it is important for leaders to collect feedback from colleagues or subordinates to identify inappropriate behaviors. There should be processes in place so that employees can raise concerns and file complaints. In a culture where multi-party feedback is par for the course, this process is easier to facilitate. Feedback systems are good ways to signal the presence of psychopathic executives and detect dysfunctional behavior before it has graver consequences. Because SOBs are often included among high potentials, organizations should be on their guard for incongruities at an early career phase and insist on rigorous cross-checking with previous and current colleagues.

A red flag should go up if there are glaring discrepancies between how direct reports and junior employees perceive an executive, and how their peers or boss perceive them. Lower-level employees are often on the receiving end of an SOB's psychopathic behavior and usually spot a problem much sooner than senior management. Organizations should ensure that they have clear means of communication for signaling inappropriate behavior – for example, the presence of an ombudsman, an anonymous tip line, or specific whistleblower provisions. One very straightforward indicator that something is wrong is a worrying exit rate of good people from a specific project group, department, or division. This denotes the need for a closer look at that part of the organization. Another obvious signal is converging complaints received by HR.

Personal change: a losing battle?

Until now I have concentrated on how to identify and get rid of SOBs. But this begs the question of whether anything can be done to make these people change. Unfortunately, in most instances the psychopathic personality is carved in stone. "Heavy" psychopaths are impervious to change; they don't fit the basic assumption of psychotherapy or coaching, which is that the client wants to find a way of dealing with distressing or painful psychological and emotional problems.[29] In most cases, psychopaths are completely unaware that they have any psychological or emotional problems. They are quite satisfied with themselves and their inner landscape and see no need to change. They consider themselves superior to others and beyond regulatory social norms.

Psychopaths' inability to develop compassion, guilt, and remorse makes them incapable of establishing any form of working alliance with a therapist or coach. On the limited occasions when they do restrain their antisocial impulses, it's not their conscience kicking in, but because doing so suits their purpose at the time. Interventions with psychopaths are rarely effective; indeed, mental health professionals consider clinical psychopathic personality disorders untreatable. Such people may claim improvements, but often their only goal in undertaking therapy is to obtain a "good report" from the therapist or coach. Once they have that, it's back to business as usual.

"interventions with psychopaths are rarely effective"

There may be more hope, however, for people at the other end of the spectrum – the psychopath "lite," the SOB.

Coaching for personal change

Ted, the CEO of a large consumer product company, was concerned about David, one of his young high potentials who seemed to have a knack for rubbing people up the wrong way. He told David that unless he shaped up there would be no long-term future for him in the company and advised him to work with an executive coach to do something about his behavior. David seemed receptive to this idea. The coach, Robert, discovered that there were numerous complaints about David, which Ted summarized for him: his exaggerated sense of self-importance; his apparent belief that the normal rules of society didn't apply to him; his tendency to apportion blame to others when things went wrong; his refusal to accept responsibility or blame for his actions; his permanent state of denial; his selective memory; his untrustworthiness and breaches of confidence; his excessive competitiveness; and his counter-cultural inability to be a team player. On a slightly less negative note, Ted admitted that David could be very charming.

Robert realized that David's case would be a challenge but he decided to take it on. Although he had been forewarned, David's charm and evasiveness in the first session made it difficult for Robert to ask the kind of questions, and extract the kind of responses, that would help him to get a better understanding of his client. In an attempt to break the stalemate, he suggested that David undertake a 360-degree, multi-party feedback exercise that would also include feedback from family members and friends – people outside the work environment. The feedback corroborated Ted's summary of the problems with David and set the stage for a number of sessions. Robert began by asking David to interpret the feedback from the exercise himself, a form of "psychological judo." He needed to avoid arguments and head-to-head confrontations with his client. It would get him nowhere.

The theme he worked on was how to make David happier in his work and private life, which the feedback revealed was far from the case. It was important to clarify in David's mind the discrepancy between his current behavior and broader goals, as this could be a motivation for change. Robert explained that David's style of interacting with people, which may have been effective at an earlier stage in life (given the rather destructive atmosphere at home, where he always needed to be on his guard), was ineffective at his present stage of life. Something needed to change. Although Robert was up against a formidable client, gradually the interplay between the two began to have an effect, as a check-up with Ted confirmed. David seemed to have made more than a superficial change. Despite many setbacks, Robert seemed to be able to touch David. It helped that David's leadership reputation (notwithstanding his previous dysfunctional behavior) had not been totally destroyed. Colleagues in the company appreciated the progress he was making, and were willing to give him the benefit of the doubt. He showed so much progress that Ted appointed him to spearhead the Asian expansion of the company. At the same time, he continued his regular sessions with Robert, fearful of reverting to his previous dysfunctional behavior.

Nevertheless, David's case should be viewed as an exception, not the rule. Because he was a "lite" psychopath, some change was possible. Among this kind of SOB, we find daring, adventurous, unconventional people who learned to play by their own rules early in life; people who can't resist temptation and as a result often get into trouble. If they see others like them benefiting from coaching interventions, these individuals may be persuaded that there's something to be gained in asking for help. If they can build up a relationship with a therapist or coach, there is some hope that something can be done. However, changing these people's behavior patterns will not be easy.

Generally, however, when SOB executives seek treatment (often imposed from the outside or through exhaustion from the "theatre" in which they are engaged), their relationship with the therapist or coach usually takes one of two forms. Either the SOB executive will try to enlist the therapist/coach as an ally against the people who "forced" him or her to undergo coaching; or he or she will try to impress the therapist/coach to gain some other kind of advantage, usually of a legal nature.

Whichever form it takes, most therapists and coaches find working with these people extremely exasperating and frustrating. SOB executives play masterful mind games with their therapists or leadership coaches. They always find new excuses for their own behavior, and new insights into others' vulnerabilities. In many instances, these interventions only help them to become more effective at manipulating people. It's not unusual for them to become active readers of therapeutic/coaching literature, and acquire a language to rationalize why they do what they do. Some will mirror the wishes of the therapist or coach, and claim they have seen the error of their ways. They may express remorse, and then contradict themselves through their words or actions. And in the rare cases when psychotherapy or coaching does have some effect, it doesn't take much for them to turn against the person who is trying to help them. Whatever working alliance is established, it will always remain a very fragile one.

I have suggested that SOB executives in senior leadership positions can significantly alter the makeup of the organization; their dysfunctional and debilitating behavior can permeate organizations like a cancer. If we take the financial sector as an example, we have seen how the immoral actions of a relatively small number of SOBs can wreak catastrophe on the effectiveness of organizations, the profitability of industry, the performance of the economy, and the prosperity of society. The greater their power, the more dangerous the abuse.

To be able to identify the presence of SOBs in an organization, we need to move beyond a purely cognitive-rational approach to organizational and individual analysis, to a more clinical one. Taking a psychodynamic-systemic perspective will provide insights into the unconscious emotional and psychological dynamics that are barriers to organizational effectiveness, creating the kinds of interventions that reduce the negative impact of individual pathologies. The clinical paradigm brings to the surface a Dorian Gray-style portrait of what is happening. Skillful application of this knowledge will show how things really are – and expose the damage some people can inflict on others. Maintaining people's mental health should be a key value in all organizations. A zero-tolerance policy for SOB behavior will be a given for any organization. Al Capone allegedly once said, "You can get more with a kind word and a gun than you can with a kind word alone." Leaders of organizations do well to remember these words when trying to understand what SOBs are all about.

CHAPTER 6

Why Coaching?

You cannot teach a man anything. You can only help him discover it within himself.

– *Galileo Galilei*

The greatest danger for most of us is not that our aim is too high and we miss it, but that our aim is too low and we reach it.

– *Michelangelo*

Those who have immobilized and muted many of the plots and players in their internal theater, allowing them no action but to hammer on the walls of the mind, might learn to value the words of Sartre: "If you want your characters to live, then liberate them!"

– *Joyce McDougall*

In this chapter I describe the conundrum that coaches face, wanting to undertake the journey of becoming a coach, and, in particular, learning what it means to coach in a group setting. For the purpose of illumination, I have used a case history to explore some of the important issues pertaining to this kind of intervention. The case presented illustrates what coaches are up against when undertaking this venture. The first part of this chapter describes a coach's reflections on leadership group coaching, exploring his inner journey toward becoming a group coach. The second part of the chapter discusses what makes group coaching such an effective intervention technique, exploring the dynamic processes applicable to individual participants, and the "cloud" issues – themes that the group-as-a-whole brings to the table.

A coach's journey

> Peter had been asked to facilitate a group coaching session, unsupervised. For the first time he was going solo as a group coach, finally getting to do something he had looked forward to for some considerable time. So it was ironic that he felt so anxious. But one-on-one coaching is one thing; coaching in a group setting is a very different matter. He knew it was natural to be anxious – fear of the unknown is programmed into *Homo sapiens*. And of course, Peter was more of a worrier than others; it was part of his personality.

The way he felt now reminded Peter of how he had felt when he once took part in a fire walk. He recalled vividly how he had looked at the glowing embers, braced himself, taken some deep breaths to slow the beating of his heart and got himself ready to step on the glowing red coals. Taking the first step had been scary, but once he got the hang of it, the walk had been extremely exhilarating. To his great surprise he didn't get burned. Later on, he found out that heat transfer from red-hot coals happens very slowly. His feet had not been in contact with the coals for long enough to cause burns. His willingness to suspend disbelief had paid off.

Peter realized that going solo was another fire walk. Yes, he felt anxious – but he also felt exhilarated and curious. He was looking forward to the adventure. The session would be a milestone, the first step toward yet another role in his protean career. He should see it as the start of a new working identity.

Becoming

From the moment Peter had learned about coaching, he had been enthusiastic about it. As an executive, he had been on the receiving end of various coaching interventions, and every time, he had found the coaches' insights extremely useful. He believed that coaching was a great way to help people deal more effectively with their professional and personal life. He liked being part of it. What better career can you have than one where you get the best out of people? What could be better than enabling others to make decisions that would improve the quality of their life? Peter had always thrived on making people realize that they were capable of being more than they were.

But there had been obstacles to overcome. Peter realized that if he was going to be effective as a coach, he had to deal with some issues of his own. To do this kind of work, he needed a healthy balance in his own life – and there had been times when his life had been completely out of sync. He needed to work on his relationships with people close to him, which meant working on his own emotional self-mastery.

For Peter, overcoming fears, insecurity, and uncertainties had been a lifelong challenge. But we are the authors of our own misery and Peter knew that nobody could make him feel inferior without his own consent. He needed to have greater clarity about why he wanted to become a coach before he embarked on this new career. He had to ask himself some searching questions.

A state of being

What was this desire to become a leadership coach all about? Why did it excite him? Was it about helping himself or was it about helping other people? Was it to be both? To be an effective coach, he would have to be wiling to leave his ego outside the door when dealing with others. Could he do that? Could he leave himself out of the picture, and step into another person's world? Would he be empathic enough? He knew he would only be able to function authentically as a coach if he could answer "Yes" to those questions.

Peter realized that he would have to be prepared for finding out new things about himself, including his blind spots. But would he like what he found? Would he be upset to uncover things about himself that he had hidden away? Knowing more about his conflicts, wishes, desires, fears, biases, and blind spots, however, was better than not knowing. It would prevent him from projecting his own biases on his clients. Arriving at this level of self-understanding would not be easy, but it would make for an interesting journey. If he got things right, he would have a constant learning dialogue with his clients.

Of course, this would entail a mutual willingness to share perspectives, the ability to truly listen to the other, be open to new ideas, and take joint responsibility for the conversation and its outcomes. In fact, the coaching journey implied a lifelong quest for personal excellence. When Peter thought about this further, he realized that his own quest for greater self-awareness **"the coaching journey implied a lifelong quest for personal excellence"** might have been his motivation to become a leadership coach in the first place.

Peter knew that he was intuitive, better able than most to sense things about others. For as long as he could remember he had combined this talent with a natural curiosity about people. He was naturally empathic, had always been interested in understanding better the people he came across, and was very good at sense making. Peter also knew he was highly skilled at listening, not only to what other people were saying but also what they were *not* saying – at least verbally. It came naturally to him to listen with the third ear, and decipher the unspoken text behind the words. He had always paid attention to facial expressions, body language, tone of voice, and expressions of emotion.

Perhaps Peter's ability to put himself in others' shoes (without necessarily agreeing with them) was one reason for these inner dialogues. It was his way of understanding better what others were doing to him. He knew how to use himself as an instrument.[1] He was aware of his feelings, why he had certain feelings – and the impact he had on others. He was also very good at recognizing how others perceived him. These skills made it easy for him to build trustful, collaborative relationships with others, a *sine qua non* for an effective coaching relationship. But by using himself as an instrument, he also knew how to catch others off-guard. They would often be surprised when he shared his observations with them.

Peter realized that coaching had helped him to connect with himself and others at a much deeper level. The journey to becoming a coach had contributed to his own internal change and growth. It had helped him to understand himself better and taught him to be more effective at connecting to other people. His contact with a great variety of people, each with their own unique personality and their own problems to solve, had helped him continue to learn and grow. Most importantly, taking this coaching journey had made him feel much better.

One of the valuable things Peter had learned in his development as a coach was to engage every day in a process of self-evaluation and self-reflection. He believed strongly that all coaches – indeed, anyone working in a helping profession – could profit from this reflective process. After all, we all have only so many days in our life. How else can we know whether a particular day has been useful?

Peter knew that he was seen as deeply caring, perhaps because he could communicate hope and possibility to others – affirm a client's resourceful-ness, and communicate this affirmation to the client. He was very good at identifying other people's strengths and getting the best out of them. His track record showed that he had been effective in helping many of the people he encountered. It had always been one of his greatest satisfac-tions to see others achieve their goals.

With these capabilities, it is no wonder that many people had steered Peter toward the coaching profession. Even before he had begun to think about embarking on this career, people would always come to him for advice. But Peter knew that being sought out for advice was only one part of the equation. He needed to learn how to help people act on that advice, once given. He needed to learn more of the tricks of the trade.

Peter realized that the value and contribution of coaching would be achieved through facilitation, not through control. Coaches cannot be really directive. The royal road to coaching lay in asking the sort of open-ended questions that pushed people out of their comfort zone, confront-ing them with challenges, exploring options, and facilitating the discovery of new choices and possibilities.

Peter had learned that most people generally know (at least subliminally) the right thing to do when they find themselves in tricky situations. However, his challenge as a coach was to draw these responses out of the individuals with whom he dealt. He had learned from experience that it was more effective if the clients figured out the answers that would work best for them. If he gave them the answer, they would be less likely to own the solution and fully commit themselves to it.

Far too often, the people who came to Peter for advice played the help-lessness card. Peter would point out to them that they had many choices and their assumption that they had no control over their life was wrong. So many were unable to see the causal relationship between their choices, and the changes those choices would bring. Instead of recognizing their own ability to influence the course of their life they felt like victims of circumstance. This cognitive dissonance meant they drifted through life.

Of course, it was platitudinous to note that people who are going nowhere are sure of reaching their destination. The challenge was to help them assume a different mindset. Helping clients to bring out their best, discover what mattered most to them, and achieve the outcomes they desired most, was extremely rewarding work.

Peter saw that interdependence and reciprocity were at the heart of the coaching process. He knew from experience that when someone did something for him, he had a compelling urge to give something back. There was a great need to reciprocate. Paradoxically, it is when we help others without any expectation of return that we invoke the power of reciprocity. And even if reciprocity does not occur immediately, or with the same person, it is still likely to happen. Of course, the negative aspect of reciprocity – "an eye for an eye, and a tooth for a tooth" – is also true.

> "when we help others without any expectation of return that we invoke the power of reciprocity"

It was largely a matter of timing. Going the extra mile for a client gave that person an increased sense of indebtedness and loyalty. And this was exactly the moment when the client would be more receptive to different ways of looking at once insoluble difficulties. Peter knew that the coaching process worked best when it was based on trust, mutual support, and shared values. But something more was required than good timing; the coach also needed to create a safe space in which the process could unfold.

Being aware of all these things was one thing, but applying them was another. Peter was conscious of his insecurity. How good was he really compared to others? Did he really have what it takes? He often felt that others were much quicker at picking up significant themes and identifying the major drivers in a client's life. Occasionally he felt downright dumb at not picking up on something he should have seen immediately. Those experiences always made him want to do better.

It never ceased to amaze Peter how good some coaches were at highlighting important themes in people's lives, how quickly they were able to draw out the skills or talents that had been hidden, and how effective they were in helping them solve problems they previously thought unsolvable. He also marveled at the way more effective leadership coaches worked in organizations, establishing a coaching culture characterized by trust and open dialogue.

He knew the expression sounded trite, but Peter had always wanted to make a difference. Finding meaning was an important driver for him. Coaching offered that opportunity. He had seen it make a huge difference in other people's lives and he had figured out that by helping others improve the quality of their life and achieve their goals, he would feel better about himself.

Now, contemplating his next step into solo group coaching, Peter knew there was a real basis to his feelings of anxiety. A coach has to earn credibility with every new intervention. Activity and achievement were very different things and should never be confused. Peter would have to gain the respect of his clients quickly and he would be under pressure to produce immediate results, always an unrealistic expectation. Short-termism in a long-term setting could have worrying side effects.

A state of doing

Peter thought back to his first experience of a group coaching session, as a participant. He and the other members of his group had been nervous before the session started. What was it going to be about? Why did they have to do it? What benefit were they going to get from it?

Apart from his anxiety about what to expect, he had been nervous about what people would say about him. What was their feedback going to be like? Most of the people he knew who had gone through a similar experience had been very positive about it; some said that, as a review of their leadership style, it had been one of the best learning experiences they had ever had. In the end, he had felt the same. With hindsight, Peter realized that that first group intervention had been the impetus for a number of important life changes, including becoming a coach himself.

It had been a lengthy educational process. He started by taking INSEAD's Executive Master's Degree in Coaching and Consulting for Change, even though it was longer than most other programs. The program had been an enlightening experience that involved two learning journeys. One was a cognitive one, learning more about psychological theory, career dynamics, leadership, family business, and organizational behavior; the other journey involved an excursion – through an intense, personal psychotherapeutic intervention – into his own underworld. During the time in the program he learned an enormous amount about his strengths, weaknesses, personality, and drivers. It gave him the "Aha!" experience that he had always wanted to be a leadership coach.

To prepare himself even better for this new adventure, Peter began to see a psychotherapist on a regular basis and enrolled in a clinical psychology program to improve his skills. To learn more about group behavior, he participated in a few group dynamic events. Finally, he decided to take the leap and leave the organization where he had been working as head of talent management to start his own coaching practice.

It had been a very good choice. With his network, it was not long before Peter had a fully booked coaching practice. But he realized he wanted more, a greater impact. To really influence the clients he worked with, and their organizations, he needed to become more familiar with group coaching – an intervention process that was both scary and exciting. Although he had become more familiar with group dynamics through various workshops, the next step was to better understand group coaching. Through the INSEAD Global Leadership Centre (IGLC) he undertook a process of "shadow" coaching – participation in a number of group coaching sessions under the supervision of experienced group coaches – an IGLC requirement for becoming a group coach.

Preparing himself for the shadow coaching session had been interesting but it had also become clear that the process was going to be a much more complicated challenge than one-on-one coaching. Would he live up to the expectations of the group coach who was leading him? Would he able to handle the group dynamics? It seemed a bit of a tightrope: he would need to show a degree of deference toward the main coach without being a "wallflower." He would have to make insightful observations that would contribute to the success of the process – but how insightful was insightful? Being judged had never been a comfortable position for Peter.

He took comfort from the fact that he had done his homework. He knew the bio-notes of the five participants by heart. He had read up on the company's values, culture, structure, strategy, and leadership. He had also studied carefully each participant's results from a 360-degree feedback instrument, the Global Executive Leadership Inventory (GELI), paying particular attention to the written comments by anonymous raters.[2] Finally, he reflected on the outcomes of the Personality Audit (PA),[3] another 360-degree multi-feedback instrument that listed the names of the people who had done the ratings. Peter noted that the comments made by close family members were, at times, extremely revealing.

When all the participants had arrived the coach introduced herself and explained why there was a shadow coach present. Peter was asked to say a few words about himself, which he did rather humorously, despite his nerves. The coach then talked about the importance of confidentiality during the process, referring to the Hippocratic oath to "do no harm." She also pointed out the importance of time management – to ensure fair process, everybody should get an equal amount of time.

To break the ice, the coach introduced an exercise in which each participant was asked to draw a self-portrait associated with themes such as head, heart, stomach, work, leisure, future, and past. They could use only symbols, no words. At first, the participants seemed uncomfortable about the assignment – some clearly thought it was childish – but after a little encouragement, and conscious that time was ticking by (they only had 20 minutes to complete the task), they got down to it. The self-portraits, with each participant's name attached, were then hung around the room.

It was time to start the group coaching process. The leadership coach had already identified the participant she wanted to start with. She had explained to Peter that she had singled out someone with an "average" dossier, that is, his ratings were neither extremely high – which would evoke envy – nor extremely low – which could make him embarrassed or defensive. Fortunately, the volunteer didn't seem to mind, and embarked full-heartedly on the exercise, setting an excellent example.

Before the session, the group coach had advised Peter to pay attention, not only to the person who was the subject of discussion, but also to the reactions of the group-as-a-whole. Their motto should be "Welcome the neuroses." Resistance should be seen as a sign that the coaching dialogue was on track and touching on important issues. She emphasized that working with client resistance, rather than trying to ignore it, or pushing it

"Welcome the neuroses"

away, can help clients clarify their values and goals, and explore what will help or hinder them in making changes. An effective coach explores with clients (in a non-threatening way) what they don't want to hear, and makes them see what they don't want to see, so they can be what they have always known (at least, subliminally) what they could be. But the coach also cautioned that it was important to "strike when the iron is cold." When the iron is too hot, the client may not be ready to hear what is said. As on many occasions, timing is everything. Often, it can be better to keep your mouth shut even though interesting things are going on.

The shadow coaching day passed very quickly. One by one the participants took the " hot seat," starting with the self-portrait to point out highlights and lowlights in their life story, and received other people's reflections on the results of the GELI and PA. Peter saw how careful the coach was to express negative comments in a positive, sometimes humorous way – and how many positive comments were made to cancel one negative one.

As the day went on, the participants began to feel more comfortable with each other. The atmosphere in the room became less tense, even playful, and he realized that he had become part of the play. Occasionally, he asked the person in the hot seat challenging questions, to prompt greater insight. During the day, a number of skeletons came rattling out of the closet; interpersonal conflict was discussed constructively; and ideas were put forward about how the company as a whole could improve its way of working. There was even a moderated amount of discussion of the company's values; in addition, structural themes, such as organizational design, were reviewed; and even a few strategic issues were put on the table.

By the time the coach summed up, everyone in the room had a clearer idea of the issues they needed to work on. They all now had a leadership action plan signed off by everyone else. The session had helped the group members get to know each other better, even though some of them had worked together for many years. In the coffee break, some told Peter that it was the first time the members of the team had held really courageous conversations. They seemed much less guarded and to be communicating more openly with one another. The session had helped resolve ongoing issues within the team that were becoming circular and frustrating. For example, some of the themes were how to make a new IT system acceptable to a specific division, how to better integrate a newly acquired company, how to better approach meetings, how to deal with different people in more constructive ways, and how to deal with a specific top executive. A number of the participants had been aware of some of these issues for some time, but never really done anything about it. The hope was that, this time, things would be different – no more short-lived New Year's resolutions.

To help them internalize their good intentions, the coach scheduled a number of conference calls during which they would discuss their progress, as well as a follow-up session where their action plans would be re-examined. In addition, each participant chose a "peer" coach from among the other group members whose task it was to keep them on track.

After the session, the coach reviewed Peter's contribution. She complimented him on his observations during the session and also explained why she had acted the way she did at certain times. She told him that she was very satisfied with the way he had handled his role as a shadow; how it had contributed to a successful experience for the group; and that she thought he would excel at this kind of work. She encouraged him to trust his intuition more and noted his ability to tolerate ambiguity, paradox, and not knowing without having the urge to rush to closure.[4] In short, she said, "You've got what it takes."

Afterwards, Peter realized that she hadn't said anything about the remarkable fact that after nine hours, a group of relative strangers had bonded, developed greater trust in one another, and were set to have a much better working relationship in the future. He reflected on the fact how group coaching (especially in company-specific programs) was an excellent way of making organizations strategically more agile. This was a great way to create a truly networked organization and a highly effective way of minimizing the kind of paranoid thinking that was so likely to occur in virtual, highly diverse groups. A group coaching intervention could be a milestone in creating a boundaryless organization – one that would go beyond the silo mentality so prevalent in many complex organizations. From what he had witnessed he could see that this kind of intervention could lay the foundation for real information exchange. It once more dawned on him that setting up a data bank alone would not be enough to create a more agile, learning organization. Unless the data were shared – by people who trust one another – nothing would really happen.

But why had all this happened? What was it about the process that made it so effective? In the taxi to the airport, Peter was still puzzling how it was possible that the exchange of stories about the vicissitudes of five individuals' personal and professional lives could, in such a short time, be a catalyst for change.

Learning from experience

At INSEAD's Global Leadership Centre (IGLC), where I pioneered the group coaching intervention method, we have all been very agreeably surprised by its success. The outcomes have been much more impressive than we had originally imagined. The leadership coaches connected with the center (and other institutions interested in the group coaching intervention process) have been delighted with the impact of this intervention method, which goes far beyond the creation of individual action plans, particularly for company-specific programs.

In its early days, I was quite concerned that getting people to talk about their life relatively intimately could have negative consequences; there was bound to be fear of self-exposure and lack of reciprocity, and possibly a variety of paranoid reactions. But my concerns turned out to be unwarranted. Group coaching at INSEAD (and other institutions) is a numbers game – by now tens of thousands of executives (from all over the world) have gone through the experience – and looking back at a long history of interventions, the problems encountered have been minuscule.

One extremely gratifying experience for the coaches has been the participants' reactions. Very often, they have hailed the leadership group coaching intervention as the best thing that happened to them during the entire executive program. Even better, they complained that the intervention had been too short. If the ratings and written feedback are to be believed, it seems to be an excellent learning experience for almost all the participants who have gone through the process. In many cases, the executives contact the coaches much later to thank them, saying how instrumental the event had been in creating a tipping point for making major career and life decisions.

When the coaches would get together at the end of the day to discuss what had happened, often, they would express their surprise at people's revelations; they would talk about feeling privileged to help these people move forward in their life. However, I rarely used to hear them talk about why this particular process worked so well. Rarely was much insight provided about its dynamics.

Because I was very pleased with the results, for many years, I didn't explore the matter any further. Why question success? Why bother when the clients are so satisfied? Without really knowing what we were doing, we seemed to have stumbled on an intervention technique that proved extremely effective at creating inflection points in executives' lives. But after a while I started to feel uncomfortably dissatisfied. The reason why this process worked needed to be explored further. Were there elements of the design of the intervention process that made a difference?

Sense making

When I started the group coaching intervention method on a larger scale, I would tell other leadership coaches that I didn't believe in a cookie-cutter approach to coaching. Although standardization has its advantages, I felt strongly that all coaches should approach group coaching in the way that best suited their personality; they should do what they were most comfortable doing. One recommendation I made (particularly in the case of very short interventions) was to use one or two multi-party feedback questionnaires to help jump-start the coaching process. The first is the Global Executive Leadership Inventory (GELI), which I developed at INSEAD and touches on the dimensions that most organizations list among their specific leadership competences. Another is the Personality Audit (PA), which combines feedback from people at work with feedback from close spouses, siblings, children, and close friends. Their feedback could have great emotional impact and become a tipping point for change. I also recommended ice-breaking exercises, like the self-portrait, which help create a safe space "to play."[5] I had always been interested in how Winnicott used the squiggle game, a pencil-and-paper technique he devised as a method of communicating with children to elicit their thoughts and feelings. The self-portrait was a logical continuation of this game. But apart from these suggestions, it was up to the coach to make the day a memorable learning experience.

> "I didn't believe in a cookie-cutter approach to coaching"

Plato's cave: the clinical paradigm

I also strongly advocated applying the clinical paradigm to group coaching whenever appropriate. As I described in the Preface (p. 10–12), the clinical paradigm is a specific way of looking at human phenomena; metaphorically, it is a lens through which to explore people's inner theater. To elaborate, many of our thoughts, feelings, and memories float in a twilight zone between reality and fantasy; they may be blocked from consciousness and beyond our immediate awareness. The question becomes, how to bring these aspects of human functioning to the surface. I have found the clinical paradigm a highly effective way to go beyond the obvious and make them visible. It can help us understand better the irrational, sometimes darker aspects of personality functioning.

> "many of our thoughts, feelings, and memories float in a twilight zone between reality and fantasy"

When the clinical paradigm is used as a conceptual framework to promote insight and change, people are made aware of a whole other world that coexists with the world of reality and rationality – a world that may not yet be part of conscious awareness. Looking through this clinical lens helps us discover a world of fantasy, dreams, and daydreams, all representing forces that create another reality. Applying this lens adds a deeper and more nuanced understanding to intrapersonal, interpersonal, group, and organizational phenomena.

Twenty-four centuries ago, Plato alluded to this twilight zone between reality and fantasy in his fable of the prisoners in the cave. In this story (found in *The Republic*), he presents one of the most famous images in the history of philosophy to illustrate how to differentiate between reality and fantasy.

Plato compares most people to prisoners who are chained in a cave in such a way that they cannot turn their head. They are completely ignorant of the world beyond the cave and all they can see is the blank wall in front of them. Behind them, a fire burns and puppeteers walk between the fire and the prisoners holding up puppets that cast shadows on the wall of the cave. Because they know no better, and are unable to see the puppets passing behind them, the prisoners ascribe forms to the shadows.

According to Plato, the shadows are all the prisoners know of reality – a one-dimensional, shadowy appearance. However, if the prisoners were suddenly to be free of their chains, and could stand up, turn round, and walk toward the fire, they would recognize the puppets and puppeteers as real and solid, even though before they had been only shadows. And when they left the cave altogether, and stepped into a new, exciting outside world, they would see colors and shapes. They would, literally, see the light and it would all make perfect sense.

Unfortunately, if those prisoners who had seen the light went back to the cave to share their new knowledge with the others, they would find it difficult to explain what they had seen. Nobody would understand or believe them. How can the prisoners in the cave become aware of a world of light beyond the shadows they perceive? How can they be made aware of another reality?

The chained prisoners in Plato's cave are symbolic of the human condition. Most people are relatively ignorant about human behavior and like the prisoners in the cave, we are comfortable with our ignorance, because it's all we know. Some of us, however, are not satisfied to remain in this state. We want to penetrate the darkness. We want to be unchained, to turn their head, and leave the cave.

When we first begin to distinguish reality from illusion, it can be frightening, and because of this there will always be some people who prefer to stay chained and choose to remain ignorant. But most of us, once we discover it, opt for exploring a multidimensional life in glorious Technicolor.

In the context of leadership development, if we want to help people change their actions or behaviors, we need to step out of Plato's cave into the light. This is what happens when we apply the clinical paradigm. It helps us examine and reflect on our own behavior, the behavior of others, and the interrelationship between the two. We all possess a rich inner theater, in which the key figures and experiences that influence the development of our personality take center stage. The insights provided by a journey into that inner theater can become stepping stones to change.

"We all possess a rich inner theater, in which the key figures and experiences that influence the development of our personality take center stage"

Applying the clinical paradigm in coaching situations helped me to tease out the central interpersonal role in which clients consciously and unconsciously cast themselves. It also gave me an investigative method of identifying self-defeating expectations and negative self-appraisal, as well as outdated perceptions of the self. In coaching situations, I needed to make clients realize that what may have been effective behavior at the age of 12, could be highly destructive at the age of 40. The clinical lens also enabled me to make sense of the prevailing group dynamics – the defensive patterns that manifested themselves within the group-as-a-whole.

Although the clinical paradigm was a great help in better understanding intrapersonal, interpersonal, and group dynamics, I started to wonder about other possible levers for change. What were some of the variables that made group coaching interventions such a success? What was the X factor that group coaching provided?

"what was the X factor that group coaching provided?"

To help me better understand the process I embarked (with the help of a number of colleagues) on various research projects. I was trying to capture the intuitive knowledge of the coaches – the unknown knowns. The results of these projects was a series of edited books on coaching[6] – books in which many coaches using the group intervention method reflected on their experiences. I also wrote The Hedgehog Effect,[7] which focused on the dynamics of group intervention. My work on these four titles helped me to identify several forms of intercession that all of us had been practicing in the group coaching process.

"I was trying to capture the intuitive knowledge of the coaches – the unknown knowns"

The power of groups

Working in groups can be like navigating a way through a field of icebergs: much of the danger lies hidden below the surface. The iceberg is a very appropriate metaphor as it helps people visualize the overt and covert interpersonal dynamics that affect group work. While one-on-one coaching can be complex enough, the challenges become much more pronounced in a group coaching setting. The coach has to digest and metabolize a myriad of dynamic, fluctuating, and multidimensional projections that represent group members' intersubjective experiences at various developmental levels. If the group is going to progress (not regress), the coach needs to act as a safe container for all this emotional and cognitive debris and create an ambiance where participants can explore their feelings and challenges without the fear of judgment or rejection. The coach has to construct a safe, transitional space for the participants, where they have permission to talk about issues they never had the opportunity to confront before.

If this containment is satisfactory, the participants will be able to fully experience themselves, having found a space where the intolerable is tolerated. Such a safe space allows them to be in touch with *all* of what they really are in an honest and authentic manner. Being in such a safe space encourages participants to let go of previously repressed parts of themselves. It also makes them realize that their lives are not solely determined by fate, their personal history, or their genetic inheritance; it is also *self*-determined through their own free will. They have a say in the matter.

I have learned from experience that two dynamics occur simultaneously in group interventions. In the first place there are the dynamic processes applicable to the person in the hot seat whose life and career is being discussed. Simultaneously, there are also "cloud" issues in the room – by this I mean the themes that the group-as-a-whole brings to the table,[8] themes that as it were float in the clouds. Often these cloud issues remain untouched. However, I observed that some of the more sensitive (and more effective) coaches would address these cloud issues during a group session, when appropriate: this often happened when the group discussion seemed to have come to a halt. Cloud issues would usually involve the unfinished business of one or more of the participants, issues that had become contagious like envy, jealousy, lust, rivalry, fear of abandonment, shame, guilt, and fear of engulfment.

I began to realize other psychodynamic processes were taking place during a group coaching process, consciously or unconsciously – processes that produced tipping points for change. For example, if a relatively safe, playful space has been established, a number of things can occur.

1. A group or team intervention provides a context for cathartic experiences. For some members, a group is an audience as they get

things off their chest; it can become a forum, at least figuratively, for emotional cleansing. Some participants are instrumental in bringing repressed feelings and fears to consciousness. Expressing the things that trouble us, instead of stubbornly holding them back, can be an extremely powerful emotional experience. However, proper containment of these emotions by the group coach and members of the group is essential to making such a catharsis a significant experience.

But there has to be a caveat here. Catharsis may not in itself have a beneficial effect. There are occasions when it can be counterproductive, in particular if it occurs at the wrong time or place. Under the right circumstances, however, it provides an opportunity to re-experience and transform deeply troubling or repetitive life experiences, helping an individual understand better why certain psychological wounds have been so troublesome. From psychotherapy research we know how important simple listening is in helping clients to move forward.

2. While listening to other people's life stories, participants may come to realize that they are not alone in their confusion and that others, too, struggle with similar problems. This realization can bring a great sense of relief. The "join the human race" effect has great benefits. Mutual identification with specific problems offers many opportunities to discuss alternative ways of dealing with them. **"the 'join the human race' effect has great benefits"**

3. Use of the clinical paradigm can set in motion a whole process of association about why the participants have been doing things in certain ways. Is that the only way? Is a behavioral repertoire that was extremely appropriate at one point in time, still effective now? Encouraged by the group members, these kinds of reflection can lead to a willingness to experiment in doing things differently and create new hope for the future. Participants realize that there are ways to get unstuck. In many instances, this kind of self-understanding and insight moves people a long way along the road to change.

4. Every presentation, not just only their own, offers participants the opportunity for vicarious learning. They soon realize that learning does not only occur through direct participation in dialogue; they can also learn vicariously, by observing and listening to others' stories. This kind of learning implies retaining and replicating effective behavior observed in others.

5. The interpersonal learning process can also be instrumental in detecting and correcting distortions in self-perception. There are always team members who are admired because of the way they deal with life's adversities. They become role models, the kind of people we would like to emulate. Imitative behavior – or identification with the other – is an important part of the interpersonal learning process and a force for change. Identification involves our associating with or taking on the qualities, characteristics, or views of another person or group. In this way we may assimilate an aspect, quality, or attribute of the other, and be transformed, wholly or partially, following the model the other provides. However, we need to be aware of the fact that identification is not necessarily a conscious process.

6. Participants become a real community, members of a tribe that has gone through the same emotional experience. Tribespeople draw on a great deal of mutual support whenever one of them embarks on a new challenge. This feeling of social belonging can be a very powerful catalyst for change.

7. A group setting is also an opportunity to disseminate information about different aspects of human functioning. Occasionally didactic instruction by the leadership coach can be beneficial, although it should be given sparingly. Explanation, clarification, and even direct advice about certain events within the team can reduce anxiety, and establish a modicum of control when there is a troublesome problem.

   However, it is not just the coach who will offer suggestions; members of the team will do the same. And here again, the process of vicarious experience can be very powerful. As I suggested before, it is inevitable that members of the group will find associations with their own situation in individual members' presentations. They might suggest taking a different approach and exploring other ways of going about things. Within the team setting, information can be shared about psychological problems, illness, and attaining a healthier work-life balance. By giving advice, they also help themselves and guidance activities can make the team function better.

8. A further positive force for change can be the altruistic motive, or the desire to put the needs of others above our own. While helping for helping's sake – the genuine desire to make things better for others – may seem selfless, ironically it can have some selfish side effects. The

act of giving to others can have numerous personal benefits. It feels good to be important to others, but more than that, there seems to be a link between being helpful to others, and living a longer, healthier, happier life. Helping others – offering support, reassurance, suggestions, and insights – can have a therapeutic effect, contributing to our sense of self-respect and well-being. Having something of value to offer to others can be a heartening experience. The initial rush from the helper's high may be followed by a longer-lasting period of improved emotional health.

Altruism prompts team members to credit fellow members for having helped them to deal better with life's adversities. Learning through the influence of interpersonal relationships plays an essential role in making teams and individual members more effective. The willingness of team members to have courageous conversations with each other can be extremely illuminating. Team members are very well placed to point out others' dysfunctional character patterns. Offering to work on these with other members of the team can be a great incentive for change. Constructing our self-regard through the positive appraisals of others is an important component of learning.

Many of these psychological dynamics seemed to be contributing to the effectiveness of group coaching. In getting the process off the ground, however, much depends on the ability of coaches to use the clinical lens effectively and discreetly. They need to be very skilled at using themselves as instruments.

Many years ago, I was engaged in a research project that necessitated a visit to the island of Newfoundland in Canada. The fauna and flora on the island is quite something. Just offshore there are a number of small islands that rise like citadels out of the sea and house millions of seabirds. Among these are the common murres, birds that fly quite fast but are not very agile due to their short wings; they move better underwater, and are excellent divers. Each female murre lays one egg on a tiny ledge of rock, hundreds or even thousands of feet above the sea. The ledges that form these breeding colonies are packed with murres, each pair guarding their one egg. After three weeks, the eggs hatch. Now the murre parents have a new challenge: feeding a chick that likes its fish fresh, not regurgitated.

Four weeks later, the ledges are getting very crowded; it's clear there's no future there for the fledglings, which have literally to make a leap of faith. Encouraged by the parent birds below in the sea (they choose a time when it is almost dark so that they are safer from predators), the young murres are expected to jump off these high ledges, and become seafarers. I see a strong parallel here with group coaching; like the murre parents, leadership group coaches need to help their clients get off that ledge, take a leap of faith, and create a better life.

CHAPTER 7

Creating Safe Places for Executive Play

We don't stop playing because we grow old; we grow old because we stop playing.

– George Bernard Shaw

Without this playing with fantasy no creative work has ever yet come to birth. The debt we owe to the play of the imagination is incalculable.

– Carl Jung

Word and idea are not born of scientific or logical thinking but of creative language, which means of innumerable languages – for this act of "conception" has taken place over and over again.

– Johan Huizinga

All work and no play makes Jack a dull boy.

– Proverb

Scattered through southwestern France and northeastern Spain are more than 200 caves that contain some of the oldest and finest prehistoric artworks in the world. One of these places, Les Trois Frères cave, contains some spectacular drawings, including the famous "sorcerer," a man with owl's eyes, a wizard's beard, a horse's tail, hands like paws, antlers for headgear, and a reindeer skin. The images in these caves open a window to a world long past; not only do they show us beasts that are now extinct but they also reveal the work of talented artists at play.

These drawings are true marvels of emotional expressiveness and eloquence. Contrary to expectations, they express the kind of aesthetic care associated with symbolic and playful behavior. But what enticed our ancestors to create these drawings? Was it mere playfulness, or was there more to it? Were these ancient scrapings and paintings the sophisticated creations of serious artists or merely the playful graffiti of Paleolithic teenagers?

From a more epistemological point of view, taking a long-term perspective of the developmental history of *Homo sapiens*, what is the significance of play? Is it just a frivolous activity, or is it an essential part of our evolutionary development? Does play have an important role in the transmission of culture?

Play and human development

These cave paintings demonstrate that play has been with us since the dawn of time. It may even predate culture; animals and children play instinctively. Play is engraved in our species as part of our genetic makeup.[1] We can go further, and argue that the human urge to create comes from the play impulse. But whatever its roots, biological or social, play is anything but frivolous. Play has been an intricate part of the evolution of *Homo sapiens* and through it we have developed as a species. Through play we learn to recognize colors, shapes, tastes, and sounds – the building blocks of reality.[2] Play also provides pathways to love and social connection. Moreover, play is the foundation of language, myths, rituals, behavior, and meaning. In play, connections between the individual and the environment unfold or emerge, helping the individual to develop effective learning strategies. Play accentuates our biological tendency to symbolize and create meaning in order to understand the world around us.

Homo sapiens' development and progress may have been shaped less by what people needed to do to survive than by what they did in more playful moments. Planning would have been pretty much unknown to our Paleolithic ancestors. They relied on opportunity, intercepting prey, finding roots, or collecting fruit as and when they could. Prehistoric humans had no concept of "work," as we do; even the collaborative search for food in the rainforest could have been a relatively playful, pleasurable activity. Problem solving and decision making were spontaneous and opportunistic, and these behavioral necessities would have created a foundation for intuition, improvisation, exploration, and adaptation. From an evolutionary perspective, it can even be argued (considering the relatively short time that *Homo sapiens* has been "civilized") that our brain is actually best suited to a more playful style of living. Play, artistic expression, creativity, and evolutionary human development are closely allied.

We might question whether our ancestors were happier than humans living in contemporary society. The Paleolithic body and mind were well adapted to the prevailing hunter-gatherer lifestyle. Has there been sufficient time for humans to adapt to the changes contingent on farming, industrialization, and digitization – changes that may have led to a misfit between our modern lifestyle and our evolutionary makeup? Have we had enough time to catch up? Are the present-day diseases of civilization (obesity, cardiovascular disorders, metabolic disturbances, allergies, depression, chronic stress) due to a hitch in our evolutionary progression over time?

For our ancestors, the capacity to play was an essential element of survival and this is still true today. If our life is all work and no play, we are in trouble. The lack of play is an invitation to stress disorders and mental health problems. Would we be happier, and more effective, if we could recapture the spontaneity imperative of Paleolithic times?

Civilization has been accompanied by many drawbacks, among them the negative effects of evolutionary "progress" vis-à-vis our ability to play. Perhaps the current default mode of workaholism has had adverse affects on our creative development. To what extent is playfulness the oxygen we need to develop further as a species? Are we stifling our potential for self-development by suppressing our innate playfulness?

Child's play

Recently, I watched my grandchildren playing in the attic. First (like their cave artist ancestors before them), they produced a stream of figurative, creative drawings. They changed tack when an empty cardboard box attracted their interest. In no time, this box was transformed into a cave, an airplane, and the stage of a puppet theatre. I marveled at the magic appearing before my eyes but I have to confess that I also felt envious of their ability to create such make-believe worlds. They seemed to have an uncanny capacity to function at the boundaries of fantasy and reality – to enter without hesitation into this transitional space.[3] I also envied their evident intoxication and excitement while they played.

Where does this talent for play go, once we become adults? Does it just dissipate? Does it die? My grandchildren's joy made me reflect on the price of adulthood – the shrinking of the world of the impossible. At the same time, I wondered how today's new toys like iPhones, iPads, Nintendo, and video games will affect their fantasy life. Will this electronic gadgetry, with all its pre-programmed gaming wizardry, destroy their imaginative abilities?

Watching the children, I wondered whether I still had what it took to join in with them. Would I still be able to play for the joy of playing? Or would I feel compelled to guide them toward a purposeful task? Was I too purpose-driven? Would their lack of a real task orientation disturb me? Or would my entry in the game stop it dead and explode their magical, imaginary world? I recalled a cartoon in New Yorker magazine, where a man instructs his cat, seated next to a litter tray, "Never, ever, think outside the box." Was I like the man in the cartoon? Would I be compelled to tell the children, "Don't do this, don't do that, what you are doing now is wrong"? And to be honest, I'm not a stranger to this urge.

The rules of play may seem simple but they are actually quite complex. As adults, we tend to crash through these rules, having unlearned them while growing up. We are drawn to structure rather than creative freedom; we forget the importance of spontaneity – how to accept the unexpected. And we may no longer recall that some of the best moments in life have been the unexpected ones. This is the adult paradox: we like to stimulate our playful selves but we cannot direct them.

"we like to stimulate our playful selves but we cannot direct them"

I am worried that the playfulness inside me has dissipated due to a variety of cultural indoctrinations – my strong urge to tell the children what to do, even though I know that children need the freedom and time to play, is a signifier of this. I keep telling myself that play is not a luxury, that it is a necessity. While I realize the costs of the transition from childhood to adulthood, I still miss the bygone world of make-believe, mystery, and magic. But I am also well aware that remnants of this world still exist within me. My Paleolithic ancestors are very much part of my DNA – and so is the child I was. I am grateful to my grandchildren for reminding me of the forgotten worlds of wonder that were once very much part of me. But that reflection also forces me to realize that, as an adult, I am guilty of destroying them, through my urge to control my grandchildren's free flow of activities.

As a psychoanalyst and educator I know that children learn through play and that play has a purpose. It can be viewed as the royal road to human development. Like our Paleolithic ancestors before us, children's play substitutes for what they can't yet verbalize; symbols substitute for language. Play helps children to develop mentally, physically, and socially. In play, affective, cognitive, and motivational processes are set into motion. Play ignites creativity and spontaneity.

Modern findings in neuroscience suggest that play also promotes mental flexibility, including adaptive practices such as discovering multiple ways to achieve a desired result, creative ways to improve or reorganize a given situation, or alternative ways of decision making.[4] Play facilitates expressive language and divergent thinking. It is essential to the physical development of children's motor skills. It helps them to bridge the gap between concrete experience and abstract thought. Play also offers the opportunity to act out negative emotions and control impulsive behavior. It's a chance to experiment with new roles and explore the intricacies of interpersonal relationships. It helps the developing child understand empathy. The give-and-take of play is a context for learning cooperation, initiative, and social and leadership skills. Through play, children learn how to work together, to follow mutually agreed rules, and how to socialize in groups. Compassion, trust, and the capacity for intimacy come to the fore through regular play. Play can work wonders for interpersonal relationships. It's difficult to stay mad at someone with whom you play. Some forms of play are rehearsals or trials for later life events, such as "play fighting," imaginary social encounters (such as tea parties with dolls, or playing doctor

"Play can work wonders for interpersonal relationships"

and nurse), or even flirting. Through play we learn how to transform emotionally difficult situations into manageable ones. Play stimulates children's imagination and rouses their curiosity, which leads to discovery, creativity, and innovation.

Play helps relieve stress. When we play vigorously, we trigger a mix of endorphins that lift our spirits and help us cope with pain, fear, and anxiety. Play can also have a restorative function in managing grief. But above all, we play for the pure pleasure of it. In fact, the benefits of play for both children and adults are too many to mention, which makes play not only a frivolous but also a very serious business. Some of us continue to refine these skills in adulthood through play and playful communication; as the old saying goes, "Scratch the adult and find the child."

Play or purpose?

Childhood play is largely play for its own sake, an intrinsic activity that has no direct external purpose, or significant outcome. When children play, they focus mostly on the means, not the ends. Unfortunately, as we grow up, play becomes increasingly viewed as unimportant and is sidelined. Play for its own sake becomes more difficult to achieve in adulthood.

For example, at work, most of us have a very instrumental approach to what we do and typically opt for the shortest, least effortful means of achieving whatever target has been set. Workaholics do everything they can to get the best results. Their goal is to be seen to have done a good job. Any activity that is not related to that goal is a wasted effort. Workaholics seem to have forgotten that many of the things we do in life have play behavior at their core. Why bother to make art, make love, or have fun, without an intrinsic component of playfulness? These activities may seem purposeful, but they are not utilitarian.

Of course, we can also ask ourselves whether it is appropriate to be playful when so much of "civilized" life is serious, stressful, difficult, and no fun at all. Natural as play may be for children, for adults dealing with the vicissitudes of contemporary society, it becomes much less natural. When we do play, logic interferes all too often, telling us that what we are doing may not be the best use of our time. Playing with empty boxes in the attic is not something to recount to others with pride. In adulthood, purposefulness overrides everything. Even while watching our children playing in the attic, an inner voice tells us that it's high time to clean up the mess and get rid of all those empty boxes. Adults are easily confused by the seriousness of children's play and by children's refusal, while playing, to acknowledge that they are playing. We may worry that our children are unable to distinguish fantasy from reality. But of course they are well aware of the difference. The fictional mode of thinking, and our ability to keep it distinct from the literal mode, are innate capacities of the human mind. Fortunately, children are not (yet) troubled by that inner voice that says they need a reason for doing what they are doing. They follow a different type of logic. They play for the sheer joy of it and they don't even think about tidying up the attic.

Watching my grandchildren mess about happily, I realize that I may need to learn how to play again, or relearn how to let things simply be. Perhaps I need to unlearn the need to look at my email and scan my phone, and learn instead to leave my phone behind and close my computer.

"the opposite of play is not work – it's more like depression"

It's high time I realized that the opposite of play is not work. It's more like depression.

But do I still have the capacity to play? Adult play rarely involves cardboard boxes – but am I still capable of sitting in a café and just watching the traffic and people pass by? Can I still take a walk and simply look at the scenery? Or is this too much of a challenge? Sitting or walking, will I find myself preoccupied with the next errand to be done or the next goal to pursue?

What happens on the road to adulthood? What goes wrong? When I look back at my personal history, and what energized me when I was younger, I seem to have strayed from the things that gave me playful pleasure. Despite the powerfulness of the play impulse, somewhere between childhood and adulthood I stopped playing. At some point I exchanged play for work and responsibilities. Even now, when I do have some leisure time, I tend to zone out in front of the TV or computer screen, instead of reverting to the more creative, brain-stimulating play activities of the past. I am far from alone in this. Is play neglected in our fast-paced, task-driven society?

We know that children who continue to be playful are likely to be more successful at school and more socially content than their work-driven counterparts. We know that there is a strong relationship between playfulness and creativity.[5] But do we pay enough attention to this knowledge? Do we recognize the importance of play for our continuing personal development? If we could rediscover play as adults, we might be much more creatively effective. Playing together also brings greater joy, vitality, and resilience to relationships, work associations included. Through regular play, we learn to trust each other more, which enables us to work better together, opens us to intimacy, and enables us to try new things.

Some of these questions may be answered by the fact that we fail to realize how much we do actually play in adulthood, when it is more common to find purposefulness and playfulness combined. In childhood, play is principally a separate activity in time and space; in adulthood it is a much less overt, transparent process and is more imbedded in our daily activities. Perhaps our main difficulty is recognizing when we are at play, rather than our failure to play – because play is not a lost cause in adulthood. It takes many forms, from storytelling, mimicry, and games, to extreme sports like skydiving, high-speed racing, mountain hunting, and so on. Some professions – architecture, design, and acting for example – are really creative play at work. If we give ourselves conscious permission to play with the joyful abandon of childhood, we will continue to reap the benefits throughout our life.

Play and flow

As children or adults, we seem never to be more fully alive, or deeply engrossed in anything, than when we are playing. One major reason for this is that play facilitates feelings of embodiment, meaning it locates us in our bodies and places us in the present moment. Through play, we generate and attend to sensation, and we move in ways that both nurture and challenge our whole bodily system. That system, in turn, generates endorphins and dopamine, our internal pleasure-inducing neurotransmitters. These induce a state of mind that some researchers call "flow."[6] Flow occurs when we are totally attuned to a specific activity. While in flow, there is reduced consciousness of self and time – a state of consciousness that is in harmony with our surroundings and feelings. While in this state, we are deeply immersed in the present, and feel at our best. Nothing else seems to matter. We experience a sense of bliss and positive detachment from everyday reality – an inner state of being that brings us peace and fulfillment. Whatever the worries and frustrations of everyday life, they fade into the background. At the same time, we have the confidence that whatever we are doing is doable – that our skills are up to the task. In flow, there is intrinsic motivation and understanding about what needs to be done and a desire to keep up the momentum.

The rules of the game

Understanding "flow" may help us understand the significance of play, but we are still faced with the question of what differentiates play from other activities. What are its key characteristics?

To start with, play is a freely chosen activity, but it is not a free-form activity. Although play has structure, it's one that derives from rules in the player's mind. Importantly, these rules are self-chosen. Even rough and tumble play, which may look wild from the outside, has its rules. The most complex forms of play, socio-dramatic play – the acting out of roles or scenes, like playing "house," or acting out a marriage, or pretending to be superheroes – can be quite rule bound, with the players setting the rules as they go along, consistent with their shared understanding of the roles that are being acted out.

Although imagination and fantasy are most obvious in socio-dramatic play, where the players create characters and plot, they are also present to some degree in all other forms of human play. For example, a rough and tumble fight is a pretend fight, not a real one. In more constructive, elaborate play, the players may say that they are building a castle, but they know it is a pretend castle, not a real one. Clearly, play presents a conundrum – there are no rules yet there are also many rules, all self-imposed.

The contradictions embedded in play are a theme of a classic text in the field of play studies, the book *Homo Ludens*, written by one of the founders of modern cultural history, Johan Huizinga. He defined play as follows:

> Summing up the formal characteristic of play, we might call it a free activity standing quite consciously outside "ordinary" life as being "not serious" but at the same time absorbing the player intensely and utterly. It is an activity connected with no material interest, and no profit can

be gained by it. It proceeds within its own proper boundaries of time and space according to fixed rules and in an orderly manner. It promotes the formation of social groupings that tend to surround themselves with secrecy and to stress the difference from the common world by disguise or other means.[7]

Building on Huizinga's work, I have devised a highly simplified way of identifying some of the innate characteristics of play – MMMM, four Ms that stand for me-time, make-believe, mastery, and meaning.

1. The need for me-time

Me-time is one of the basic ingredients of play, which is, first and foremost, a representation of freedom. For example, when we have a great deal of freedom about how and when we do our work, work is experienced as play, even (in fact, especially) when the work to be done is difficult. Me-time implies having autonomy, a free choice. Formally, it can be defined as having an internally perceived locus of causality – that is, being able to do what we want to do, rather than what others expect us to do. In situations when we have to do what others tell us, we rarely experience such work as play.

As play is done for its own sake, it gives us a special feeling of liberty. Playing means being self-governed – being able to make our own informed decisions and choosing to act according to our own values and beliefs. It also implies taking responsibility for our actions, and experiencing the knowledge that those actions are the result of our own choices. While play represents spontaneous and voluntary action, it also implies involvement. Play is anything but a spectator sport. For example, sitting in front of television may be relaxation or time out but it is not play. Players not only choose to play or not to play, but also direct their own actions during play.

Play draws and fascinates players precisely because it is structured by rules we invent or accept. The ultimate freedom in play, and a crucial aspect of its definition, is the freedom to quit. Without that, the rules of play would be intolerable.

2. The need for make-believe

As Shakespeare famously wrote, "All the world's a stage, and all the men and women merely players: they have their exits and their entrances; and one man in his time plays many parts."[8] An apparent paradox of play is that it is serious yet not serious, real yet not real. Play is centered on make-believe, the pretense that what is not real, is. Make-believe play lies at the intersection of cognitive development and social experience. In this way it creates a double consciousness that consists of reality and the representation of reality needed for make-believe play. For example, we cannot ride an elephant unless there is a real elephant available for us to ride. But when we are playing, if the rules of the game designate the arm of the sofa as an elephant, we can ride an elephant to our heart's content. In reality, a rug is a piece of material covering the floor, but in play it can be a flying carpet. The fictional situation dictates the rules of the game; the actual physical world within which the game is played becomes secondary. Because play takes place in a fantasy world, it is governed by the rules in the minds of the players rather than externally imposed rules.

This make-believe world offers great developmental opportunities. Within it, children can override their fears; they can fight off dragons with magical swords; they can vanquish the monsters under the bed; they can be masters of the universe. Through play children acquire control of the world, as opposed to being subject to its vagaries. Make-believe play can have a huge cognitive and emotional impact, allowing children to experiment with social roles and interactions. They can walk in others' shoes. They can practice being surgeons, pilots, firefighters, or racecar drivers. The leaps of imagination that occur during play are powerful tools in the development of young minds because they encourage children to resolve problems on their own.

"Through play children acquire control of the world, as opposed to being subject to its vagaries"

Daydreaming

Make-believe and daydreaming are closely linked. As the wealth of myths, legends, and fairy tales handed down to us over time illustrates, we have been the creators of a huge variety of heroes and heroines. Yet behind the diversity of our dreaming, there is communality. Two of the more common daydream narratives focus on the "conquering hero," and the "suffering martyr." These are universal stories; they touch and motivate us, and, like many other daydreams, they offer plenty of playful space for the creative process.

These two themes – starting in childhood and continuing in adulthood – reflect our great need for mastery and for escape from the frustrations and compromises of everyday life. We want to believe; we make-believe. The urge to make-believe accompanies us throughout life. Just as in childhood, our daydreams help us define future plans and aspirations by allowing us to play with various roles, lifestyles, and occupations. These daydreams are fundamental to the creative process.

"The urge to make-believe accompanies us throughout life"

3. The need for mastery

The personality psychologist Robert White introduced the concept of "effectance motivation," describing it as our tendency to explore and influence our environment.[9] He suggested that the human "master reinforcer" is a sense of competence, the ability to interact effectively with the environment. This desire can be seen very clearly in child's play. Children will gravitate to areas in which they perceive competence and avoid areas where success is hit or miss, or there is no sense of accomplishment. As might be expected, successful and failed attempts at mastery result in reinforcement of the domain towards which a person migrates. Interactive play and games provide opportunities for experimentation and are a way of achieving a sense of mastery over the environment. Again, this motivation to play exists *within* the individual rather than being dependent on any external pressure. The goals are experienced as an intrinsic part of the game, not as the sole reason for engaging in the game's actions. Thus the main objective in such play is creating the object, not having it. For example, when my children were playing on the beach, making a sand castle, they would not be pleased if I told them "I'll make the castle for you." That would spoil their fun. They would be motivated by the process, not the product. It is the mastery of making sand castles that counts; the significant thing is the efficacy of doing it.

4. The need for meaning

Some of the most fundamental questions we ask ourselves are "Who am I?," "Where do I come from?," and "What is the purpose of my life?," questions that can be transcribed into "How meaningful is the life I am currently living?" This is a personalization of the more general and philosophical question, "What is the meaning of life, the universe, and everything?" These questions are interconnected, because behind them all, of course, looms the specter of death.

All meaning in life is self-defined and as might be expected, the meaning of life is different for different people: it is not this, or that – it depends who you are. Things and situations in our lives have no meaning by themselves; we attribute meaning to them, depending on our perspective, reality, and belief system.[10] Something that has deep meaning for me might be meaningless to other people, or have different meanings to them at different times in their lives, depending on their experiences, motivations, beliefs, and perspectives.

Meaning implies experiencing the world by interacting authentically with our environment and with others – giving something to the world through self-expression. We may become depressed when there is a mismatch between our lived experience and our desired experience; between the meaninglessness of everyday life and our innate drive to search for meaning, to self-actualize, to be all that we can be. Play takes on an essential role in the search for meaning. It is critical to our exploration of facets of our identity and the various roles we might undertake or consider undertaking. In that respect, meaning is both created and found. However, what we construe as meaningful will always be highly subjective.

Transitional processes

Meaning has its origins in the early developmental trajectory formed through the interaction of mothers (or other caregivers) and infants.[11] We can observe how mother and child create a play zone – a stage for helping the developing infant deal with the vicissitudes of life. If the mother is "good enough" she will both be attuned to, and inevitably frustrate, her infant's needs and desires. This interplay is a meaning-making activity and as such will spark the development of the infant's mind. It provides a sense of continuity, and helps the child create a self-defined identity distinct from that of the mother.

Winnicott used the term *transitional* to describe the "intermediate" or "third area" between the thumb that is sucked and the teddy bear.[12] For example, a first manifestation of "primitive" play is children's ability to create transitional objects – items that are invested with aspects of mother/caregiver and themselves. These items are at once "me" and "not-me," and are transitional in that they facilitate the transition from the omnipotence of the tiny infant (for whom external objects have not yet separated out), to the capacity to relate to "objectively perceived" objects. We are – to illustrate the meaning-making process – quite familiar with children carrying around blankets, teddy bears, or other stuffed toys that are deeply treasured. These transitional objects, which are imbued with meaning, help the child make the transition from feelings of ownership and oneness with mother/caregiver to a stage of separateness and individuation. Over time, with growth and development, these transitional objects lose their meaning and are given up.

Transitional objects are associated with transitional space, the area where fantasy and reality overlap, and the terrain where creativity and play originate, laying the basis for our adult cultural life. In creating and contributing to this transitional space, children and parents are involved in a deep form of meaning-making play. These play activities are highly effective ways of finding creative solutions to the fact that we all must come to terms with our lack of omnipotence and omniscience; that we all have limitations.

Playing in this transitional space becomes a basic meaning-making activity. It allows for the continuing discovery and construction of meaning of the self and its place in the world. This kind of play involves the coming together of inner psychic reality with the objective external world via the positive use of "illusion." Such play is a very serious but also a very joyous activity. Through playing in this intermediate space, children are able to manipulate external phenomena in the service of their imagination, and invest this imagery with meaning and feeling. Through play, they can actualize their internal imaginary experiences by enacting them in the real world. We can recognize such play in the work of artists and writers, but also on a broader, more institutional scale, such as in religions and ideologies.

However, when play in this transitional space is stifled, it may negatively affect developing children's future ability to play – which will have consequences for their future search for meaning. People who experience difficulties in play may have difficulties in constructing meaning in their lives. An inability to play fully, or at all, may lead to difficulty in constructing a coherent narrative or story about themselves around which they can organize a robust sense of self. Highly effective leaders – like Nelson Mandela, Mother Teresa, or Aung San Suu Kyi – have a great ability to create meaning for themselves and for others. There is often a kind of playfulness to these people, as if their equanimity has its source in this playfulness, or vice versa. They use their playful gifts to create something bigger than themselves.

> **"People who experience difficulties in play may have difficulties in constructing meaning in their lives"**

The price of adulthood

Friedrich Nietzsche once said, "In the true man there is a child concealed – who wants to play." But a lot of adult behavior suggests that that inner child is well hidden. Play is no longer what it used to be; we live in an unforgiving, relentless, achievement-oriented society in which play is turned into work. Not even children have time to play; they are expected to perform, from the minute they set foot in nursery school. One way or another, children are expected to fulfill adults' expectations. Their parents are compelled to send them on a "mission impossible" and too many teachers collude in this, with their faulty attitude that children are immature adults. Better and more respectful teaching would follow if they thought of adults as atrophied children.

It is unfortunate that adults who engage overtly in forms of play find themselves described as "childish" by their less playful peers. People who use this as a derogatory term fail to realize that play retains its importance, regardless of age. Play can function as a protective mechanism against the high demands work makes on us – for example, a well-timed joke can alleviate a stressful situation. Articulating the fundamental absurdity of all forms of human endeavor – which is the essence of all comedy and informs every joke ever told – can help even the most committed workaholic get things into perspective and liberate some mental space.

But appearances can be deceptive, because as we move through the life cycle, the proclivity to play remains an essential part of our makeup. Even though our capacity for play may not be so visible once we are grown up, it is there, albeit dormant. Make-believe and fantasy continue to play a significant role in much, if not most, of what we do as adults. Play is an invaluable mode of learning and source of creative production, and work without play will not get the best out of people. To quote the actor and comic writer John Cleese, "If you want creative workers, give them enough time to play." If we are prepared to go beyond narrow, task-driven concerns of the traditional work environment and give people "play time," the effects can be remarkable. Concerns with outcome are reduced and people's enjoyment of the task for its own sake is increased.

Are you playing?

If you were told you could leave your job and still have the same income and level of satisfaction, what would you decide? If you would jump at the offer, there can be very little play involved in what you do. If you would quit reluctantly, or not at all, your job is something that you enjoy doing independently of its extrinsic rewards. You are playing as well as working.

Today, people in work are working longer and harder, in the belief that this makes them more productive. Instead, they fall behind, become chronically overwhelmed, and suffer from a variety of stress disorders. Critically, success depends less on the amount of time we spend at work and more on the quality of the work we produce. And the quality of our work is highly dependent on our mental well-being. This is why it is especially important for us to play while we work. Without playtime, our work will suffer. In the words of Albert Einstein, "To stimulate creativity, one must develop the childlike inclination for play and the childlike desire for recognition."

"from a career perspective, the capacity for play can work wonders"

From a career perspective, the capacity for play can work wonders. I have discovered, again and again, that when I reach an impasse in a project, doing something completely different, like having lunch with a friend, or going to the beach with my grandchildren, does a lot more than take my mind off the problem. It stimulates creativity. Creating a change of mindset helps me to get a new perspective on things.

So, as adults, how can we practice self-control and still be open to play, free from self-censorship? How can we become sufficiently self-aware to remain playful, without that self-awareness (and the accompanying sense of responsibility) inhibiting that very playfulness? How can we make play a central part of our lives once more? One way to find the answers to these questions is to work within a transitional space.

As an educator, my primary task is to bring my clients to a place where they can play more fully; where they can engage in a dialectic, interactive process that enables them to experience and to have both the freedom and the discipline to cultivate a sense of possibility and enhanced meaning. In practical terms, this means one of a number of executive workshops and programs that take a psychodynamic approach. But even in that context it's not easy. Executives have to summon up a considerable degree of courage in order to play. While I try to help them rediscover their child-like willingness to try something new, they are held back by their fear of making a fool of themselves. There is a lot of posturing in adulthood. Worse is the way many adults consciously suppress their playful self, on the grounds that the world is a vale of tears, life is not a bed of roses, and we are all on a hiding to nothing. This may be existentially true, but we don't get anywhere if we are caught up in such negative projections. This state of mind destroys the capacity for playfulness.

Organizational play therapy

Play therapy is a very common form of intervention when dealing with children.[13] It is used to help them better understand confused feelings or traumatic events that they have not had the opportunity or the skills to sort out properly. Through play therapy, they are given the chance to "manipulate" the world on a smaller scale, something that may not be possible in their day-to-day environment.

Using play therapy with adults is very different. One explanation for the reluctance of adults to play is that it is considered childish and inappropri-ate behavior. But people who take this view do not recognize that a lot of adult behavior, like making art or making love, is play, and what's more play at its best. The point cannot be overemphasized: adults (overtly and/ or covertly) benefit from playful exploration. Educational settings are particularly suitable for playful interventions that foster learning, enhance relationships, and improve health and well-being. They provide a safe space in which adults can take the opportunity to experiment, embark on new life experiences, rediscover their creativity, and even reinvent and renew themselves.

In the executive programs for which I am responsible I use the technology of educational play to further the creative development of participants. These programs are given greater impetus by the fact that many people enroll because they sense that something is going on in their lives that they want time out to explore. They are mentally ready to do things differently. They have not only come to the realization that they are at a dead end, they also want to do something about it.

The CEO "recycling" seminar

Once a year, I run a workshop at INSEAD called "The Challenge of Leadership: Creating Reflective Leaders." Twenty very senior executives (most of them CEOs from the private and public sector and from all over the world) are invited to participate. These executives apply to the program for a variety of reasons. The guiding themes may have to do with seemingly insoluble dilemmas, negative feelings about themselves, being bored, or feeling like an impostor. They may be suffering from various stress symptoms, or struggling with the existential dilemmas of life. Typically, however, these issues are not clearly articulated in the candidates' mind when they apply to the program.

To be accepted on the program, each potential participant has to complete a complex application form. The information provided helps me to make an initial assessment about the candidate's suitability for the program. In addition, I interview each future participant—whatever their location—in person (or over the phone) to see if they have what it takes to go through such a challenging seminar, where the "life" case study will be a main source of interpretive material. In these interviews I look for signs of psychological mindedness, their capacity to be open and responsive, their degree of defensiveness, their sense of who they are, their capacity for reality testing, and their preparedness to really understand themselves better.

The workshop consists of three five-day modules with breaks of approximately two months in between. Six months after the last of these modules, a fourth four-day module assesses how well the participants have enacted the life decisions they made over the duration of the first three modules. The expectation is that during each module the participants learn more about themselves, agree a "contract" on what to work on in the workplace and at home during the time they are away from the workshop; and return to the workshop to deepen their understanding. I share responsibility for monitoring the "homework" assignments with fellow participants. Mutual coaching is part of the program design. Participants write reflection papers after each module. These are sent to me, and provide essential feedback on the participants' experience; but they also serve another function, in that writing about our experiences is a life-structuring exercise in itself.

The first module is the most structured of the four. During this module I give a number of interactive mini-lectures on high performance organizations, organizational culture, leadership (exemplary and dysfunctional), the career life cycle, cross-cultural management, organizational stress, and the dynamics of individual and organizational change. However, the central model of psychological activity and organization within the program is the personal case history. At some point, each participant is expected to volunteer to sit in the "hot seat" to discuss his or her salient life issues and dilemmas. This part of the program is extremely important, as experiences and decisions, including successes and setbacks, become organized when people narrate their personal life story. The presentation becomes a process of self-discovery, and also helps the other participants to better understand the problems they have in their own public or private life.

During the second module a considerable amount of time is devoted to processing a number of 360-degree feedback instruments that I have developed. All of these have both an organizational and personal focus, including feedback gathered from spouses/partners or significant other(s).[14] Additional information is collected from other family members and close friends. This information provides the basis for a more refined action plan in the period between the second and third modules. The main focus of the third module is the consolidation of acquired insights, the creation of tipping points for change, and experimentation with future action plans.

Throughout the program, a key element is nurturing a sense of play among the participants. To enable this playfulness to come to the fore, an essential task for the program facilitator is to create a safe, transitional space that is characterized by trust and reciprocity. This space will provide a kind of holding environment in which the participants (depending on the dysfunctionalities they have to overcome) can be contained and mirrored. A holding environment of this kind is necessary to be able to begin experimentation, play, and working through their issues.

By the third module of this program, most of the participants know each other better than many of their family members do. At this point the interchange in the plenary session has become extremely free-flowing with much less intervention required from me. The group of participants is turning into a self-analyzing community. Finally, the fourth module of the program becomes like a built-in alumni session, providing an opportunity to see if all the learning has been internalized.

A key factor in this kind of educational organizational therapy program is creating the opportunity for participants to "play." A very effective way to start this "play" is to ask each of them to draw a self-portrait. It enables the participants to reflect on how they would portray their life in images. After an initial hesitation, this exercise has proven to be extremely helpful in having the participants enter a different world – a world of make-believe. To create the safe, transitional space this requires, it is important to demonstrate authenticity, directed empathy, and unconditional positive regard.[15] Once such a space has been created, it will support a learning community in which the participating executives will dare to experiment with new possibilities and life strategies.

A transitional space is vital for the development of the self, whether this emerges as inhibition or the capacity to create, and for individual creativity and cultural experience. This space will also provide a container for participants. Only when they feel this containment is adequate – having acquired trust in the process – will they feel secure enough to begin experimentation, and play; only then, will they be able to work through their issues. Experimenting with alternatives, and experiencing satisfactory results, will enable them to make connections between inner and outer reality. These links will create a greater sense of authenticity, and efficacy.

These experimentations for new beginnings are helped by the fact that the participants spend a considerable amount of time in small groups in and outside the classroom. These playful interactions are extremely valuable as these encounters serve to consolidate newly acquired behavioral patterns. Learning from the others is essential to making this process of change work. Eventually, the participants in these organizational group therapy sessions form an intense learning community in which each of them gives the others constructive feedback (nobody should get hurt but no "love bombing" either) whenever they fall back into behavior patterns they are trying to unlearn. The important challenge is to turn the participating groups into self-analyzing communities.

In the later stages of the workshop, the members of this playful learning community demonstrate a remarkable level of emotional intelligence, compared with their abilities in the first module. In many instances, the program learning becomes even more consolidated through follow-up sessions year after year, which offers the opportunity to assess the degree to which new behavior patterns have become part of their modus operandi.

The psychological dance

When teaching executives how to play, it's important that they focus their attention on the sensations, feelings, and thoughts they had not previously acknowledged. My challenge as a facilitator is to create greater awareness of their actions. But this facilitation goes both ways. To be sufficiently susceptible to what is happening to them, I also need to be highly vigilant about my own counter-transference reactions.[16] Listening to the narratives that emerge, I also need to listen to what is not being said. The process is a playful dance between the person whose issues are being discussed, the observations of the group-as-a-whole, and the way I experience this interplay. The free play of attention stimulates cognitive flow, emotional resilience, and physical alertness. While the dance is played out, I try to ensure that every speaker is listened to respectfully and that everyone has the opportunity to be heard. I also encourage everyone to articulate what they really think and what they feel should be said. This means that there will be negative reflections and the elephants in the room will have to be named. The participants are encouraged to express their feelings about the forum, which will range between sadness, anger, joy, despondency, disgust, excitement, and envy.

> "Listening to the narratives that emerge, I also need to listen to what is not being said"

Everyone enters a process like these workshops in order to be seen and understood, but at the same time we fear criticism and exposure. We may also not know how to pay the same attention to others, without projecting our positive and negative fantasies onto them. Play practices that cultivate high-quality attention and awareness, both of oneself and others, are an essential part of an adult educational playgroup.

As the program progresses, the participants take deep personal responsibility for themselves and for what the group presents to them. Within the safe space of the workshop, unconscious and unrecognized material, including long-repressed fears and longings, will surface, prompting classic forms of resistance, such as splitting, projection, denial, displacement, dissociation, and depression. As time goes on, these defenses become less effective. The group context creates feelings of intimacy, belonging, and social healing and becomes a container for individuals' cathartic experiences.

When the seminar is over, the participants have to re-enter their daily lives, taking their new insights and learning with them, and find a new fit for these in the outside environment. This means using their thoughts, feelings, and even their bodies differently, and demonstrating this difference in their daily behavior. Change has to be manifested if it is to be real but it has to be practiced until it is lodged in each participant's behavioral repertoire. If not, it will dissipate, like a mirage.

Playology redux

The Greek playwright Aeschylus once said, "It is a profitable thing, if one is wise, to seem foolish." In this chapter, I have suggested that our ability to play is an essential part of our makeup. Play is not merely a child's game; it is also a vital part of adulthood. There is no learning or creativity without play. Play is our brain's favorite learning mode. We need to play so that we can discover and rediscover the magic around us.

"there is no learning or creativity without play"

As I have found for myself, the best inspiration comes from watching how children play. Like we were once as children, we shouldn't turn away from the playful child within us, but let it lead us through life as we play, explore, and try out new things. In our time, we will all experience the deadening effect of routines, plans, rules, and the expectations of others. We should remind ourselves that we have it within us to be playful and spontaneous, to experiment with new challenges, and explore new places, ideas, and activities.

Our playfulness underwrites our willingness to learn new skills and readiness to take up unexpected opportunities. It is also a powerful defense against boredom, worry, and depression. If we can free our minds to play, we can often solve apparently insoluble problems. And we can only laugh at life's absurdities if we retain a playful mindset. As the Monty Python team said, encouraging us to always look on the bright side of life, "If life seems jolly rotten, there's something you've forgotten, and that's to laugh and smile and dance and sing." Perhaps we should try to see the world as a great sandbox, like the ones we played in as children. We should give ourselves permission to play in this sandbox, to create new adventures of self-exploration and to reinvent ourselves.

CHAPTER 8

Creating Tipping Points

It is only with the heart that one can see rightly; what is essential is invisible to the eye.

– Antoine de Saint-Exupéry

When you change the way you look at things, the things you look at change.

– Max Planck

People think of these eureka moments and my feeling is that they tend to be little things, a little realization and then a little realization built on that.

– Roger Penrose

Introduction

Many people view leadership coaching as an arcane and dubious process, evoking notions of occult exchanges between people who are basically strangers to each other. This unfortunate and inaccurate image has been perpetuated by the popular media: we have all seen therapists or coaches depicted as aloof, grey-bearded men with Viennese accents, who say nothing as their clients writhe miserably on old-fashioned upholstered couches, fighting their demons unaided. This classic scenario can be the background to some very funny cartoons; however, more disingenuously, it encourages negative imagery and stereotyping.

Coaching practitioners worry about this public image of the client-coach interchange, which is far removed from reality. Such characterizations, however amusing, do little to help people grasp what really occurs within a coaching context and belittle the hard work coaches engage in to help their clients create incremental and transformational change.

Unsurprisingly, given this negative and suspect imagery, there is often great hesitancy about asking for help from someone in a helping profession. But I have learned from my own experience as a leadership coach that when the coach-client interface works well, great things can happen. Effective coaches operate like seasoned jazz musicians: using their talent for reconstruction, reformulation, and respectful listening they improvise on the themes their clients present, recasting motifs, phrases, and statements to re-create experiences in new and interesting ways. Their clients may come to see things differently; they may feel able to take greater control over their lives; and, most importantly, they may even reinvent themselves.

"Effective coaches operate like seasoned jazz musicians"

It is true that coaching often awakens old demons, reminding clients of past traumas and unhappy situations. But when the coaching process is done well, it can be greatly empowering, improving self-awareness and self-expression, and prompting self-exploration. Effective coaching also stimulates the creative process, encourages psychological risk-taking, helps clients attain deeper levels of emotional intelligence, and may create a greater sense of realism about what life has to offer. Coaching can resolve wide-ranging problems, including self-esteem issues, persistent anxiety, stress symptoms, sexual dysfunction, depression, dealing with envy and jealousy, lack of purpose, and many others that trouble clients at various stages of the life cycle.

"Aha!" moments

We all recognize "Aha!" or "Eureka!" moments, times when we suddenly find the answer to a riddle, or when, out of the blue, we understand the solution to a problem and a light bulb goes on in our head. These moments are often referred to as tipping points,[1] signaling events of great significance that contribute to meaningful life changes.

As some of the most famous accounts of eureka moments illustrate, the profound insights they stimulate can be triggered by very banal experiences. According to legend, Archimedes, the Greek mathematician and scientist, was challenged to find a way to prove whether the king's crown was really made of solid gold or had been adulterated with silver. It was when he got into his bath and noticed how the level of the water rose that Archimedes suddenly realized that he could use the volume of displaced water to work out the density of the king's crown. The story goes that Archimedes was so excited by his discovery that he ran naked into the street, crying "Eureka! Eureka!" ("I have found it").

Another famous "Aha!" moment that has become the stuff of legend is the tale of the 17th-century English physicist Isaac Newton and the apple. It is said that Newton was lying under tree in an orchard, and saw an apple fall to the ground. Wondering idly why apples fall down rather than up, and why we walk on the ground rather than float in the air, Newton realized that the large mass of the earth must pull objects toward it – and so his theory of a specific kind of motion, gravity, began to take shape.

Compared to these two glorious examples, the insights produced by "Aha!" moments in coaching may seem relatively banal – however, the incidents that provoke them may be similarly humdrum, yet, on a personal level, prove to be important tipping points. Generally speaking, coaches expect to see incremental changes in their clients, but we are occasionally privy to "Aha!" moments and, when they happen, they are very different from the small successes that characterize the "normal" coaching experience.

Linear versus quantum change

The kinds of experience that cause change of a discontinuous and non-linear nature[2] can be quite dramatic. "Aha!" moments may be triggered by traumatic events and major life challenges that cause significant emotional distress, unbalancing someone's mental state. This phenomenon has been described as "quantum change," a sudden, unexpected form of change, signified by an enduring and deep shift in core values, attitudes, or actions, moments that are vividly remembered and, I should stress, that can occur both within and outside a psychotherapeutic context. According to Miller and C'de Baca,[3] such experiences affect a broad range of personal emotion, cognition, and behavior. Their survey revealed that these quantum change experiences are neither as uncommon as we might think, nor easily dismissed as wishful thinking or passing delusions.

Miller and C'de Baca liken quantum change to "a bolt from the blue" or "seeing the light." Individuals who had had such a life-changing experience almost universally described it as becoming aware of a new, meaningful reality. Suddenly, an important truth was revealed to them.[4] They realized that they had a considerable amount of untapped potential. When these thoughts took hold, they realized that living authentically was all that mattered, and peacefulness and inner strength ensued, contributing to a positive shift in their core values. They experienced a greater sense of meaning in life, having freed themselves from unhealthy, dysfunctional patterns of behavior. They were also less likely to bemoan unpleasant past experiences. Instead, they cherished the present, and looked forward to the future.

In their hypothesis, Miller and C'de Baca[5] refer to two types of quantum change: sudden insights and more mystical epiphanies. Some of the participants in their study accepted what they had experienced as a product of rarely tapped inner resources; others saw it as a gift from a higher power. Yet Miller and C'de Baca reckon that mystical experiences and quantum changes have much in common.

Mystical experiences have been described since the dawn of psychology, most notably by William James in *The Varieties of Religious Experience*.[6] According to James, mystical states of consciousness are central to religious experiences, which come in many different forms, and can vary in intensity. In their simplest form they appear to the individual as a sudden burst of intelligence or insight (as Archimedes and Newton experienced). But they differ considerably.

In a sublime mystical state, achieved through meditation, the individual experiences the ecstasy of being in union with the Absolute (God). This direct non-rational encounter with ultimate divine reality engenders a deep sense of unity, and a sense of living at a higher level of being. For people who go in search of these experiences, their mystical journey can become life long, culminating in a direct encounter with the unknown – a path into the hidden regions of the mind that are not open to rational explanation but dependent on direct experience.

Miller and C'de Baca have tried to deconstruct the non-mystical forms of quantum change by referring to "self-regulation." They argue that it "is conceivable that quantum changes represent a major and enduring change of behavior triggered by highly significant discrepancies, involving goals that are central to meaning and identity."[7] They also suggest the effect of a "perception shift" – our initial perceptions dominate our attention and inhibit our way of looking at things, blocking alternative perceptions. An additional factor is "value conflict" – a coach or consultant can induce a value conflict that has lasting consequences. Finally, they mention "transcendence." Such changes may even occur without conscious effort or desire by the individual, as in unexpected and uninvited transformations."[8] In these instances, it can seem as if an external agent or force is involved in the transformation, which is like an act of God. Such changes have a transcendent, but very powerful quality (markedly different from ordinary experiences), to paraphrase William James and others. Again, we arrive at the boundary of spirituality and psychology.

This is rather murky terrain. Reading the testimonies of people subjected to these quantum changes, these sudden insights are often attributed to faith, revelation, intuition, instinct, ESP, and many other quasi-spiritual events, which have no place within a scientific view of human development. There has always been a chasm of sorts between more rational research approaches and the mystical nature of religious experience.

To shift from a study of mystical processes to more "objective" research studies of human nature, we can make an excursion into neurology. Studies of brain functioning have suggested that there may be a neurological foundation to these dramatic transformational experiences. Apparently, our brain activity when solving problems requiring creative insight differs from the way it behaves when we are engaged in more linear problem-solving activities.

A neurological excursion

Neuroscientists have always been intrigued by tipping points and wondered whether specific neural activities are associated with transformational experiences. From their research, they have discovered that strong affective experiences are linked to neurophysiological processes[9] that seem to become activated during coach-client exchanges in which coaches play a role in reformulating stuck, or stalled, situations.

To elaborate, while the left hemisphere of the brain is critical for more routine, cognitive processing activities, the more dramatic tipping point moments seem to be linked to the right hemisphere – the intuitive, spontaneous, emotional, and imagistic part of the brain that allows access to the unconscious. The right hemisphere is critical to the exploratory processing of novel, cognitive situations to which no pre-existing codes or strategies in our cognitive repertoire readily apply, that is, the spontaneous surprise that accompanies a new or different idea. From a neurophysiological point of view, the left side of the brain seems to be circumvented during tipping point moments. Clearly, if we are looking for dramatic insights, we have to rely on the right side of the brain – and trust it to function out of awareness.

Neuroscientists have also discovered that the amygdala shows a significant increase in activity during moments of real insight, when there is a sudden reorganization of information in our brain (a sudden shift in perception).[10] The amygdala signals to different cortical regions that an internal event of significant neural reorganization has occurred, playing a critical role in higher order thinking.

Information that results from moments of insight is, almost by definition, incorporated in long-term memory and the amygdala performs a primary role in the formation and storage of memories associated with highly emotional events. Once we have realized a new way to solve a problem, or perform a task better and faster, the amygdala assures that we are unlikely to forget it. The amygdala promotes the long-term memory of the sudden reorganization of these new, internal representations.[11] In this new state, body physiology, information processing, affect, memory, cognition, and communication, as well as subjective self-experience, are organized in a fashion that is optimally conducive to effective therapeutic work.

We can infer that these transformational experiences are very closely related to basic physiological processes derived from our Paleolithic heritage. The kinds of life-threatening events our prehistoric ancestors routinely faced molded our modern nervous system to respond powerfully and fully when we perceive that our survival is threatened. To this day, if we find ourselves in similar situations, we feel exhilarated, more alive, powerful, full of energy, and ready to take on any challenge. Clearly, feeling threatened (or being in love) engages our deepest resources and allows us to experience our fullest potential as human beings. Significantly, it reinforces the observation that some form of discomfort is needed to set a tipping point in motion when coupled with a willingness to look at stuck situations with a different eye.

Real change versus pseudo-change

These neurological studies affirm that an "Aha!" moment (in any situation, including coaching) is a distinct shift in awareness about important issues in our life that signals new insights and the possibility of change. A tipping point occurs when worries and concerns – the negative thoughts that may have previously bothered a coaching client – suddenly evaporate.

But just how real are tipping points? Are they merely transitory phenomena? Do the acquired insights last? In therapeutic circles, a perennial theme of discussion is the "transference cure," a phenomenon whereby clients (consciously or unconsciously) do what a therapist wants in exchange for the gratification of their emotional needs. The transference cure is a form of collusion whereby the client claims to experience miraculous change in an effort to please the therapist, while the therapist (as a reward) ignores troubling symptoms or behavior patterns that are an issue for the client.

The success of this Faustian bargain depends on how good clients are at detaching their symptoms or behavior patterns from other areas of functioning. In the context of a transference cure, clients often try to please the therapist by demonstrating intellectual understanding.[12] This will almost certainly prove to be a transitory solution, and the clients will relapse into their original state.

Regression in the service of the ego

The psychoanalyst and art historian Ernst Kris differentiated between two kinds of regression that can occur during a therapy session. In the first, the patient is overwhelmed, prompting pathological reactions. In the second, regression is more controlled, and enhances the patient's creative capabilities.[13] Kris described a session in which positive regressive processes occurred as the "good hour."

And although psychoanalysts had long known that some sessions turned out to be especially productive for both patient and analyst, Kris was the first to examine these sessions systematically. In the "good hour," patients would not be straining for new memories; on the contrary, they would appear unbidden. Previous defensive reactions would be reduced. The capacity to uncover new memories would coincide with the capacity to grasp the significance of what had been uncovered. In the "good hour" the therapist would be totally attuned to the patient's affective state; memories would appear in context, symbolizing significant events, and resulting in a reorientation of the psychic structure of the patient's life. Kris calls this process regression in the service of the ego,[14] and it closely resembles "Aha!" moments or tipping points. One challenge to anyone in a helping profession is to create "good hours," the kinds of exchange that make tipping points more likely.

However, aware of the dangers of the transference cure, Kris differentiated between the "good hour" and the "deceptively good hour." In the latter the patient wanted the therapist's love and so produced associations the therapist would appreciate. In instances when such collusion occurs, both patient and therapist take the easy way out, and create pseudo-change; the therapist sacrifices real hope of growth and lasting change in favor of short-term good feelings. However, this still begs the question of what these quantum changes are all about.

The anatomy of the tipping point

As a leadership coach and psychotherapist I am regularly confronted with tipping points – sudden moments of insight that make everything click in a client's life and result in positive life changes. A tipping point is the moment when all the pieces of the great puzzle of someone's life fall into place, a moment of extreme clarity, elation, realization, and relief. But as I emphasized earlier, such moments don't occur very frequently – and also may not be reported until sometime after the event. But when they happen, I have seen people put in place dramatic life changes in ways that do not necessarily fit their previous patterns of behavior.

At a tipping point, clients' self-limiting beliefs and negative conditioning (products of their past history) unexpectedly evaporate. They suddenly recognize the distorted notions that have kept them from living life to the full and connecting to their authentic self. They realize that they have been stuck in automatic patterns of thinking and behaving. Now, however, they are prepared to look at things in a new, and more constructive way; they are prepared to live life with greater authenticity and purpose.

Many variables come together at tipping point moments and warrant closer analysis. Apart from a neurological connection, cognitive, emotive, and behavioral variables also play a role in the process, and may serve as catalysts for change. How does this process come about? Does a tipping point come out of the blue or are there preliminary processes at work?

My own observations, and those of many of my colleagues, suggest that there is a sequence that leads up to "Aha!" moments, beginning with the frustration many clients report, the feeling that something is lacking in their lives. On the surface they seem quite content and to have everything that really matters – health, family, friends, and a good job – yet in their quieter moments, they are aware of an emptiness, a sense that things are not how they would like them to be. Without specifically expressing it, clients often have a deep, intense longing for something more – something that they cannot name. While they realize that they should confront this state of mind, they don't know what to do, or how to do it. They may be vaguely aware of behavior they need to change, but not motivated to take the next step. Somehow, somewhere, they know they have a lot of untapped potential and that it should be possible to be more aligned with what is really important to them.

In most instances, coaching enhances an incremental change process during which clients' awareness of their feelings and patterns of thinking and behaving gradually increases. Clients become more and more aware of the everyday frustrations that hold them back. Once these are acknowledged, what follows are micro "Aha!" moments, small daily victories that are frequently overlooked. These small victories over life's adversities, or the expression of pent-up frustration – leading to "mad as hell, can't take it anymore" moments – create the momentum that leads to an almost magical tipping point.

In his studies of people who have experienced dramatic life transformations, Roy Baumeister[15] identifies a phenomenon that he calls "crystallization of discontent," which resonates with the tipping point sequence. Baumeister describes a process whereby incongruent and potentially disturbing information and experiences can be dismissed or minimized if they arise from single, one-off events. In contrast, the accumulation of negative, dissonant thoughts arising from a number of events increases feelings of discontent and acts as a catalyst for significant and often dramatic life transitions. As the saying goes, if someone says you have ears like a donkey, ignore him; but when several people tell you, it's time to buy a saddle. After a period of intense and enduring negative affect that culminates in a new perspective, change will be inevitable. But it is the prior crystallization of discontent that creates a sudden revelation.

All these observations tell us that **"tipping points do not just** tipping points do not just come out **come out of the blue"** of the blue; "Aha!" moments grow out of hours of thought, reflection, and preparation. Tipping points, like chance, favor only the prepared mind. Although the visible effects of deep change may seem out of the ordinary, they are the result of many small, often unremarkable, preparatory interventions. Small changes combine to produce big changes because they lay down new cognitive, emotive, and behavioral pathways. The visible "effects," however, seem rapid and dramatic because we don't see all the work going on behind the scenes, before deep change occurs.

Conceptually, we can distinguish a *preparation phase* during which relevant psychological material is collected, and affective, cognitive, and behavioral issues are worked through (aside from the various neurological processes at work). Given the relative stability of individual personality, getting the process of change into motion usually requires a strong inducement in the form of pain or distress – discomfort that outweighs the pleasure of the "secondary gains"[16] in the current situation that create immunity to change.[17] Whether the trigger is family tension, bereavement, divorce or separation, health problems, negative social sanctions, an accident, feelings of isolation, problem behavior, distressing life events affecting someone close, or simply everyday hassles and frustrations, people must experience a sense of concern about their present situation to kick-start the change process. Many of the executives in the Challenge of Leadership program I mentioned in the previous chapter report a high level of negative emotions in the period just prior to change, generally precipitated by experiences like these that make them aware of the serious negative consequences of continuing their current dysfunctional behavior patterns. They are ready to confront the opposing psychological forces that are responsible for maintaining the status quo. The stage is set for a tipping point. People who report major change say that they reach a point where it is increasingly difficult to maintain the status quo. Their situation increasingly unsettles their psychological well-being. The traditional defense mechanisms – denial, repression, and projection – are no longer working.

This period is followed by an *incubation phase*, a period of very private, creative, inner work. During the incubation period, some kind of information processing keeps going, even when people are not aware of it – including the information processing that happens while we are asleep (and dreaming). When people realize that their bad days are turning into a bad year – in other words, that isolated incidents of discontent have transformed into a steady pattern of unhappiness – they are no longer able to deny that something has to be done. From this point on, every new disturbance is recognized as part of the general pattern of dissatisfaction. People are finally prepared to see that neither the passage of time nor minor changes in behavior will improve the situation – indeed, the situation is likely to become even worse if nothing drastic is done about it.

However, even the insight that drastic measures are required does not automatically compel people to take action. The defenses that are in place to maintain equilibrium can be hard to break down. Nonetheless, it typically sets into motion a mental process whereby people start to consider alternatives to the adverse situation. Having made the transition from denial (implying that their defensive system is changing) to realizing that all is not well, they are then able to move on from a situation in which every alternative appears more frightening than the status quo to a position where they can undertake a reappraisal process. They are starting to play with their ambivalence, having an inner dialogue about the advantages and disadvantages of taking some sort of action. They may start to experiment with small change efforts.

This is followed by the *illumination phase*, the "Aha!" moment, when all the pieces of the puzzle come together. Accepting the need for change is an essential first step, but on its own is no guarantee of action. Usually, at this point in the process (helped by the many confrontational and clarification questions posed by the coach), the many discontents merge into a coherent entity (or focal event) that is viewed retrospectively as a milestone.[18] With hindsight, this focal event will be seen as the tipping point, even though it is often only a minor occurrence. It is seen as focal simply because it enables a discontented person to take that long-delayed first step toward change. It becomes the catalyst in the change process, whether an outside observer perceives it as major or minor.

Some focal events – such as divorce, separation, illness – are objectively and subjectively significant and serious. But many focal events seem trivial at first glance. However, they can be indicators of a whole range of incidents that symbolize the essence of the problem. Although objectively perceived as minor, subjectively they will be significant, because they call attention to problems that have existed for a long time. They precipitate moments of insight and lead to reinterpretation of people's lives.

It is at this point in the process that people start to become prepared to take action. Their resistance to change begins to break down. Their habitual defenses no longer work as they used to. Disequilibrium sets in. Clients acquire new insights about their situation and see new possibilities, whereas before they knew only helplessness and hopelessness. Their emotional energy has been transferred from past concerns (such as dysfunctional behaviors) to the present and future. They feel as if a heavy burden has been lifted, and they are mentally ready to tackle a more constructive future. The client is ready to take new initiatives and engage in behavioral experimentation.

At this point the toughest challenges of the change process have been met. Personal resolutions have laid the groundwork for a thoughtful, detailed reappraisal of goals. There will be experimentation with the new alternatives that have been envisioned. Ideas and plans become clearer and more definite. The destination of this sometimes painful inner journey is increased self-knowledge and a new beginning. As clients progress through the various phases of successful personal change they demonstrate a growing ability to give up their old identifications and roles and to adopt new ones. They begin to reorganize the world in which they live in a significant way. They re-evaluate their life's goals and meanings, letting go of the old, and accepting the new.

Finally, there is the *verification phase*, when these new ways of looking at the world are reintegrated and stabilized. We all tend to talk big when it comes to change. But how many of the hundreds of new pages we promise to turn do we ever lay a finger on? The only true sign that change has been achieved is a new mindset. The final part of the individual change process involves reshaping the internal world and accepting a new identity, or (more modestly), rediscovering and validating an older, more authentic one. The client becomes proactive. Past patterns of thinking, feeling, and acting are discarded as the client begins to turn toward the future. A shift in attitude and behavior has culminated in the redefinition, and even reinvention, of the self or parts of the self that have been dormant for a very long time. Exhibit 8.1 summarizes the stages of the tipping point sequence.

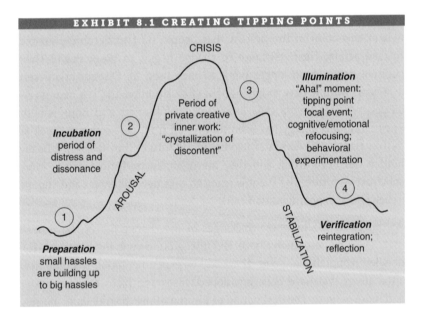

EXHIBIT 8.1 CREATING TIPPING POINTS

CRISIS

Period of private creative inner work: "crystallization of discontent"

Illumination "Aha!" moment: tipping point focal event; cognitive/emotional refocusing; behavioral experimentation

Incubation period of distress and dissonance

AROUSAL

STABILIZATION

Preparation small hassles are building up to big hassles

Verification reintegration; reflection

While "Aha!" moments cannot be engineered, coaches can create an ambiance that becomes conducive to such transformations. They can help to create discontinuous transformational experiences, as the following case example illustrates.

Peter had been a student in a short executive program I ran a number of years ago. I remembered him as a talented, active participant who often took a lead in the discussions – and, most importantly, made a lot of sense. He was the CEO of a successful global IT firm, a company he had taken over when his father retired from the business. I had worked with Peter on a number of occasions after that initial program, helping him to make his top executive team more effective.

Now I had received an email from him asking me whether we could see each other, the sooner the better. I made an appointment to meet him at his office, a week later. As his assistant ushered me into his office, I saw immediately that Peter was not his usual lively self. His complexion was grayish, his face drawn, and his speech slow – very different from the Peter I knew.

After exchanging a few pleasantries, I asked Peter how his various businesses were coming along; his responses were perfunctory and confusing. I had no idea where he was going. But my confusion set into motion an inner dialogue about the themes that were floating around in our bi-personal field. Why was Peter going round in circles? As I always do when I ask these questions, I kept a general road map to our discussions (a contractual agreement) in mind: Where is the client presently? Where does the client want to be? What road should I take to get him there? And of course, because I am also a psychoanalyst, I am always aware of the psychodynamic dimension.

Peter gave me a harangue about the rapid technological changes in the industry; he was extremely worried about the future and wondered, in particular, whether he had the right people in place to deal with the company's rapidly changing strategic landscape. In a lament that lasted quite some time, he described the members of his top team and their fallibilities. Were they the right people for these positions? Had he made a mistake in giving them so many responsibilities?

While he talked, I listened but I was also trying to hear the background track to what Peter was saying. However, I was drowning in his words and overwhelmed by his barrage of complaints. I lost the thread of the conversation. On a whim (if there is such a thing), I asked him to rate on a scale of one to 10 (10 being the highest, and one the lowest), how he felt right now. Peter's immediate response was "Four," which he then corrected to three. I responded that such a low figure should be a cause of some concern. Could he explain to me why he rated himself so miserably? Peter then tried to explain his state of mind, reporting, for my benefit and for his own understanding, recent events that had contributed to his agitation and unhappiness.

First, he was concerned about the business. Peter felt his key executives had become too complacent, and feared that the competition was catching up. In brief, he thought that the company was losing its competitive edge and that unless some drastic measures were taken soon, the company would find itself in deep trouble. He even mentioned bankruptcy as a not-so-remote possibility. Wallowing in his misery, he carried on in this way for quite a while. When I prompted him to elaborate on this idea of bankruptcy, he changed the topic and began talking about his relationship with his wife. Things were not going very well between them. He felt they were living parallel lives; the only issues they shared were rather vacuous exchanges about their children. Apart from the children, they seemed to have very little in common. There were very few things they enjoyed doing together.

I subtly encouraged Peter to voice all the issues that troubled him until I felt satisfied that most of the important facts had been vocalized and expressed accurately. There is something to be said about catharsis, at least when there is a sympathetic audience. It was not difficult to see that Peter felt relieved to get everything off his chest to a non-judgmental listener. This information-gathering process was the first phase of our interchange.

While I listened to Peter's story, I tried to make sense of my own feelings (I have described this elsewhere as the technique of "using myself as an instrument").[19] At one point, when I felt so overwhelmed by the avalanche of material Peter presented me with, I found myself wondering whether I was competent enough to help him. Would I be able to unravel the complex strands that made up his story? Were the complexities of the industry just too much for me? Could I really add some value? Or was I just an impostor, pretending to be able to help him solve such an impossible task? These thoughts made me wonder what Peter was doing to me. Was he using me as a translator of his knotty problems or as a toxic dump for all the unwanted, confusing, or threatened parts of himself that he was unable to cope with? Was he, through projective identification, helping me to become familiar with the themes in his inner theater?

Projective identification is a psychological process whereby one person projects thoughts, feelings, or behaviors onto another, invoking precisely those thoughts, feelings, or behaviors in the other. The other person will be influenced by the projection and begin to behave in accordance with the projected thoughts or beliefs. Projective identification differs from simple projection, the latter being a process whereby individuals subconsciously deny their own attributes, thoughts, and emotions, ascribing them instead to the outside world, usually to other people.[20]

In the second phase of our encounter, I tuned in to those feelings and asked Peter if he sometimes felt like an impostor, given all the challenges he faced on a daily basis. This question led to a flow of associations about Peter's life history, starting with the way he had been treated within his family, where he never felt good enough. In particular, Peter felt he never had been able to live up to his father's high expectations. His father always pooh-poohed any successes he had in life. Interestingly enough, while Peter was discussing his memories of the past, he simultaneously arrived at new insights. He made fresh associations between the past and the present, leading to new observations about his relationships with women, specifically his mother. It dawned on him only now that that she had been too self-involved and self-centered to help him feel better about himself. She hadn't helped him build up his self-esteem. He had to thank his grandfather for that. He was very thankful for the many good times he had spent with him.

Given the psychodynamics of the exchange between us, I felt it was time to experiment with the Pygmalion effect,[21] and communicate to Peter my belief in his capabilities – to treat him as a competent, responsible person, very much as his grandfather had done – to counter his self-image as an incompetent. A considerable body of research has shown that the greater the expectations placed upon a person, the better they perform.[22] I thought that supportive observations would be helpful at this point. I was very aware that, as a leadership coach, I needed to take care of Peter's deep and profound need for support, comfort, and connectedness. I needed to empathize with his subjective experience and pay attention to the central, repetitive, conflictual transference configurations. Could I be the good father or mother Peter never had? Could I be the supportive grandfather?

This positive re-experiencing would be a more constructive way of dealing with Peter's past demons than transforming into his non-caring, irresponsible parents – not that these negative parental experiences should remain suppressed; on the contrary, they would have to be dealt with. But accentuating the negative would not be very constructive.

Generally, emphasizing self-competence strengthens the working alliance between coach and client and enhances self-esteem, becoming a self-fulfilling prophecy. Clients often respond to high performance

expectations and a sense of self-efficacy may be an important consequence. But in acting as I did, I remained aware of the danger of creating
a transference cure. Of course, only time would tell whether any of the
professed changes Peter made were of a lasting nature. This was the third
phase of our encounter.

At my prompting Peter came to the realization that he might be overly
pessimistic about parts of his life. He had overlooked a lot of positive things.
His reflective stance provided me with the opportunity to ask him about the
good things his father and mother had done for him – he was now in a very
different situation than his position as a child; he was an adult who should
take responsibility for his life in the present. I also made clear to Peter that
(consciously or unconsciously) change can be scary and confusing. Entering
this exchange, Peter began to realize that he should count his blessings. If
he took a hard look at things, business was not so bad after all. He had an
affectionate wife and healthy children who were doing very well in life. There
was no reason to put himself in such a dark hole and give himself such low
happiness ratings. There was no real reason to regress into misery.

Reflecting on these matters – turning negative to positive – Peter's mood
shifted dramatically. It was as if a light had switched on inside him, creating some kind of "Aha!" moment that was connected emotionally with a
deep sense of relief. Clearly, Peter had cognitively and emotionally come to
a profound re-evaluation of his present situation. He had become unstuck.
Suddenly, he saw solutions where before there had been only problems.
He identified new action steps in his business that he hadn't seen before
or had been at a loss to deal with. He also saw new ways of getting closer
to his wife and finding things they both enjoyed doing.

While he was talking, I noticed physical signs of Peter's emotional change.
His dejected demeanor disappeared. His sense of illumination and relief,
and a new hopefulness about the future, became visible. We were moving
into the fourth phase of our encounter. Peter had experienced a tipping
point moment, an experience of powerful knowing, an instant in which
solutions to knotty issues suddenly became clear. He felt that he had
reached a turning point, a point of inner clarity. We discussed how he
might proceed, what he could do to actualize his new insights. A follow-up
phone call a week later proved that the action steps we talked about during
our previous encounter were not merely fantasies. Peter took a significant
number of actions concerning both his company and his private life.

Epilogue

With Peter, I was presented with someone who felt tired and depressed. The stress and anxiety of the fast-paced environment in which he operated had been getting the better of him. The demands of others, the endless stream of emails and phone messages, and a nagging question of whether he was really living his life as he wished were all factors that contributed to his feeling overwhelmed, stressed out, and anxiety-ridden.

An intense workload (as a result of his assistant's departure) had overwhelmed Peter's mind with all the responsibilities he had to deal with. He found himself in a vicious circle of doom. An argument he had had with his wife the previous day was the proverbial straw that broke the camel's back, adding to his feelings of disconnection, frustration, and depression. By the time Peter reached his office, he was ready to explode or implode. These feelings manifested themselves in thoughts of how much he hated his job and the faulty perception that the company was on the edge of a precipice. These fears, combined with his feelings about his wife, made him feel his life was coming apart.

In Peter's case, the various strands of his life were working on each other without conscious awareness. By asking Peter some questions, listening to him, and making supportive comments (when timely), I was able to help him become more aware of his confused feelings and cognitive distortions. He became more cognizant of the forces that were building upon one another, contributing to this distressed state of mind.

The observations I offered Peter had helped him shift the pendulum of discouragement toward hope. I had created some kind of tipping point. In one short encounter (although I had held many previous sessions with him), I had helped him see life in a very different light, full of new possibilities and opportunities. In Peter's case, as in many others of a similar nature, this one "good hour" could be seen as the culmination of a whole series of frustrating experiences that came to a head, and resulted in his "Aha!" experience. All my previous sessions with Peter had laid the foundation for this tipping point experience.

The "good" session

As my intervention with Peter demonstrates, coaching is a Socratic process, not a didactic exercise. During our encounter I was faced with an overwhelming mass of information. I asked clarification questions and occasionally confronted him with a few contradictions and non-sensible ideas. I was aware that Peter was haunted by a number of cognitive distortions. For example, he seemed to accept the notion that "We have absolutely no control over our happiness. It is all a question of chance" – a helplessness fallacy that is *not* a recipe for happiness. Peter had always had a tendency to disqualify the positive, quickly seeing things through a negative filter. In addition, his father had imbued him with the notion that "One should reach perfection in whatever one does." This may be a worthwhile theme to live by, but it is very hard to live up to. It makes for too many "shoulds." Satisficing instead of optimizing would be a much better slogan to live by.

"Satisficing instead of optimizing would be a much better slogan to live by"

Peter also had a tendency toward catastrophizing, expecting disaster to strike at any moment. The bankruptcy scenarios he dwelt on were predictable. In hindsight, I realized that I had often been rather puzzled by the cheerful comments Peter had made during our previous interactions. It was as if he was covering his negative feelings with a layer of defenses. On occasions, I had felt that many things were being left unsaid. But with limited time at our disposal, I had decided that it was not appropriate to probe any further. Now, some of his past behavior made much more sense.

A final cognitive distortion that made Peter's life difficult was the idea that "Because something happened in the past, it is impossible to make changes in the present situation." Helplessness and hopelessness are the likely consequences of this kind of fatalistic outlook on life.

Clearly, Peter's perceptions of himself and the world around him needed to change. I had to make him realize how irrational his thoughts were. I needed to create for Peter a greater sense of optimism, more hope for the future, a greater sense of self-efficacy, and self-confidence.[23] When the timing was right, I offered a few ideas about the material he presented, not forgetting to pay heed to his feelings, his past experiences, and his own theories about life. I also engaged in supportive behavior, when appropriate. I was not only trying to get him out of his funk; my challenge was to help him to delve deeper into his life, and his feelings – to enable him to make the changes needed to make him function more satisfactorily. I helped him reframe his outlook toward his life and attack his cognitive distortions head-on. I was trying to bring about meaningful change – if possible, to create a tipping point to help him see other ways of looking at life.

As coaches, we should never forget that coaching is all about the client. It is the task of coaches to do their utmost to help clients seek and reach the goals they are pursuing. It is all about helping clients make the kinds of choices that fit them; to make them realize that they are not passive subjects of life's vicissitudes. They need to recognize that they can be active players in the game of life. Surprisingly enough, for many clients, being in a position to make significant choices about their own well-being is a novel experience. Creating this kind of awareness is important, however, as is being a sounding board for the client. When these issues are dealt with in an appropriate manner, they can release an extraordinary amount of pressure and alleviate stress, enabling clients to become much more content, and much more centered.

It is worth noting that tipping points are often preceded by increased resistance. As coaches we need to be able to tolerate and deal with this. Although it is not pleasant to be used as a toxic dump, we need to be able to contain the negative feelings and thoughts that are projected toward us. We must also be able to help clients recognize their defensive patterns and recast them. One of the talents coaches need is the ability to take something familiar, intuitive, and ubiquitous and modify it in a manner that will redefine its use to drive profound change.

"tipping points are often preceded by increased resistance"

Awareness precedes and follows any tipping point moment and is a key ingredient in human growth. After all, we don't know what we don't know; we can't change our behavior if we aren't aware of how our behavior affects others. In becoming aware, we need to become cognizant of the effects of our behavior and the things that get in the way of our reaching our full potential as human beings. Awareness breeds tipping points that, in turn, breed more awareness about what makes us tick, what makes us happy, and what prevents us from experiencing our life to the fullest.

The working alliance

The quality of the relationship between coach and client is essential in creating tipping points, and just as important to effective coaching interventions as the techniques or tools that are used. A considerable body of research has shown that relationship skills and personal style have a much greater impact in creating "Aha!" moments than theoretical conceptualizations of treatment.[24] What happens between the client and coach – the kind of relationship that is established – is *the* deciding factor in creating meaningful change. Clients need to feel safe, understood, and appreciated. Empathy and sensitivity toward the client is the bedrock of any coaching experience.

"Empathy and sensitivity toward the client is the bedrock of any coaching experience"

Clearly, Peter and I had a very solid working alliance, built on our previous student-teacher history. There was a great amount of trust between us. During the session, I provided Peter with a safe and secure space where he could talk to another person without the fear of ridicule, shame, or judgment. We were operating in a kind of transitional space that allowed him to voice concerns, find new knowledge, and explore new, creative ways of doing things, free from external pressures. It was a space where he could "play." Play generates positive affect, which, in its turn, increases cognitive flexibility and the ability to organize ideas in a different way. All this is positively linked to the creative process, enabling divergent thinking.

However, coaches must take care when creating these transitional spaces. The interpersonal magic between client and coach is very delicate, and can evaporate quickly. Even the slightest negative comment or interpretive mistake can be perceived as threatening, or judgmental – and may jeopardize the working alliance. Clients who feel judged withhold information, which impedes progress. This implies that observations should be made in a very sensitive, perhaps interrogative, manner, so that clients do not feel they have their back to the wall.

Because of the excellent working alliance between us that enabled a transitional space, Peter was more inclined to present his vulnerability. He was prepared to talk about his fears and anxieties, rather than assume the mantle of the business tycoon he was, and reduce the conversation to general, abstract management babble. Many people go into a coaching session highly anxious about "letting their guard down." They fear ridicule, are afraid that people will laugh at them, and so they maintain their defenses. But if they are unable to open up to their coach, they will not get much out of the session.

Affect, cognitions, and defenses

We all know that cognition alone is not enough to help people change. Cognition has to be combined with affect. Understanding affect is the royal road to the unconscious. To be effective – to create tipping point moments – coaches need to be totally attuned to their clients' affective experiences. When there is real attunement, memories, feelings, and fantasies that have long been defended can be unlocked. The original template for this emotional attunement is the nature of the attachment relationship between mother and child, the archetypical example of regulating affective states and creating feelings of safety and resonance.[25] This dyadic affect pattern will remain important from cradle to grave, and will very much influence the kind of working alliance the coach is able to establish.[26] The degree of security of these original attachment patterns will determine the ease with which a working alliance can be established in the present. As a coach, there are times when these childhood attachment patterns are worth revisiting.

Coaches have to go out of their way to identify with, or vicariously experience their clients' feelings, thoughts, or attitudes, whatever the previous attachment patterns may be. They need empathy, yet they must remain independent of their clients' ways of functioning. Empathic resonance is the process of understanding the other's subjective experience by sharing it vicariously, while simultaneously maintaining an observant stance. This balanced curiosity will lead to a deeper understanding of the other.

Empathic resonance is one of the forces that enable tipping point moments. Another is helping clients to change their defensive patterns of behavior. Coaches need to "unlock the unconscious" and help their clients overcome resistances to experiencing true feelings about the present and the past.[27] These feelings are likely to have been warded off because they are either too frightening or too painful. Clients need to free themselves from often crippling, deep-rooted patterns of self-sabotage. They have to find ways to deal with dysfunctional defense mechanisms. As I have said before, what may have been an effective way of dealing with a situation at the age of 10 may no longer be appropriate at the age of 40. And coaches can play a major role in helping their clients on this journey. They can help them to find new ways of dealing with the vicissitudes of daily life.

The corrective emotional experience

Coaches also need to be prepared to engage in the reparative process of affirmation of the self.[28] They have to help their clients to see themselves in a different light. The inner voice that is full of "should haves" or "could

"clients should focus on what they have and can do"

haves" needs to be corrected. Instead of plaguing themselves constantly by emphasizing what they don't have, or haven't done, clients should focus on what they have and can do. Coaches need to help their clients not to expect too much of themselves. A "good enough" performance should be good enough. They need to work on and accept a different self-image.

To change self-image, it is essential "to re-expose the client, under more favorable circumstances, to emotional situations which he or she could not handle in the past. The client, in order to be helped, must undergo a corrective emotional experience suitable to repair the traumatic influence of previous experiences."[29] These encounters in the bi-personal field help clients give up old behavior patterns and learn or relearn new patterns by re-experiencing early, unresolved feelings and needs. A good session becomes a truly "good hour" when clients are willing to push themselves out of their comfort zone and try things that are new, unfamiliar, and even scary. They need to try out different behavior patterns. When the coach-client dyad functions optimally, reparative efforts will become a reality.

It should be noted that clients sometimes start to feel worse during the course of a good session in which long-buried feelings and resentments are dredged up, uncovering regrets, setbacks, and failures. The challenge for the coach is to reframe these feelings, thoughts, and memories in a positive, constructive manner. And when the working alliance is really working – inducing a corrective emotional experience – there is the possibility for a real tipping point moment.

A greater sense of authenticity

At times, in an effort to make these corrective emotional experiences a reality, effective coaches may appear somewhat confrontational, interpretive, and corrective. They need to help their clients to get in touch with what feels "right" to them – the only way their clients will achieve a heightened sense of authenticity and vitality. This sense of rightness comes with the capacity for self-observation. Clients need to have the capacity to report on their conscious inner thoughts, desires, and feelings. They need to recognize what their behavior is all about. Helped by their coaches' reparative attitude, clients will have the experience of being affirmed, recognized, understood, and appreciated. They will receive from the coach the sort of response they always wanted but were previously too frightened to allow.

The positive signs of heightened sensations and new perceptions are indications that this bi-personal exchange is working, creating a form of interpersonal communion whereby coaches (unconsciously) respond to their client in a very personal and improvisational manner. By tuning in affectively and cognitively, dysfunctional patterns of behavior are illuminated and at the same time, the ways in which they can be changed become clearer. Discovering and practicing new ways of behaving becomes a realistic option.

This playful engagement, in a freely associative manner, opens the client affectively, cognitively, and defensively to more possibilities. Through experiencing and reflection, a co-construction (by the client and coach) of new life strategies emerges. Defensive patterns will be redefined or

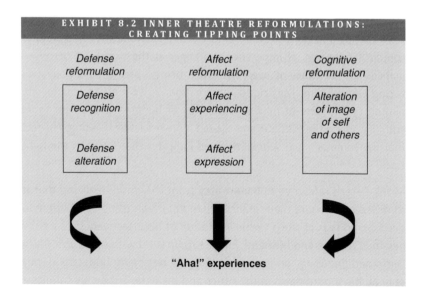

EXHIBIT 8.2 INNER THEATRE REFORMULATIONS: CREATING TIPPING POINTS

Defense reformulation	Affect reformulation	Cognitive reformulation
Defense recognition	Affect experiencing	Alteration of image of self and others
Defense alteration	Affect expression	

"Aha!" experiences

altered. Modifications will take place in the inner theater of the client, contributing to changes in the client's self-image. Exhibit 8.2 gives a description of these defensively, affective, and cognitive processes.

"Cloud" observations

On occasions in this process, coaches may resort to "cloud" observations. Comparable to cloud computing, where a network is used as a means to connect a user to resources based in the "cloud" (as opposed to actually possessing them), cloud psychodynamics refers to themes in the client-coach dyad that are brought out during the interface as the pair creates a collective unconsciousness. The "cloud" contains partially metabolized material from both coach and client, bits and pieces of thoughts, moods, behavior, and actions (including bodily sensations) that invisibly influence the behavior and interactions between the two parties. In the cloud, we will find the dyad's evaluations and judgments, its labels of good and bad, and the resulting neurophysiological sensations that accompany each of them. These cloud snippets are usually left untouched in the discussion, even though the cloud themes have a (conscious and unconscious) influence on the nature of the interchange. At times, however, a cloud intervention can make the day.

I resorted to cloud observations at times in my discussions with Peter. When he overwhelmed me with a barrage of complaints (using me as a toxic dump), I needed to be a more effective "container," to find ways to contain his feelings of impotence and anger at the world, his perceived inability to take care of everyone while being upset that nobody was taking care of him. My "cloud" observation, when I asked him to rate himself on his state of misery, was a way of bringing this lament to an end. It stopped the outpour, and elicited more reflective thinking. The fact that my comment was so well received indicates that I was on the right track.

I took Peter's reference to bankruptcy from the cloud, realizing that it signified much more than financial ruin. Peter was using bankruptcy to describe his fear of the possible implosion of his effectiveness as a businessman, father, and husband. His preoccupation with bankruptcy also contained lingering, unresolved feelings of not being understood, not only by his subordinates in the office and his wife, but by his parents.

The impostor theme in our exchange was another cloud observation. Although Peter didn't say the word explicitly, I picked the impostor theme out of the cloud. While Peter was overloading me with all his complaints, I felt helpless; I didn't know what to do. Eventually, I began to feel like an impostor – exactly the feeling of low self-esteem he was experiencing himself. It was my task to help him acquire greater clarity about how he felt about himself, his role in the company, and his role as a father and husband. After I had made the implicit explicit through this cloud interpretation, Peter felt much better understood.

The client-coach dyad co-created this shared unconscious, or "cloud," which contained multiple anxieties, fantasies, defenses, myths, memories, and shared cultural prohibitions. Feelings of anxiety, anger, contempt, disgust, envy, jealousy, remorse, shame, guilt, rivalry, boredom, pride, joy, or awe can all be viewed as parts of cloud phenomena. These feelings are remnants of memorable, even traumatic experiences – representations that can reawaken during a dyadic or group interface. As coaches, our role is to see that these themes are addressed when appropriate. Cloud observations can be particularly helpful when a coach-client interchange (or work with a group) has ground to a halt.

EXHIBIT 8.3 "CLOUD" ISSUES

1. *Physiological* hunger, thirst, respiration, excretion, etc.

2. *Sexual/sensual* lust

3. *Attachment/affiliation* wanting to care/wanting to be loved/fear of abandonment/fear of loneliness/fear of emotional closeness (engulfment)/dealing with mourning/grief

4. *Fearful* self-esteem issues/not feeling worthy of approval/fear of being hurt/being shamed/feeling embarrassed/feeling guilty/not feeling safe/being fearful/being distrustful

5. *Anger* rage/resentment/envy/jealousy/losing control/panic

6. *Exploratory* play/social joy

A cloud observation can go a long way toward breaking a stalemate in the coaching encounter. Some of the most common basic cloud concerns are listed in Exhibit 8.3. These basic concerns will be metabolized, assuming more concrete forms as we saw in the case of Peter (i.e., loneliness, helplessness, panic).

In Exhibit 8.3, I summarize cloud issues in terms of six major concerns – physiological, sexual/sensual, attachment, fear, anger, and exploration – that touch all of us, and range from basic evolutionary, psychological fight-flight mechanisms (including sexuality), to basic emotional experiences (joy, disgust, anger, surprise, fear, distress), to their emotional derivatives (guilt, envy, jealousy, shame, aggressiveness, sadness, remorse, disappointment, optimism, pride, awe, contempt, submission), to various relational patterns (basic trust, need for control, sense of self-esteem, fear of loneliness/ abandonment), to exploratory concerns such as play and social joy.

Feeding the wolves

There is a tale of an old Cherokee Indian who told his grandson about the battle that continues constantly inside us all. He said, "This battle is between two wolves. One is Evil. It is anger, envy, jealousy, sorrow, regret, greed, arrogance, self-pity, resentment, inferiority, lies, false pride, and superiority; it is Ego. The other is Good. It is joy, peace, love, hope, serenity, humility, kindness, benevolence, empathy, generosity, truth, compassion, and faith; it is Spirit."

The boy thought for about a minute and then asked, "Grandfather, which wolf wins?"

The old Cherokee simply replied, "The one you feed."

The task of coaches is to help their clients sort out the wolves inside them and feed the right one. It is their responsibility to facilitate greater awareness of their clients' inner theater and life journey. It is their challenge to make clients feel better; to liberate clients from the shackles that bind them. Coaches need to help their clients to accept what they do know, don't know, don't want to know, and will never know. Coaches need to address their clients' cognitive distortions. Effective coaches also need to be masters of affect management, to be able to tune in to their clients' mood states. As masters of cloud management, they need to know how to integrate multiple ideas, fantasies, feelings, representations, and relationship patterns.

The nature of the client-coach interface (if carried out effectively) will make for experiential relearning through which clients can safely alter rigid relational patterns by being exposed to new interpersonal experiences. In assuming this challenge, coaches become guides who enable more favorable perceptions of the self and others, helping the client acquire a very different *Weltanschauung*. As a client's self-image determines who he or she is, the turbulence in the intersubjective field between coaches and clients will be the matrix to work through distorted self-perceptions. If coaches can help their clients to make changes in their self-image, they have a chance to make some modifications in their clients' way of functioning. After all, it is not who they are that holds them back; it is what they think they are not.

In helping clients on their life journey, coaches facilitate the transformational process. They make them realize that they are not at the mercy of previous life events, that mental health means having a choice. By seeing things in perspective, by showing their clients that there are other ways to deal with life's adversities, they co-create a better future. And if such experiences add up, and transform into tipping points, so much the better.

The American social writer and philosopher, Eric Hoffer once noted: "No matter what our achievements might be, we think well of ourselves only in rare moments. We need people to bear witness against our inner judge, who keeps book on our shortcomings and transgressions. We need people to convince us that we are not as bad as we think we are." If we are able to do this as coaches, we stand a good chance of creating the tipping points that effect real change.

Conclusion

I wish that strife would vanish away from among gods and mortals, and gall, which makes a man grow angry for all his great mind, that gall of anger that swarms like smoke inside of a man's heart and becomes a thing sweeter to him by far than the dripping of honey.

— Homer, the Iliad

I am indebted to my father for living, but to my teacher for living well.

— Alexander the Great

The mind is not a vessel to be filled, but a fire to be kindled.

— Plutarch

Coaching Alexander

Perhaps the most famous coach-client relationship in history has been that of the philosopher Aristotle with Alexander the Great – King of Macedonia, and conqueror of the Persian Empire, one of the greatest military geniuses that has ever lived. When Alexander the Great was 13 years old, his father Philip II, King of Macedon, decided that his son needed a tutor. Aristotle was appointed as the head of the Royal Academy of Macedon. The temple where the academy was based was turned into a kind of boarding school for Alexander and the children of Macedonian nobles. Many of his fellow pupils would become Alexander's friends and future generals, including two future kings, Ptolemy and Cassander, and are often referred to as the "Companions."

Plutarch dwells on this coaching relationship in his biography of Alexander. He tells us how Philip arranged the location: "As a place for the pursuit of their studies and exercises, he assigned the temple of the Nymphs, near Mieza, where, to this very day, they show you Aristotle's stone seats, and the shady walks which he was wont to frequent."[1]

Aristotle proved to be a brilliant tutor of rhetoric and the art of effective public speaking. He coached Alexander for a number of years, from around 343 BCE. Under Aristotle's leadership coaching, Alexander blossomed, and his nascent talents came to fruition. Encouraged by Aristotle, Alexander embarked on a classic Greek education, which included history, logic, psychology, political theory, and ethics. According to Plutarch, Alexander was such a good student that later on he was able to give Aristotle a lesson or two.

Alexander also developed a passion for the works of Homer, in particular the *Iliad*, of which Aristotle gave him an annotated copy. He carried it with him always, placing it "with his dagger under his pillow." Poetry led him to take Achilles as a role model for living a life of greatness. Alexander allegedly said, "I would rather live a short life of glory than a long life of obscurity."

During his coaching sessions with Aristotle, Alexander also displayed an interest in medicine and the treatments for the sick. This interest became a passion for him later in his life. On many occasions, the medical knowledge he acquired from Aristotle may have saved his life and the lives of his troops. When later he set off on the conquest of Asia, he took zoologists and botanists with him.

Though perhaps best known for his scientific treatises, Aristotle also published his *Ethics* and *Politics*, and his coaching in these areas greatly influenced Alexander, who was particularly attracted by Aristotle's ethical and political views of social hierarchies. Aristotle believed that "barbarians" or "non-Greeks" were meant to be slaves due to natural selection, and were to be treated as beasts, whereas Greeks were considered close friends. "Barbarians" were fierce, brutal, cruel, insensitive, and uncultured, living only through and for their senses, incapable of rising above hedonism. Alexander was already anti-Persian (the result of his father's influence), but Aristotle's coaching provided him with the intellectual justification for his inherited and fated mission.

Encouraged by Aristotle, Alexander placed great value on honor, and the virtues of self-control and self-denial. He was to set the heroic Greek template and be the antithesis of the base barbarians. In this respect, Alexander was departing from his father as a role model. Philip was a hedonist, had fathered many children by many different women, and had generally lived a life of excess. Alexander would follow in his father's footsteps by conquering cities, but he would also challenge his father by achieving greater goals. Aristotle's leadership coaching laid the foundation for Alexander's eventual greatness. He became a self-disciplined, powerful soldier, and a generous leader who honored the deserving for their service. In his short life, Alexander conquered almost half the globe, leaving an indelible mark on the history of human civilization.

The case of Alexander the Great illustrates how coaching can get the best out of an individual, and by extension teams, organizations, institutions, and societies. As a result, an increasing number of business and public organizations recognize the value of leadership coaching as important sources of managerial learning and career development.

Future concerns

Despite the remarkable success of leadership coaching in helping leaders develop their talent, looking forward, I have a number of concerns. There are several issues in the field of coaching that warrant more attention.

As organizations become more complex, new demands are placed on their leadership to attain strategic agility. These demands put pressure not only on the organizations' leaders but also on leadership coaches, who will be expected to help make these organizations function satisfactorily. I predict that this will mean that team coaching will become increasingly important. But will there be a sufficient number of well-trained leadership coaches who can handle the complexity of team dynamics – and the complications that come from dealing with issues of the group-as-a-whole?[2]

In the same vein, given the increasing importance of corporate governance, the need to provide some form of leadership coaching for these groups will increase. Not everyone has the skills to develop and implement effective organizational governance, strategy and risk oversight, stakeholder communication, board organization and process, executive compensation policies, board assessments and evaluations, board/management relationships, and group dynamics. Specially trained leadership coaches will be needed to deal with these complexities. Such work will require a deep understanding of board dynamics, decision making processes, conflict resolution patterns, and other factors – skills that are not necessarily available and are certainly not universal.

I am also deeply worried by the ease with which just about anybody can practice as a coach. Coaching is still an unregulated field. Anyone can call themselves a coach; the only criterion seems to be the coach's ability to solicit clients. With the number of practitioners referring to themselves as "executive" or "leadership" coaches increasing so rapidly, the question becomes whether professional standards or guidelines for coaches and the coaching process are needed. What kind of certification or licensing should be introduced for quality control? Standards and criteria for effective coaching are hard to find. Currently, leadership coaches are not subject to any form of regulation or licensing requirements but I foresee an increasing number of barriers to entry, despite significant challenges.

I am also concerned about the ever-present ethical dilemmas in coaching, in particular, the many possibilities of boundary violation. In psychotherapy and psychiatry the boundaries are quite clear, but the same cannot be said for leadership coaching. Confidentiality is a major issue. What are the ethical implications of executive coaching initiatives? How should assessment data (the results of personality tests and multi-party feedback instruments) be used? What are the dangers of leadership coaching turning into a form of ersatz psychotherapy? All these questions need to be addressed.

"what are the ethical implications of executive coaching initiatives?"

This brings me to the issue of the difference between coaching and psychotherapy. The boundaries are frequently unclear. As the scale and scope of leadership coaching grows, clear guidelines will be needed. To illustrate, in psychotherapy, the clinician functions primarily in a process-oriented and non-directive role. A leadership coach, however, will emphasize more immediate practical concerns. But there are many other thorny questions: who is the client, the person coached or the organization paying for the coaching? And if the latter, who in the organization? There are also questions concerning factors such as methodology (time-limited approaches, cognitive or psychodynamic), length of session, and duration. The fuzzy boundaries between leadership coaching and psychotherapy may necessitate greater collaboration between coaches and mental health professionals.

These concerns also raise the question of whether leadership coaches are sufficiently equipped to deal with truly complex psychological issues. Can they tell when they are getting into deep water? What kinds of leadership coaching qualities (and training) are needed to ensure professional and effective interactions? In this context, supervision is highly important as a fail-safe measure to prevent disaster.

Predictably, most coaching targets the kinds of people for whom the payback is greatest. Seen in terms of return on investment, this means that leadership coaching will be directed toward the development of selected key individuals, particularly those faced with a significant increase in the complexity of their roles. Given the high cost of coaching, the logical consequence of this strategic decision is that coaching delivered to middle- or lower-level executives will be in the form of peer coaching, or internal mentorship programs. In all these cases, a suitable match between coach and client will be essential. A good "fit" is a critical condition for making leadership coaching work – a topic that needs greater exploration.

The lack of regulation has led to concerns about the quality and effectiveness of leadership coaching. The future of leadership coaching as a legitimate and effective professional service will depend on credible empirical data that support its effectiveness as a developmental tool for executive talent. Some research has started but is still in its infancy. Scholars in various disciplines (psychology, behavioral science, social work, business management, education, counseling, organizational development) need to find ways to collect, study, and interpret such information. HR and learning development professionals should also evaluate the business impact of leadership coaching. They need to determine the goals of the initiative and evaluate the success or failure of leadership coaching on the basis of those goals. There should be established metrics to assess the effectiveness of coaching interventions. Tipping-point analysis would also be an interesting avenue for further research.

There is also going to be a greater need for leadership coaches who are comfortable operating across cultures to meet the demands of today's diverse and international workplace. They will need the skill to facilitate culturally relevant ways to unleash people's potential. Far too often, leadership coaches fail to tap into the richness of cultural diversity. Cultural differences become a source of misunderstanding and frustration, leading to serious conflict, missed opportunities, and financial losses. Leadership coaches who can work across cultures will be better equipped to compete in the global marketplace by leveraging cultural differences.

For example, a high percentage of strategic alliances and mergers and acquisitions break down prematurely, failing to deliver the expected strategic benefits and inflicting financial damage on the various partners. The main reason for failure is usually the human factor in general and national and organizational culture in particular. When understood and used constructively, however, these differences can provide a remarkable source of richness for interactions, learning, and growth.

Finally, the leadership of today's increasingly complex organizations would do well to invest in a pool of leadership coaches who have a deep knowledge of the organization, its leadership, culture, and processes. I foresee that systemic interventions will grow in importance and that this kind of investment will be even more vital. In this context, leadership coaching will be used more as a catalyst for change. Through leadership coaching, a coaching culture can be established, building organizations that will set the standard in the 21st century. These are the authentizotic organizations I mentioned earlier in Chapter 2.

> "leadership coaching will be used more as a catalyst for change"

This term is derived from two Greek words: *authenteekos* and *zoteekos*. In its broadest sense, the word *authentic* describes something and someone worthy of trust, being genuine. As a workplace label, *authenticity* implies that the organization has a compelling connective quality for its employees in its vision, mission, culture, and structure. The term *zoteekos* means "vital to life." In the organizational context, it describes the way in which people are invigorated by their work, organizations that provide a sense of effectiveness and competency, of autonomy, initiative, creativity, entrepreneurship, and industry – organizations that have an Ouroboros quality, an ability to contribute to people's renewal and reinvention.

The road toward renewal and authenticity

The mythical Ouroboros eats its own tail to sustain its life, in an eternal cycle of renewal. Symbolically, the Ouroboros stands for self-reflexivity, cyclicality, and re-creation. It suggests that opposites not only coexist but are also related in a cyclical manner. Continuity, completion, repetition, self-sufficiency, and rebirth can all be seen within the circular boundary of the Ouroboros.

In leadership coaching, the theme of change or metamorphosis is especially prevalent. Leaders need to be equipped with a variety of leadership skills to be able to adapt to whatever setting or environment they are in. Although change evokes anxiety, it's better to opt for change than to be stuck in a psychic prison. But, like it or not, as human beings, we are continually subjected to various forms of change. Simply leafing through a photo album shows us our physical metamorphosis in fast-forward: the baby of six months, the child of six, the 16-year-old adolescent, the 36-year-old parent, and the senior citizen of 66 meet between its pages. Looking at the images of our various selves, what has changed? It isn't only our physical appearance. We're not the same people we were at each of these stages. We've changed; we've grown. But do we digest these changes? The self has to deal with the ambiguity of metamorphosis, overcoming self-transformation. Some people look forward to change; others get stuck.

Like it or not, we are all subject to change. But how will we welcome it? How will we experience it? Our obvious external change needs to be matched with inner change. The only way to make sense of change is to plunge into it, move with it, and join it, because change is the only constant. Those of us who are reluctant to accept the evidence and need for change become stuck in a state of quiet desperation.

We all know that if you do what you have always done, most likely, you will get what you have always got. But to go where you really want to go, you need to do something different. To go somewhere different, I have shown in this book how effective coaches will ask the people with whom they work the kinds of insightful and challenging questions that will get them out of their comfort zone. I have demonstrated how individuals who engage in a coaching relationship can expect to experience fresh perspectives on personal challenges and opportunities, thereby acquiring enhanced thinking and decision making skills, greater interpersonal effectiveness, and increased confidence in carrying out their chosen work and life roles. Consistent with a commitment to enhancing their personal effectiveness, I have also pointed out that such development will contribute to appreciable results in the areas of productivity, satisfaction with life and work, and the achievement of personally relevant goals. My hope is that many of the people that are being coached have discovered more options than they thought were ever possible.

In this book, I hope to have demonstrated that coaching provides an invaluable space that allows executives to resolve issues and concerns within the boundaries of a trusted and confidential relationship. When a coaching relationship works, it can help reduce frustrations on a personal level and improve the quality of the coachee's working and personal life. Furthermore, I have shown how effective coaching will improve the functioning of a team, and even an entire organization. I hope I have also made evident how limiting beliefs can give people low confidence and insecurities that become obstacles to achieving what's really possible. We may have come to realize that understanding both our own motivational factors and those of others can have a huge impact on how we work together and how effective we are. What's more, I have shown how the development of greater self-awareness helps people to take ownership and responsibility, provides the opportunity to correct behavior and performance difficulties, and will contribute to increased creativity, learning, and knowledge.

Finally, I have pointed out that for organizations, leadership coaching is a long-term investment in higher business performance. It can be the most cost-effective way of getting better performance from key individuals. Coaching also provides evidence of the organization's commitment to develop its people and create the kind of coaching culture where people are at their best.

This book deals with the yin and yang of resisting and welcoming change. It has examined how human attitudes to change translate into many of the diverse challenges experienced in the coaching world. It is my hope that some of the lessons of this book can be applied to your own life. In the words of Leo Tolstoy, "Everyone thinks of changing the world, but no one thinks of changing himself."

Notes

Introduction

1. Mahler, A. (1940). *Gustav Mahler: Memories and Letters*. Seattle: University of Washington Press.
2. Jones, E. (1953–1957). *Sigmund Freud: Life and Work*. London: Hogarth Press; Kuehn, J. L. (1965). "Encounter at Leiden: Gustav Mahler consults Sigmund Freud," *Psychoanalytic Review*, 52, 345–364.
3. Reik, T. (1953). *The Haunting Melody: Psychoanalytic Experiences in Life and Music*. New York: Farrar, Straus and Young.
4. Mitchell, D. (1958). *Gustav Mahler: The Early Years*. London: Rockliff; La Grange, H-L. de (1973). *Gustav Mahler*, Vol. 3: *Le génie Foudroyé, 1907–1911*. Paris: Fayard.
5. Reik, *The Haunting Melody*.
6. Mahler, *Gustav Mahler*.
7. Cardus, N. (1972). *Gustav Mahler: His Mind and His Music*. London: Victor Gollancz Ltd.
8. Freud, S. (1905). "Fragment of an analysis of a case of hysteria," *Standard Edition of the Complete Psychological Works of Sigmund Freud*, Vol. 7, London: Hogarth Press and the Institute of Psychoanalysis; Kets de Vries, M. F. R. (2007). "Are you feeling mad, bad, sad, or glad?" *INSEAD Research papers*, 2007/ 09/ EFE.
9. Freud, S. (1912). "Ratschläge für den Arzt bei der psychoanalytischen Behandlung," *Zentralblatt für Psycho-analyse*, II, 483–489 ("Recommendations to physicians practising psycho-analysis." *Standard Edition of the Complete Psychological Works of Sigmund Freud*, Vol. 12, (pp. 111–120). London: Hogarth Press and the Institute of Psychoanalysis.
10. Freud, "Fragment of an analysis of a case of hysteria"; Racker, H. (1957). "The Meaning and Uses of Countertransference," *Psychoanalytic Quarterly*, 26, 303–357; Kets de Vries, "Are you feeling mad, bad, sad, or glad?"

11. James, W. (1902). *The Varieties of Religious Experience, a Study of Human Nature: – A Psychology Classic on Religious Impulse* (2008). New York: Exposure Publishers.

1   The Attachment Imperative: The Hedgehog's Kiss

1. Main, M., Kaplan, N. and Cassidy, J. (1985). "Security in infancy, childhood, and adulthood: A move to the level of representation." In I. Bretherton and E. Waters (Eds), *Monographs of the Society for Research in Child Development*. Vol. 50: Growing points in attachment theory and research (pp. 66–106). (1–2, Serial No. 209); Karen, R. (1998) *Becoming Attached: First Relationships and How They Shape Our Capacity to Love*. New York: Oxford University Press; Grossman, K., Grossman, K. and Kindler, H. (2005). "Early care and the roots of attachment and partnership representation in the Bielefeld and Regensburg longitudinal studies." In *Attachment from Infancy to Adulthood: The Major Longitudinal Studies*. New York: Guilford; Caspi, A. and Elder, G. H. (1988). "Emergent family patterns: The intergenerational construction of problem behavior and relationships." In R. A. Hinde and J. Stevenson-Hinde (Eds), *Relationships within Families* (pp. 218–240). London: Oxford Clarendon Press; Sroufe, L. A. (2005). "Attachment and development: A prospective, longitudinal study from birth to adulthood," *Attachment and Human Development*, 7(4), 349–367; Steele, H. and Steele, M. (2005). "Understanding and resolving emotional conflict: The London Parent-Child Project." In K. E. Grossman, K. Grossman and E. Waters (Eds), *Attachment from Infancy to Adulthood: The Major Longitudinal Studies* (pp. 137–164). New York: Guilford.
2. Cassidy, J. and Shaver, P. (Eds). (1999). *Handbook of Attachment: Theory, Research, and Clinical Applications*. New York: Guilford Press; Egeland, B. and Sroufe, L. A. (1981). "Attachment and early maltreatment," *Child Development*, 52, 44–52.
3. Parkes, C. M., Stevenson-Hinde, J. and Marris, P. (Eds) (1991). *Attachment across the Life Cycle*. New York: Routledge; Karen, *Becoming Attached*; Cassidy and Shaver, *Handbook of Attachment*.
4. Bowlby, J. (1969). *Attachment*. Second Edition (Attachment and Loss Series, Vol. 1). New York: Basic Books; Bowlby, J. (1973). *Separation: Anxiety and Anger* (Attachment and Loss Series, Vol. 2). New York: Basic Books; Bowlby, J. (1980). *Loss: Sadness And Depression* (Attachment and Loss Series, Vol. 3). New York: Basic Books.
5. Miller, L. C. and Fishkin, S. A. (1997). "On the dynamics of human bonding and reproductive success: Seeking windows on the adapted-for

human–environmental interface." In J. A. Simpson and D. T. Kenrick (Eds), *Evolutionary Social Psychology* (pp. 197–235). Mahwah, NJ: Erlbaum; Kirkpatrick, L. A. (1998). "Evolution, pair bonding, and reproductive strategies: A reconceptualization of adult attachment." In J. A. Simpson and W. S. Rholes (Eds), *Attachment Theory and Close Relationships* (pp. 353–393). New York: Guilford Press; Simpson, J. A. (1999). "Attachment theory in modern evolutionary perspective." In J. Cassidy and P. R. Shaver (Eds), *Handbook of Attachment: Theory, Research, and Clinical Applications* (pp. 123–150). New York: Guilford Press.

6. Belsky, J. (1999). "Modern evolutionary theory and patterns of attachment." In J. Cassidy and P. Shaver (Eds), *Handbook of Attachment: Theory, Research, and Clinical Applications* (pp. 151–173). New York: Guilford Press.

7. Bowlby, *Attachment*, p. 129.

8. Hazan, C. and Shaver, P. R. (1994). "Attachment as an organizational framework for research on close relationships," *Psychological Inquiry*, 5, 1–22; Hazan, C. and Shaver, P. R. (1990). "Love and work: An attachment theoretical perspective," *Journal of Personality and Social Psychology*, 270–280; Hazan, C. and Shaver P. R. (1987)." Romantic love conceptualized as an attachment process," *Journal of Personality and Social Psychology*, 52 (3): 511–24; Feeney, J. A. (1999). "Adult romantic attachment and couple relationships." In J. Cassidy and P. Shaver (Eds), *Handbook of Attachment: Theory, Research, and Clinical Applications* (pp. 355–377). New York: Guilford Press; Fraley, R. C. and Shaver, P. R. (2000). "Adult romantic attachment: Theoretical developments, emerging controversies, and unanswered questions," *Review of General Psychology*, 4, 132–154; Teyber, E. and McClure, F. H. (2011). *Interpersonal Process in Therapy: An Integrative Model*. (6th ed., pp. 232–279). Belmont, CA: Brooks/Cole.

9. Ainsworth, M. and Bowlby, J. (1965). *Child Care and the Growth of Love*. London: Penguin Books; Ainsworth, M. D. S. (1969). "Object relations, dependency, and attachment: A theoretical review of the infant-mother relationship." *Child Development*, 40, 969–1025; Ainsworth, M., Blehar, M., Waters, E. and Wall, S. (1978). *Patterns of Attachment*. Hillsdale, NJ: Erlbaum; Ainsworth, M. D. S. (1982). Attachment: Retrospect and prospect. In C. M. Parkes and J. Stevenson-Hinde (Eds), *The Place* of *Attachment in Human Behavior* (pp. 3–30). New York: Basic Books; Main, M. and Solomon, J. (1986). "Discovery of an insecure-disorganized disoriented attachment pattern." In T. B. Brazelton and M. W. Yogman (Eds), *Affective Development in Infancy*. Norwood, NJ: Ablex.

10. Mikulincer, M. and Shaver, P. R. (2007). *Attachment in Adulthood: Structure, Dynamics, and Change*. New York: Guilford; Parkes, Stevenson-Hinde and Marris, *Attachment Across The Life Cycle*.

11. Hazan and Shaver, "Attachment as an organizational framework"; Sroufe, "Attachment and development," 349–367.

12. Bartholomew, K. (1990). "Avoidance of intimacy: An attachment perspective," *Journal* of *Social and Personal Relationships*, 7, 147–178; Bartholomew, K. and Horowitz, L. M. (1991). "Attachment styles among young adults: a test of a four-category model," *Journal of Personality and Social Psychology*, 61 (2): 226–44; Feeney, "Adult romantic attachment and couple relationships"; Pietromonaco, P. R. and Barrett, L. F. (2000). "The internal working models concept: What do we really know about the self in relation to others?" *Review of General Psychology*, 4, 155–175; Rholes, W. S. and Simpson, J. A. (2004). "Attachment theory: Basic concepts and contemporary questions." In W. S. Rholes and J. A. Simpson (Eds), *Adult Attachment: Theory, Research, and Clinical Implications*, pp. 3–14. New York, NY: Guilford Press.

13. Ainsworth et al., *Patterns of Attachment*.

14. Bartholomew, "Avoidance of intimacy"; Bartholomew and Horowitz, "Attachment styles among young adults"; Brennan, K. A., Clark, C. L. and Shaver, P. R. (1998). "Self-report measurement of adult romantic attachment: An integrative overview." In J. A. Simpson and W. S. Rholes (Eds), *Attachment Theory and Close Relationships* (pp. 46–76). New York: Guilford Press; Fraley and Shaver, "Adult romantic attachment"; Mikulincer, M. and Shaver, P. R. (2003). "The attachment behavioral system in adulthood: Activation, psychodynamics, and interpersonal processes." In M. P. Zanna (Ed.), *Advances in Experimental Social Psychology* (Vol. 35, pp. 53–152). San Diego, CA: Academic Press.

15. Hazan and Shaver, "Love and work."

16. Millon, T. with Davis, R. D. (1996). *Disorders of Personality: DSM-IV and Beyond* (2nd edn). New York: John Wiley and Sons.

17. Hazan and Shaver, "Romantic love conceptualized as an attachment process"; Hendrick, S. S., Dicke, A. and Hendrick, C. (1998). "The relationship assessment scale," *Journal of Social and Personal Relationships*, 15, 137–142; Hesse, E. (1999). "The adult attachment interview: Historical and current perspectives," In J. Cassidy and P. R. Shaver (Eds), *Handbook of Attachment: Theory, Research, and Clinical Applications*; Collins, N. L. and Read, S. J. (1990). "Adult attachment, working models, and relationship quality in dating couples," *Journal of Personality and Social Psychology*, 58 (4), 644–663; Crowell, J. A. and Treboux, D. (1995). "A review of adult attachment measures: Implications for theory and research," *Social Development*, 4, 294–327.

18. Hesse, "The adult attachment interview"; 1999: 575–594; Sable, P. (2000). *Attachment and Adult Psychotherapy*. Northvale, NJ: Jason Aronson; Davis, D., Shaver, P. R. and Vernon, M. L. (2003). "Physical, emotional, and behavioral reactions to breaking up: The roles of gender, age, emotional involvement, and attachment styles," *Personality and Social Psychology Bulletin*, 29, 871–884.

19. Vaillant, G. E. (1992). *Ego Mechanisms of Defense: A Guide to Clinicians and Researchers*. New York: American Psychiatric Publishing.

20. Byng-Hall, J. (1999). "Family and Couple Therapy: Toward Greater Security." In J. Cassidy and P. R. Shaver, *Handbook of Attachment: Theory, Research, and Clinical Applications* (pp. 707–731). New York: Guilford Press; Holmes, J. (1999). "Defensive and creative uses of narrative in psychotherapy: an attachment perspective." In G. Roberts and J. Holmes (Eds), *Healing Stories* (pp. 49–66). New York: Oxford University Press; Holmes, J. (2001) *The Search for the Secure Base: Attachment Theory and Psychotherapy*. London: Brunner-Routledge; Sable, *Attachment and Adult Psychotherapy*; Sable, P. (2004). "Attachment, ethology and adult psychotherapy," *Attachment and Human Development, 6*, 3–19; Teyber and McClure, *Interpersonal Process in Therapy*.

21. Eagle, M. N. (2000). "A critical evaluation of current conceptions of transference and countertransference," *Psychoanalytic Psychology*, 17 (1), 24–37; Kets de Vries, M. F. R. (2011). *The Hedgehog Effect: The Secrets of Building High Performance Teams*. New York: Wiley.

22. Bowlby, *Loss*; Collins, N. L. and Read S. J. (1994)." Representations of attachment: The structure and function of working models." In K. Bartholomew and D. Perlman (Eds) *Advances in Personal Relationships Vol. 5: Attachment Process in Adulthood* (pp. 53–90). London: Jessica Kingsley Publishers; Scharfe, E. and Bartholomew, K. (1994). "Reliability and stability of adult attachment patterns," *Personal Relationships, 1*, 23–43.

23. Collins and Read, "Adult attachment, working models, and relationship quality in dating couples"; Collins and Read, "Representations of attachment"; Feeney, "Adult romantic attachment and couple relationships."

2 The Art of Forgiveness: Differentiating Transformational Leaders

1. Fehr, R. and Gelfand, M. J. (2012). "The forgiving organization: A multilevel model of forgiveness at work," *Academy of Management Review*, 37 (4), 664–688.

2. Kets de Vries, M. F. R. (2001). "Creating authentizotic organizations: Well functioning individuals in vibrant companies," *Human Relations*, 54 (1), 101–111.

3. Ehrenreich, B. (1997). *Blood Rites: Origins and history of the passions of war*. New York: Metropolitan Books; Enright, R. D. and North, J. (Eds) (1998). *Exploring forgiveness*. Madison: University of Wisconsin Press; Exline, J. J., Worthington, E. L. Jr., Hill, P. and McCullough, M. E. (2003). "Forgiveness and justice: A research agenda for social and personality psychology," *Personality and Social Psychology Review*, 7, 337–348; Tabibnia, G., Satpute, A. B. and Lieberman, M. D. (2008). "The sunny side of fairness: preference for fairness

activates reward circuitry (and disregarding unfairness activates self-control circuitry)," *Psychological Science*, 19 (4), 339–347.

4. De Waal, F. (1996). *Good Natured: The Origins of Right and Wrong in Humans and Other Animals.* Cambridge, MA: Harvard University Press.

5. Witvliet, C. V. O., Ludwig, T. E. and Vander Laan, K. L. (2001). "Granting forgiveness or harboring grudges: Implications for emotion, physiology, and health," *Psychological Science, 12*(2), 117–123; Worthington, E. L. Jr. and Scherer, M. (2004). "Forgiveness is an emotion-focused coping strategy that can reduce health risks and promote health resilience: Theory, review, and hypotheses," *Psychology and Health*, 19, 385–405; Worthington Jr, E. L., Witvliet, C. V. O., Pietrini, P. and Miller, A. J. (2007). "Forgiveness, health, and well-being: A review of evidence for emotional versus decisional forgiveness, dispositional forgivingness, and reduced unforgiveness," *Journal of Behavioral Medicine*, 30:291–302.

6. Lyubomirsky, S. (2008). *The How of Happiness.* New York: Penguin Press.

7. Witvliet, C. V. O. et al., "Granting forgiveness or harboring grudges."

8. Batson, C. D. (1990). "How social an animal: The human capacity for caring," *American Psychologist*, 45, 336–346; Lyubomirsky, *The How of Happiness*; Mullet, E., Neto, F. and Riviere, S. (2005). "Personality and its effects on resentment, revenge, and forgiveness and on self-forgiveness." In E. L. Worthington Jr. (Ed.), *Handbook of Forgiveness* (pp. 159–182). New York: Brunner-Routledge; Witvliet, C. V. O. et al., "Granting forgiveness or harboring grudges."

9. Luskin, F. (2002). *Forgive for Good: A Proven Prescription for Health and Happiness.* New York: Harper.

10. McCullough, M. E., Pargament, K. J. and Thoresen, C. E. (2000). "The psychology of forgiveness. History, conceptual issues, and overview." In M. E. McCullough, K. J. Pargament and C. E. Thoresen (Eds), *Forgiveness: Theory, Research, and Practice*, 1–14. New York: Guilford Press.

11. Griswold, C. (2007). *Forgiveness: a Philosophical Exploration.* Cambridge: Cambridge University Press; Konstan, D. (2010). *Before Forgiveness: The Origins of a Moral Idea.* Cambridge: Cambridge University Press; Roberts, R. C. (1995). "Forgivingness," *American Philosophical Quarterly, 32,* 289–306; Worthington, E. L. Jr. (Ed.) (2005). *Handbook of Forgiveness.* New York: Brunner-Routledge; Worthington, E. L. Jr. (2006). *Forgiveness and Reconciliation: Theory and Application.* New York: Brunner-Routledge.

12. Griswold, *Forgiveness.*

13. Ashton, M. C., Paunonen, S. V., Helmes, E. and Jackson, D. N. (1998). "Kin altruism, reciprocal altruism, and the Big Five personality factors," *Evolution and Human Behavior, 19,* 243–255; Berry, J. W., Worthington, E.L, Jr., O'Connor, L. E., Parrott, L., III and Wade, N. G. (2005). "Forgiveness, vengeful rumination, and affective traits," *Journal of Personality, 73,* 183–229; Brown, R. P. (2003). "Measuring individual differences in the tendency to

forgive: Construct validity and links with depression," *Personality and Social Psychology Bulletin, 29*, 759–771; Lawler-Row, K. A. and Piferi, R. L. (2006). "The forgiving personality: Describing a life well lived?" *Personality and Individual Differences*, 41 (6), 1009–1020; Maltby, J., Wood, A. M., Day, L., Kon, T. W. H., Colley, A. and Linley, P. A. (2008). "Personality predictors of levels of forgiveness two and a half years after the transgression," *Journal of Research in Personality*, 42, 1088–1094; McCullough, M. E. and Hoyt, W. T. (2002). "Transgression-related motivational dispositions: Personality substrates of forgiveness and their links to the big five," *Personality and Social Psychology Bulletin*, 28, 1556–1573.; Younger, J. W., Piferi, R. L., Jobe, R. L. and Lawler, K. A. (2004). "Dimensions of forgiveness: The views of laypersons," *Journal of Social and Personal Relationships*, 21, 837–855.

14. Komorita, S. S., Hilty, J. A. and Parks, C. D. (1991). "Reciprocity and cooperation in social dilemmas," *Journal of Conflict Resolution, 35*, 494–518; McCullough, M. E., Exline, J. J. and Banmeister, R. E. (1998). "An annotated bibliography of research on forgiveness and related concepts." In E. L. Worthington, Jr. (Ed.), *Dimensions of forgiveness* (pp. 193– 317). Radnor, PA: Templeton Foundation Press.

15. Costa, P. T. and McCrae, R. R. (1992). *NEO PI-R. Professional Manual*. Odessa, FL: Psychological Assessment Resources, Inc.

16. Berry, J. W., Worthington, E. L., Jr., Parrott, L., O'Connor, L. E. and Wade, N. E. (2001). "Dispositional forgivingness: Development and construct validity of the Transgression Narrative Test of Forgivingness (TNTF)," *Personality and Social Psychology Bulletin, 27*, 1277–1290; Brose, L. A., Rye, M. S., Lutz-Zois, C. and Ross, S. R. (2005). "Forgiveness and personality traits," *Personality and Individual Differences, 39*, 35–46; McCullough and Hoyt, "Transgression-related motivational dispositions"; McCullough, M. E., Bellah, C. G., Kilpatrick, S. D. and Johnson, J. L. (2001). "Vengefulness: Relationships with forgiveness, rumination, well-being and the big five," *Personality and Social Psychology Bulletin*, 27, 601–610; Walker, D. F. and Gorsuch, R. L. (2002). "Forgiveness within the Big Five model of personality," *Personality and Individual Differences*, 32, 1127–1137.

17. McCullough, M. E. and Witvliet, C. O. (2002). "The psychology of forgiveness." In C. R. Snyder and S. J. Lopez (Eds), *Handbook of Positive Psychology*. (pp. 446–458). New York: Oxford University Press.

18. Griswold, *Forgiveness*; Gorsuch, R. L. and Hao, J. Y. (1993). "Forgiveness: An exploratory factor analysis and its relationship to religious variables," *Review of Religious Research, 34*, 333–347; McCullough, M. E. (2001). "Forgiveness: Who does it and how do they do it?" *Current Directions in Psychological Science, 10* (6), 194–197; McCullough, M. E. and Worthington, E. L. Jr. (1999). "Religion and the forgiving personality," *Journal of Personality*, 67 (6), 1141–1164.

19. Acklin, M. W. (1992). "Psychodiagnosis of personality structure. Psychotic personality organization," *Journal of Personality Assessment*, 58, 454–463;

Acklin, M. W. (1993). "Psychodiagnosis of personality structure II. Borderline personality organization," *Journal of Personality Assessment*, 61, 329–341; Acklin, M. W. (1994). "Psychodiagnosis of personality structure III. Neurotic personality organization," *Journal of Personality Assessment*, 63 (1), 1–9; Waldron, S., Moscovitz, S. Lundin, J., Helm, F. L., Jemerin, J. and Gorman, B. (2011). "Evaluating the outcomes of psychotherapies," *Psychoanalytic Psychology*, 28 (3), 363–388.

20. Berry et al., "Forgiveness, vengeful rumination, and affective traits."
21. Freud, S. (1923), *Das Ich und das Es*, Internationaler Psycho-analytischer Verlag, Leipzig, Vienna, and Zurich. English translation, *The Ego and the Id. The Standard Edition of the Complete Psychological Works of Sigmund Freud*, Vol. XIX, James Strachey (ed.), Hogarth Press and Institute of Psycho-analysis, London, UK, 1927.
22. Bloom, S. L. (2001) "Commentary: Reflections on the desire for revenge." *Journal of Emotional Abuse*, 2 (4), 61–94.
23. Batson, C. D. and Shaw, L. L. (1991). "Evidence for altruism: Toward a pluralism of prosocial motives," *Psychological Inquiry, 2*, 107–122.
24. De Waal, *Good Natured*; Toi, M. and Batson, C. D. (1982). "More evidence that empathy is a source of altruistic motivation," *Journal of Personality and Social Psychology, 43*, 281–292.
25. McCullough, M. E., Sandage, S. J. and Worthington, E.L., Jr. (1997). *To Forgive is Human*. Downers Grove, IL: InterVarsity; McCullough, M. E., Worthington, E. L. and Rachal, K. C. (1997). "Interpersonal forgiving in close relationships," *Journal of Personality and Social Psychology, 73*, 321–336.
26. Baumeister, R. F., Exline, J. J. and Sommer, K. L. (1998). "The victim role, grudge theory, and two dimensions of forgiveness." In E. L. Worthington (Ed.), *Dimensions of forgiveness: Psychological research and theological perspectives* (pp. 79–104). Philadelphia: Templeton Foundation Press; Tangney, J. P, Miller, R. S, Flicker, L. and Barlow D. H. (1996). "Are shame, guilt and embarrassment distinct emotions?" *Journal of Personality and Social Psychology* 70, 1256–69.
27. Feldman, R. (2007). "Mother-infant synchrony and the development of moral orientation in childhood and adolescence: Direct and indirect mechanisms of developmental continuity," *American Journal of Orthopsychiatry* 77, 582–597.
28. Bowlby, J. (1968). *Attachment and Loss, Vol. 1: Attachment*. New York: Basic Books; Bowlby, J. (1973). *Attachment and Loss, Vol. 2: Separation, Anxiety, and Anger*. New York: Basic Books; Bowlby, J. (1980). *Attachment and Loss, Vol. 3: Loss: Sadness and Depression*. New York: Basic Books.
29. Calkings, S. D. (1994). "Origins and outcomes of individual differences in emotion regulation," *Monographs of the Society for Research in Child Development*, Volume 59, Issue 2–3, 53–72; Rosario Rueda, M., Posner, M. I. and Rothbart, M. K. (2005). "The development of executive attention: Contributions to the emergence of self-regulation," *Developmental Neuropsychology*, 28 (2), 573–594.

30. Prince, M. (2009). "Revenge and the people who seek it," *Monitor*, 40 (6), p. 34 (http://www.apa.org/monitor/2009/06/revenge.aspx)

31. Bowlby, *Attachment and Loss, Vol. 1*; Bowlby, *Attachment and Loss, Vol. 2*; Bowlby, *Attachment and Loss, Vol. 3*; Bowlby, J. and Parkes, C. M. (1970). "Separation and loss within the family," In F. J. Anthony and C. Koupernik (Eds). The Child in the Family, *International Yearbook of Child Psychiatry and Allied Professions*, New York: John Wiley.

32. Anderson, M. C., Ochsner, K. N., Kuhl, B., Cooper, J., Robertson, E., Gabrieli, S. W., Glover, G. H. and Gabrieli, J. D. E. (2004). "Neural systems underlying the suppression of unwanted memories," *Science*, 9 January, 232–235.

33. Fincham, F. D. (2000). "The kiss of the porcupines: From attributing responsibility to forgiving," *Personal Relationships*, 7, 1–23; Karen, R. (2003). *The Forgiving Self: The Road from Resentment to Connection*. New York: Anchor; Wade, N. G. and Worthington, E. L., Jr. (2005). "In search of a common core: Content analysis of interventions to promote forgiveness," *Psychotherapy: Theory, Research, Practice, Training*, 42, 160–177; Wade, N. G., Worthington, E. L., Jr. and Haake, S. (2009). "Comparison of explicit forgiveness interventions with an alternative treatment: A randomized clinical trial," *Journal of Counseling and Development*, 87, 143–151.

3   Are You a Victim of the Victim Syndrome?

1. Fenichel, O. (1945). *The Psychoanalytic Theory of Neurosis*. New York: Norton; Zur, O. (1994). "Rethinking 'don't blame the victim': Psychology of victimhood," *Journal of Couple Therapy*, 4 (3/4), 15–36.

2. American Psychiatric Association (2000). *Diagnostic and Statistical Manual of Mental Disorders (DSM-IV-TR)*. Washington, DC: APA; Millon, T. (2004). *Personality Disorders in Modern Life*. New York: John Wiley.

3. Simon, G. K. (1996). *In Sheep's Clothing: Understanding and Dealing with Manipulative People*. Little Rock: A. J. Christopher & Company.

4. Millon, *Personality Disorders in Modern Life*.

5. Rotter, J. B. (1966). "Generalized expectancies for internal versus external control of reinforcement," *Psychological Monographs*, 80 (1, Whole No. 609).

6. Schaef, A. W. (1986). *Co-dependency: Misunderstood-mistreated*. New York: Harper and Row; Zimberoff, D. (1989). *Breaking Free from the Victim Trap: Reclaiming your Personal Power*. Issaquah: Wellness Press.

7. Berry, C. R. and Baker, M. W. (1996). *Who's to Blame? Escape the Victim Trap and Gain Personal Power in your Relationship*. Colorado Springs: Pinon; Maher, C. A., Zins, J. and Elias, M. (2006). *Bullying, Victimization, and Peer*

Harassment: A Handbook of Prevention and Intervention. London: Routledge; Doerner, W. and Lab, S. P. (2011). *Victimology*. Burlington, MA: Elsevier.

8. Worchel, S. (1984). The darker side of helping. In E. Staub et al. (Ed.). *The development and maintenance of prosocial behavior*. New York: Plenum; Kets de Vries, M. F. R. (2010). Leadership Coaching and the Rescuer Syndrome: How to Manage both Sides of the Couch, INSEAD Working Papers, 2010/ 204/ EFE/ IGLC.

9. Fenichel, *The Psychoanalytic Theory of Neurosis*; Freud, S. (1959). Inhibitions, symptoms, and anxiety. In J. Strachey (Ed. & Trans.) *The Standard Edition of the Complete Psychological works of Sigmund Freud* (Vol. 20, pp. 75–175). London: Hogarth Press, 1926; Leahy, R. L. (2001). *Overcoming Resistance in Cognitive Therapy*. New York: Guilford Press.

10. Hawker, D. S. J. and Boulton, M. J. (2000). "Twenty years' research on peer victimization and psychosocial maladjustment: a meta-analytic review of cross-sectional studies," *Journal of Child Psychology and Psychiatry*, 41(4), 441–455; Mullings, J., Marquart, J. and Hartley, D. (2004) *The Victimization of Children: Emerging Issues*. London: Routledge; Harris, M. J. (2009). *Bullying, Rejection and Peer Victimization: A Social Cognitive Neuroscience Perspective*. New York: Springer.

11. Seligman, M. E. P. (1975). *Helplessness: On Depression, Development and Death*. San Francisco: W. H. Freeman; Abrahamson, L., Seligman, M. and Teasdale, J. (1978). "Learned helplessness in humans: Critique and reformulation," *Journal of Abnormal Psychology*, 87, 49–74.

12. Ochberg, F. M. and Willis, D. J. (Eds) (1991). Psychotherapy with victims. *Psychotherapy* (special issue) 28 (1).

13. Abrahamson et al., "Learned helplessness in humans."

4   Are You in the Rescuing Business?

1. Shipman, P. (2010). "The animal connection and human evolution," *Current Anthropology*, 51, 519–538.

2. Braiker, H. B. (2001). *The Disease to Please*. New York: McGraw-Hill; Lamia, M. C. and Krieger, M. J. (2009). *The White Knight Syndrome*. Oakland, CA: New Harbinger Publications; McWilliams, N. (1984). "The psychology of the altruist," *Psychoanalytic Psychology*, 1, 193–213; Seelig, B. J. and Rosof, L. S. (2001). "Normal and pathological altruism," *Journal of the American Psychoanalytic Association*, 49, 933–958.

3. Maroda, K. J. (2004). *The Power of Countertransference*. Hillsdale NJ: Analytic Press; Marshall, R. J. and Marshall, S. V. (1988). *The Transference Countertransference Matrix*. New York: Columbia University Press; Racker, H.

(1968). *Transference and Countertransference*. New York: International Universities Press; Epstein, L. and Feiner, A. H. (Eds) (1979). *Countertransference*. New York: Jason Aronson.

4. Ainsworth, M., Blehar, M., Waters, E. and Wall, S. (1978). *Patterns of Attachment*. Hillsdale, NJ: Erlbaum; Flores, P. J. (2004). *Addiction as an Attachment Disorder*. Lanham, MD: Jason Aronson; Gordon, J. R. and Barrett, K. (1993). "The codependency movement: Issues of context and differentiation," In Baer, J. S, Marlatt, A. and McMahon, R. J. (Eds) *Addictive Behaviors across the Life Span*. Newburry Park: Sage; Hale, R. (1997). "How our patients make us ill," *Advances in Psychiatric Treatment*, 3, 254–258; Mellody, P. (1989). *Facing Codependence: What it is, Where it comes from, How it Sabotages our Lives*. New York: HarperCollins.

5. Edelwich, J. and Brodsky, A. (1980). *Burn-out: Stages of Disillusionment in the Helping Professions*. New York: Human Sciences Press; Feifel, H., Hanson, S. and Jones, R. (1967). "Physicians consider death," *Proceedings of 75th Annual Convention of the American Psychological Association*. Washington, DC: American Psychological Association; Gabbard, G. (1985). "The Role of compulsiveness in the normal physician," *Journal of the American Psychiatric Association*, 254, 2926–2929; Heim, E. (1991). "Job stressors and coping in health professions," *Psychotherapy and Psychosomatics*, 55, 90–99; Lakin, P. E. (1983). *Stress, Health and Psychological Problems in the Major Professions*. Washington, D.C.: University Press of America; O'Connor, M. F. (2001). "On the etiology and effective management of professional distress and impairment among psychologists," *Professional Psychology: Research and Practice*, 32, 345–350; O'Halloran, T. M. and Linton, J. M. (2000). "Stress on the job: Self-care resources for counselors," *Journal of Mental Health Counseling, 22*, 354–365; Payne, R. and Firth-Cozens, J. (1987). *Stress in Health Professionals*. Chichester: John Wiley & Sons.

6. Dryden, W. and Spurling, L. (Eds) (1989). *On Becoming a Psychotherapist*. London: Routledge; Bager-Charleson, S. (2010). *Why Therapists Choose to Become Therapists*. London: Karnac.

7. Bager-Charleson, *Why Therapists Choose to Become Therapists*; Feltham, C. (Ed.) (1999). *Understanding the Counselling Relationship*. London: Sage; Kohut, H. (1977). *The Restoration of the Self*. New York: International Universities Press; Kottler, J. A. (1993). *On Being a Therapist*. San Francisco: Jossey-Bass; Miller, G. (2001). "Finding happiness for ourselves and our clients," *Journal of Counseling and Development, 79*, 382–385.

8. Ainsworth et al., *Patterns of Attachment*; Casement, P. (1985). *On Learning from the Patient*. London: Routledge; Neff, K. D., Kirkpatrick, K. and Rude, S. S. (2007). "Self-compassion and its link to adaptive psychological functioning," *Journal of Research in Personality*, 41, 139–154; Hinshelwood, R. D. (1999). "Countertransference," *International Journal of Psychoanalysis*, 4, 797–818.

5 The Psycho-Path to Disaster: Coping with SOB Executives

1. McCord, W. and McCord, J. (1964). *The Psychopath: An Essay on the Criminal Mind.* Princeton, NJ: Van Norstrand; Person, E. S. (1986). "Manipulativeness in entrepreneurs and psychopaths." In Reid, W. H., Dorr, D., Walker, J. I. and Bonner, J. W. (Eds) (1986). *Unmasking the Psychopath: Antisocial Personality and Related Syndromes* (pp. 256–274). New York: Norton; Tomb, D. A. and Christensen, D. D. (1987). *Case Studies in Psychiatry.* Baltimore: Williams & Wilkins; Davison, G. C. and Neale, J. M. (1990). *Abnormal Psychology* (5th ed.). New York: John Wiley and Sons; Millon, T., Simonsen, E. and Birket-Smith, M. (1998). "Historical conceptions of psychopathy in the United States and Europe." In Millon, T., Simonsen, E., Birket-Smith, M. and Davis, R. (Eds) *Psychopathy: Antisocial, Criminal and Violent Behavior.* New York, NY: The Guilford Press; Blair, R. J., Mitchell, D. R. and Blair, K. (2005). *The Psychopath: Emotion and the Brain.* New York: Wiley-Blackwell; Neumann, C. S. (2007). "Psychopathy," *British Journal of Psychiatry,* 191, 357–358.
2. Hare, R. D. (1996). "Psychopathy: A clinical construct whose time has come," *Criminal Justice and Behavior, 23,* 25–54; Hare, R. D. (1999). *Without Conscience: The Disturbing World of the Psychopaths among us.* New York: The Guilford Press; Babiak, B. and Hare, R. D. (2006). *Snakes in Suits: When Psychopaths Go to Work.* New York: HarperCollins; Boddy, C. R., Ladyshewsky, R. and Galvin, P. (2010). "Leaders without ethics in global business: Corporate psychopaths," *Journal of Public Affairs,* 10, 121–138.
3. McLean, B. and Elkind, P. (2004). *The Smartest Guys in the Room.* New York, NY: Penguin Books.
4. Clarke, J. (2005). *Working with Monsters. How to Identify and Protect Yourself from the Workplace Psychopath.* Random House: Sydney; Boddy, C. R. (2006). "The dark side of management decisions: organizational psychopaths," *Management Decision,* 44 (10), 1461–1475; Babiak, P., Neumann, G. S. and Hare, R. D. (2010). "Corporate psychopathy: talking the walk," *Behavioral Science & the Law,* 28 (2), 174–193; Babiak, P. (2007). "From darkness into the light: Psychopathy in industrial and organizational psychology." In Herve, H. and Yuille, J. C. (Eds), *The Psychopath: Theory, Research and Practice.* Mahwah, NJ: Lawrence Erlbaum Associates; Pech, R. J. and Slade, B. W. (2007). "Organizational sociopaths: rarely challenged, often promoted. Why?," *Society and Business Review,* 2 (3), 254–269.
5. Millon et al. *Psychopathy: Antisocial, Criminal, and Violent Behavior;* Millon et al., "Historical conceptions of psychopathy in the United States and Europe."
6. Prichard, J. C. (1835). *A Treatise on Insanity.* London: Sherwood, Gilbert and Piper.
7. Kraepelin, E. (1915). *Psychiatrie.* Leipzig: Barth.

8. Koch, J. L. (1891). *Die psychopathischen minderwertigkeiten*. Ravensburg: Maier.

9. Cleckley, H. (1941/1976). *The Mask of Sanity*. St Louis, MO: Mosby.

10. Bursten, B. (1973). *The Manipulator: A Psychoanalytic View*. New Haven, Conn.: Yale University Press.

11. American Psychiatric Association. (2000). *Diagnostic and Statistical Manual of Mental Disorders, fourth edition. (DSM-IV-TR)*. Washington, DC: American Psychiatric Association; American Psychiatric Association (2013). *Diagnostic and Statistical Manual of Mental Disorders (DSM-V)* (Fifth ed.). Arlington, VA: American Psychiatric Publishing; Millon, T. (1996). *Disorders of Personality: DSM-IV and Beyond*. New York: Wiley.

12. Millon, *Disorders of Personality*; Millon et al., *Psychopathy*; Millon et al., "Historical conceptions of psychopathy in the United States and Europe."

13. American Psychiatric Association, *Diagnostic and Statistical Manual of Mental Disorders, fourth edition. (DSM-IV-TR)*; American Psychiatric Association, *Diagnostic and Statistical Manual of Mental Disorders (DSM-V)* (Fifth ed.).

14. American Psychiatric Association, *Diagnostic and Statistical Manual of Mental Disorders, fourth edition (DSM-IV-TR)*; American Psychiatric Association, *Diagnostic and Statistical Manual of Mental Disorders (DSM-V)* (Fifth ed.); Robins, L. (1978). "Aetiological implications in studies of childhood histories relating to antisocial personality." In Hare, R. and Schalling, D. (Eds) *Psychopathic Behavior*. Chichester: Wiley.

15. McCord and McCord, *The Psychopath*; McCord, J. (1979). "Some child-rearing antecedents of criminal behavior in adult men," *Journal of Personality and Social Psychology*, 37, 1477–1486.

16. Livesley, W. J., Lang, K. L., Jackson, D. N. and Vernon, P. A. (1992). *Genetic and Environmental Contributions to Dimensions of Personality Disorder*. Paper presented at Meeting of the American Psychiatric Association, Washington, DC; Harris, G. T., Rice, M. E., and Lalumière, M. (2001). "Criminal violence: The roles of psychopathy, neurodevelopmental insults, and antisocial parenting," *Criminal Justice and Behavior*, 28 (4), 402–426.

17. Williamson, S., Harpur, T. J., and Hare, R. D. (1991). "Abnormal processing of affective words by psychopaths," *Psychophysiology*, 28, 260–273; Lynham, D. and Henry, B. (2001). "The role of neuropsychological deficits in conduct disorders." In Hill, J. and Maughan, B. (Eds), *Conduct Disorders in Childhood and Adolescence* (pp. 235–263). New York: Cambridge University Press.

18. Blair, R. J. (2008). "The amygdala and ventromedial prefontal cortex: functional contributions and dysfunction in psychopathy," *Philosophical transactions of the Royal Society*, 363 (1503), 2557–2565; Blair et al., *The Psychopath: Emotion and the Brain*; Williamson et al., "Abnormal processing of affective words by psychopaths."

19. Weber, S., Habel, U., Amunts, K. and Schneider, F. (2008). "Structural brain abnormalities in psychopaths – A review," *Behavioral Sciences & the Law*, 26 (1), 7–28.

20. Lyons, M., True, W. R., Eisen, S. A., Goldberg, J., Meyer, J. M, Faraone, S.V. and Eaves, L. J. (1995). "Differential heritability of adult and juvenile antisocial traits," *Archives of General Psychiatry*, 52, 906–915; Williamson et al., "Abnormal processing of affective words by psychopaths"; McGuffin, P. and Thapar, A. (1989). "Genetics and antisocial personality disorder." In *Psychopathy: Antisocial, Criminal, and Violent Behavior*, Millon, T. and Falconer, D. (Eds), *Introduction to Quantitative Genetics*. Edinburgh: Churchill Livingstone.

21. McCord and McCord, *The Psychopath*; Tomb and Christensen, *Case Studies in Psychiatry*; Willerman, J., Loehlin, J. and Horn, J. (1992). "An Adoption and a cross-fostering study of the Minnesota Multiphasic Personality Inventory (MMPI) Psychopathic deviate scale," *Behavior Genetics*, 22, 515–529.

22. Van Dusen, K. T., Mednick, S. A., Gabrielli, W. E. and Hutchings, D. (1983). "Social class and crime in an adoption cohort." In Van Dusen, K. T. and Mednick, S. A. (Eds), *Prospective Studies in Crime and Delinquency*. Hingham, MA: Kluwer Nijhoff; Wilson, J. Q. and Hernnstein, R. J. (1985). *Crime and Human Nature*. New York: Touchstone.

23. Bakan, J. (2004). *The Corporation: The Pathological Pursuit of Profit and Power*. New York: Free Press.

24. Kets de Vries, M. F. R. and Miller, D. (1984). *The Neurotic Organization: Diagnosing and Changing Counterproductive Styles of Management*. San Francisco, CA: Jossey-Bass.

25. Kets de Vries, M.F.R. (2001). "Creating authentizotic organizations: well-functioning individuals in vibrant companies," *Human Relations*, 54 (1), 101–111.

26. These questions are based on an adapted version of Robert Hare's 2003 Psychopathy Checklist. Hare, "Psychopathy"; Hare, R. D. (2003). *Manual for the Revised Psychopathy Checklist* (2nd ed.). Toronto, ON, Canada: Multi-Health Systems; Hare, R. D. and Neumann, C. N. (2006). "The PCL-R assessment of psychopathy: development, structural properties, and new directions." In Patrick, C. (Ed.), *Handbook of Psychopathy* (pp. 58–88). New York: The Guilford Press; Babiak and Hare, *Snakes in Suits*.

27. Kets de Vries, M.F.R. (2007). "Are you feeling mad, bad, sad, or glad?" *INSEAD Working Paper Series*, 2007/09/EFE.

28. Levinson, H. (1972). *Organizational Diagnosis*. Cambridge: Harvard University Press; Kets de Vries, M. F.R. (2006). *The Leader on the Couch*, West Sussex: John Wiley & Sons.

29. Wormith, S. J., Althouse, R., Simpson, M., Reitzel, L. R., Fagan, T. J. and Morgan, R. D. (2007). "The rehabilitation and reintegration of offenders: The current landscape and some future directions for correctional psychology," *Criminal Justice and Behavior*, 34, 879–892.

6 Why Coaching?

1. Kets de Vries, M. F. R. (2007) "Are you feeling mad, bad, glad or sad?" *INSEAD Working Paper Series*, 2007/09/EFE.
2. Kets de Vries, M. F. R. (2004a). *The Global Executive Leadership Inventory: Facilitator's Guide*. San Francisco, Pfeiffer; Kets de Vries, M. F. R. (2004b). *The Global Executive Leadership Inventory: Participant's Guide*. San Francisco/New York: Pfeiffer
3. Kets de Vries, M. F. R. (2005a). *Personality Audit: Participant Guide,* Fontaine-bleau, INSEAD Global Leadership Centre; Kets de Vries, M. F. R. (2005b). *Personality Audit: Facilitator's Guide,* Fontainebleau, INSEAD Global Leadership Centre.
4. Kets de Vries, M. F. R. (2011). *The Hedgehog Effect*. London: Wiley.
5. Winnicott, D. W. (1958), *Collected Papers: Through Paediatrics to Psychoanalysis*. London: Tavistock; Winnicott, D. W. (1971). *Playing and Reality*. London: Tavistock.
6. Kets de Vries, M. F. R., Florent-Treacy, E. and Korotov, K. (2007). *Coach and Couch: The Psychology of Making Better Leaders*, Hampshire: Palgrave Macmillan; Kets de Vries, M. F. R., Guillen, L., Korotov, K. and Florent-Treacy, E. (2010). *The Coaching Kaleidoscope: Insights from the Inside*, Hampshire: Palgrave Macmillan; Korotov, K., Florent-Treacy, E., Kets de Vries, M. F. R and Bernard, A. (2011). *Tricky Coaching*. Hampshire: Palgrave Macmillan.
7. Kets de Vries, *The Hedgehog Effect*.
8. Ibid.

7 Creating Safe Places for Executive Play

1. Darwin, C. (1872/1998). *The Expression of Emotion in Man and Animals*. New York: Oxford University Press; Levy, J. (1978). *Play Behavior*. Malabar, Florida: Krieger Publishing; Fagan, R. (1981). *Animal Play Behavior*. New York: Oxford University Press; Bekoff, M. and Allen, C. (1998). "Intentional communication and social play: How and why animals negotiate and agree to play," In Bekoff, M. and Byers, J. (Eds), *Animal Play: Evolutionary, Comparative, and Ecological Perspectives* (pp. 97–114). New York: Cambridge University Press; Nachmanovitch, S. (1990). *Free Play: Improvisation in Life and Art*. New York: Jeremy P. Tarcher; Lewis, J. (2012). "A Cross-Cultural Perspective on the Significance of Music and Dance on Culture and Society, with Insight from BaYaka Pygmies," in Michael Arbib (Ed.) *Language, Music and the Brain: A Mysterious Relationship*. Ernst Strüngman Forum. Cambridge MA: MIT Press.
2. Vygotsky, L. S. (1978). "The Role of Play in Development," In Cole, M., John-Steiner, V., Scribner, S. and Souberman, E. (Eds). *Mind in Society: The*

Development of Higher Psychological Processes, 92–104. (Original essay published in 1933); Elkind, D. (2006). *The Power of Play: How Spontaneous, Imaginative Activities Lead to Happier, Healthier Children.* New York: De Capo Press.

3. Winnicott, D. W. (1958). *Collected Papers: Through Paediatrics to Psychoanalysis,* London: Tavistock.

4. Vygotsky, "The role of play in development"; Bergen, D. and Coscia, J. (2001). *Brain Research and Childhood Education: Implications for Educators.* Olney, MD: Association for Childhood Education International; Mainemelis, C. and Ronson, S. (2006). "Ideas are born in fields of play: Towards a theory of play and creativity in organizational settings," *Research in Organizational Behavior,* 27, 81–131; Rushton, S., Juola-Rushton, A. and Larkin, E. (2009). "Neuroscience, play and early childhood education: Connections, implications and assessment." *Early Childhood Education Journal,* 37(5), 351–361.

5. Stipek, D. J., Feiler, R., Byler, P., Ryan, R., Milbuiw, S. and Salmon, J. M. (1998). "Good beginnings: What difference does the program make in preparing young children for school?," *Journal of Applied Developmental Psychology,* 19, 41–66; Stipek, D., Feiler, R., Daniels, D. and Milburn, S. (1995). "Effects of different instructional approaches on young children's achievement and motivation," *Child Development,* 66, 209–223; Singer, D. G. and Singer, J. L. (1992). *The House of Make-believe: Children's Play and the Developing Imagination.* Cambridge: Harvard University Press.; Singer, D. G and Singer, J. L. (2001). *Make Belief: Games and Activities for Imaginative Play.* Washington, DC.: Magination Press. American Psychological Association Books.

6. Csikszentmihalyi, M. (1990). *Flow: The Psychology of Optimal Experience.* New York: Harper Perennial; Csikszentmihalyi, M. (1996). *Creativity: Flow and the Psychology of Discovery and Exploration.* New York: Harper Perennial.

7. Huizinga, J. (1955). *Homo Ludens: A Study of the Play-element in Culture.* Boston: Beacon Press.

8. Shakespeare, W. *As You Like It,* Act II, sc.

9. White, R. W. (1959). "Motivation reconsidered: The concept of competence," *Psychological Review,* 66 (5), 297–333.

10. Frankl, V. (2006). *Man's Search for Meaning.* Boston: Beacon Press.

11. Winnicott, *Collected Papers.*

12. Winnicott, D. (1971). *Playing and Reality.* London: Tavistock.

13. Kottman, T. (2001). *Play Therapy: Basics and Beyond.* Alexandria, VA: American Counseling Association; Landreth, G. L. (2002). *Play Therapy: The Art of the Relationship* (2nd Ed.). New York: Brunner-Routledge; Schaefer, C. (Ed.). (2003a). *Play Therapy with Adults.* Hoboken, New Jersey: John Wiley & Sons, Inc.; Schaefer, C. (2003b). "Prescriptive play therapy," in Schaefer, C. (Ed.), *Foundations of Play Therapy,* 306–320. Hoboken, New Jersey: John Wiley & Sons, Inc.

14. Kets de Vries, M. F. R., Vrignaud, P. and Florent-Treacy, E. (2004). "The Global Leadership Life Inventory: development and psychometric properties of a 360° instrument," *International Journal of Human Resource Management*, 15 (3): 475–492; Kets de Vries, M. F. R, Vrignaud, P., Korotov, K. and Florent-Treacy, E. (2006). "The development of The Personality Audit: A psychodynamic multiple feedback assessment instrument," *International Journal of Human Resource Management*, 17 (5): 898–917; Kets de Vries, M. F. R., Vrignaud, P., Agrawal, A. and Florent-Treacy, E. (2010). "Development and application of the Leadership Archetype Questionnaire," *International Journal of Human Resource Management*, 21 (15), 2848–2863.

15. Rogers, C. (1951). *Client-centered Therapy: Its Current Practice, Implications and Theory*. London: Constable.

16. Kets de Vries, M. F. R. (2011). *The Hedgehog Effect: The Secrets of Building High Performance Teams*. San Francisco: Jossey-Bass.

8 Creating Tipping Points

1. Gladwell, M. (2000). *The Tipping Point: How Little Things can Make a Big Difference*. Boston: Little Brown; Loder, J. E. (1981). *The Transforming Moment: Understanding Convictional Experiences*. New York: Harper & Row.

2. Hayes, A. M., Laurenceau, J. P., Feldman, G., Strauss, J. L. and Cardaciotto, L. (2007). "Discontinuous patterns of change in psychotherapy," *Clinical Psychology Review*. 27, 715–723.

3. Miller, W. R. and C'de Baca, J. (2001). *Quantum Change: When Epiphanies and Sudden Insights Transform Ordinary Lives*. New York: Guilford Press.

4. Miller and C'de Baca, *Quantum Change*.

5. Miller and C'de Baca, *Quantum Change*.

6. James, W. (1902). *The Varieties of Religious Experience*. New York: Cosimo Classics, 2007.

7. Miller and C'de Baca, *Quantum Change*.

8. Miller and C'de Baca, *Quantum Change*, p. 275.

9. Beeman, M. J., Friedman, R. B., Grafman, J., Perez, E., Diamond, S. and Lindsay, M. B. (1994). "Summation priming and coarse semantic coding in the right hemisphere," *Journal of Cognitive Neuroscience*, 6, 26–45; Domash, L. (2010). "Unconscious freedom and the insight of the analyst: Exploring neuropsychological processes underlying 'Aha' moments," *Journal of the American Academy of Psychoanalysis and Dynamic Psychiatry*, 38 (2), 315–339.

10. The amygdala is more famously known as the seat of emotion in the brain, modulating our reactions to events that are important for our survival. This includes a range of emotions, including fear and love, and the many changes that they bring to the body.

11. Ludmer, R., Dudai, Y. and Rubin, N. (2011). "Uncovering camouflage: Amygdala activation predicts long-term memory of induced perceptual insight," *Neuron*, 69 (5), 1002–1014.
12. Freud, S. (1915). "Observations on transference-love (Further recommendations on the technique of psycho-analysis III)," *The Standard Edition of the Complete Psychological Works of Sigmund Freud*, Volume XII (1911–1913): The case of Schreber, papers on technique and other works, 157–171; Etchegoyen, R. H. (1991). *The Fundamentals of Psychoanalytic Technique* (New Ed., 2005). London: Karnac Books..
13. Kris, E. (1952). *Psychoanalytic Explorations in Art*. Madison, Conn.: International Universities Press.
14. Kris, E. (1944). "Art and regression," *Transactions of the New York Academy of Sciences,* 6, 236–250.
15. Baumeister, R. F. (1994). "The Crystallization of discontent in the process of major life change." In Heatherton, T. F. and Weinberger, J. L. (Eds), *Can Personality Change?* Washington, DC: American Psychological Association.
16. "Secondary gain" is a psychiatric term signifying the unconscious advantages that can accrue from an otherwise undesirable state. For example, certain advantages are derived from illness, such as rest, gifts, personal attention, or release from responsibility. Secondary gains explain some people's unconscious reluctance to change; the loss involved in giving up an undesirable state can seem far greater than the perceived gain.
17. Kegan, R. and Lahey, L. (2009). *Immunity to Change: How to Overcome It and Unlock the Potential in Yourself and Your Organization*. Boston: Harvard Business School Press.
18. Heatherton, T. F. and Nichols, P. A. (1994). "Personal accounts of successful versus failed attempts at life change," *Personality and Social Psychology Bulletin,* 20 (6), 664–675.
19. Kets de Vries, M. F. R. (2007). "Are you feeling mad, bad, sad or glad?," *INSEAD Working Paper Series*, 2007/09/EFE.
20. Ogden, T. (1982). *Projective Identification and Psychotherapeutic Technique*. New York, Jason Aronson.
21. Rosenthal, R. and Jacobson, L. (1992). *Pygmalion in the Classroom: Teacher Expectation and Pupils' Intellectual Development*. New York: Irvington Publishers.
22. Rosenthal and Jacobson, *Pygmalion in the Classroom*.
23. Seligman, M. E. P. and Csikszentmihalyi, M. (2000). "Positive psychology: An introduction," *American Psychologist*, 55 (1), 5–14.
24. Smith, M. and Glass, G. (1977). "Meta-Analysis of psychotherapy outcome studies," *American Psychologist.* 32, 752–760; Martin D. J., Garske J. P. and Davis M. K. (2000). "Relation of the therapeutic alliance with outcome and other variables: A meta-analytic review," *Journal of Consulting and Clinical Psychology*, 68: 438–450; Wampold, B. E. (2001). *The Great Psychotherapy Debate: Models, Methods and Findings*. Mahwah, NJ: Lawrence Erlbaum.

25. Bowlby, J. (1988). *A Secure Base: Parent-child Attachment and Healthy Human Development*. New York: Basic Books.
26. Fosha, D. (2005). "Emotion, true self, true other, core state: Toward a clinical theory of affective change process," *Psychoanalytic Review*, 92, 513–551.
27. Davanloo, H. (1990). *Unlocking the Unconscious: Selected Papers of Habib Davanloo*. New York: Wiley.
28. Kohut, H. (1971). *The Analysis of the Self*. New York: International Universities Press; Kohut, H. (1977). *The Restoration of the Self*. New York: International Universities Press.
29. Alexander, F. and French, T. (1946). *Psychoanalytic Therapy: Principles and Applications*. New York: Roland Press, p. 66.

Conclusion

1. Plutarch (1973). *Plutarch's Lives, Vol. II*. (The Dryden Translation), Digireads.com Publishing, p. 109.
2. Kets de Vries, M. F. R. (2011). *The Hedgehog Effect: The Secrets of Building High Performance Teams*. San Francisco: Jossey-Bass.

About the Author

Manfred F. R. Kets de Vries brings a different view to the much-studied subjects of leadership and the dynamics of individual and organizational change. Bringing to bear his knowledge and experience of economics (Econ. Drs., University of Amsterdam), management (ITP, MBA, and DBA, Harvard Business School), and psychoanalysis (Canadian Psychoanalytic Society and the International Psychoanalytic Association), Kets de Vries scrutinizes the interface between international management, psychoanalysis, psychotherapy, and dynamic psychiatry. His specific areas of interest are leadership, career dynamics, executive stress, entrepreneurship, family business, succession planning, cross-cultural management, team building, coaching, and the dynamics of corporate transformation and change.

Manfred Kets de Vries is the distinguished clinical professor of leadership development and organizational change at INSEAD, France, Singapore and Abu Dhabi. He was the Founder of INSEAD's Global Leadership Center, one of the largest leadership development centers in the world. In addition, he is program director of INSEAD's top management program, "The Challenge of Leadership: Developing Your Emotional Intelligence," and Scientific Director of the Executive Master's Program "Consulting and Coaching for Change" (and has five times received INSEAD's distinguished teacher award). He is also the Distinguished Visiting Professor of Leadership Development Research at the European School of Management and Technology (ESMT) in Berlin. He has held professorships at McGill University, the Ecole des Hautes Etudes Commerciales, Montreal, and the Harvard Business School, and he has lectured at management institutions around the world.

The Financial Times, *Le Capital*, *Wirtschaftswoche*, and *The Economist* have rated Manfred Kets de Vries among the world's leading leadership scholars. Kets de Vries is listed among the world's top 50 leading management thinkers and is among the most influential contributors to human resource management.

Kets de Vries is the author, co-author, or editor of more than 39 books, including *The Neurotic Organization, Leaders; Fools and Impostors; Life and Death in the Executive Fast Lane; The Leadership Mystique; The Happiness Equation; Are Leaders Born or Are They Made? The Case of Alexander the Great; The New Russian Business Leaders; Leadership by Terror: Finding Shaka Zulu in the Attic; The Global Executive Leadership Inventory; The Leader on the Couch; Coach and Couch; The Family Business on the Couch; Sex, Money, Happiness, and Death: The Quest for Authenticity; Reflections on Leadership and Character; Reflections on Leadership and Career; Reflections on Organizations; The Coaching Kaleidoscope;* and *The Hedgehog Effect: The Secrets of High Performance Teams.* Three further books are in preparation.

In addition, Kets de Vries has published over 350 scientific papers as chapters in books and as articles. He has also written approximately 100 case studies, including seven that received the Best Case of the Year award. He is a regular contributor to a number of magazines. His work has been featured in such publications as *The New York Times, The Wall Street Journal, The Los Angeles Times, Fortune, Business Week, The Economist, The Financial Times,* and *The International New York Times.* His books and articles have been translated into 31 languages.

In addition, Kets de Vries is a member of 17 editorial boards and has been elected a Fellow of the Academy of Management. He is a founding member of the International Society for the Psychoanalytic Study of Organizations (ISPSO), which has honored him with a lifetime membership. Kets de Vries is also the first non-American recipient of the International Leadership Association Lifetime Achievement Award for his contributions to leadership research and development; he is considered one of the world's founding professionals in the development of leadership as a field and discipline. The American Psychological Association has honored him with the Harry and Miriam Levinson Award (Organizational Consultation division) for his contributions to the field of consultation. He has been awarded the Freud Award for his contributions at the interface of management and psychoanalysis. He has also received the Vision of Excellence Award from the Harvard Institute of Coaching. In addition, he is the recipient of two honorary doctorates.

Kets de Vries is a consultant on organizational design/transformation and strategic human resource management to leading U.S., Canadian, European, African, and Asian companies. As a global consultant in executive leadership development his clients have included ABB, ABN-AMRO, Aegon, Air Liquide, Alcan, Alcatel, Accenture, Bain Consulting, Bang & Olufsen, Bonnier, BP, Cairn, Deutsche Bank, Ericsson, GE Capital, Goldman Sachs, Heineken, Hudson, HypoVereinsbank, Investec, KPMG, Lego, Liberty Life, Lufthansa, Lundbeck, McKinsey, ATIC, National Australian Bank, Novartis, Nokia, NovoNordisk, Origin, Shell, SHV, SpencerStuart, SABMiller, Standard Bank of South Africa, Unilever, and Volvo

Car Corporation. As an educator and consultant he has worked in more than 40 countries. In his role as a consultant, he is also the chairman of the Kets de Vries Institute (KDVI), a boutique organizational consulting firm.

The Dutch government has made him an Officer in the Order of Oranje Nassau. He was the first fly fisherman in Outer Mongolia and is a member of New York's Explorers Club. In his spare time he can be found in the rainforests or savannas of Central Africa, the Siberian taiga, the Pamir and Altai Mountains, Arnhemland, or within the Arctic Circle.

(email: manfred.ketsdevries@insead.edu; websites: www.ketsdevries.com; www. kdvi.com).

Index

.

Printed and bound by CPI Group (UK) Ltd, Croydon, CR0 4YY